J. (James) Rev Gregory

Puritanism in the Old World and in the New

J. (James) Rev Gregory

Puritanism in the Old World and in the New

ISBN/EAN: 9783744661065

Printed in Europe, USA, Canada, Australia, Japan

Cover: Foto ©Lupo / pixelio.de

More available books at **www.hansebooks.com**

PURITANISM

IN THE

OLD WORLD AND IN THE NEW

FROM ITS INCEPTION IN THE REIGN OF ELIZABETH
TO THE ESTABLISHMENT OF THE PURITAN
THEOCRACY IN NEW ENGLAND

A HISTORICAL HANDBOOK

BY THE
REV. J. GREGORY
EDINBURGH

INTRODUCTION BY THE
REV. AMORY H. BRADFORD, D.D.
AUTHOR OF "THE PILGRIM IN OLD ENGLAND"

NEW YORK   CHICAGO   TORONTO
FLEMING H. REVELL COMPANY
1896

Copyright, 1896, by
FLEMING H. REVELL COMPANY.

INTRODUCTION.

THE last few years have witnessed a real revival of interest in the subject of Puritanism. It has been studied with an earnestness and thoroughness which has not been equalled in the present century. It is difficult to determine the cause of this revival. Since the meeting of the International Council of Congregational Churches, which convened in London in 1891, the interest has been on the increase in England and in America, and several important works on the subject have appeared in both countries. Among them all, few, if any, have been more scholarly or comprehensive than the one which it is now my privilege to introduce to American readers. Its characteristics are perspicuity and careful scholarship. Its style is admirably clear, and the arrangement of the topics careful and discriminating, so that they may be easily read and remembered. It is essentially what its author styles it—a "handbook." I do not know any volume which, within the same limits, presents so much and such valuable information on the subject with which it deals.

The author, the Rev. J. Gregory, of Edinburgh, has not heretofore been known in this country. He belongs to the class of quiet but earnest students who are known to the world by their publications rather than by the positions which they may occupy in society or in public affairs. He is now in the prime of life, being, I believe, still under fifty years of age. He was educated at New College, London, and for a number of years was pastor of a prominent church in Leeds. From that he was called to succeed the Rev. Dr. Lindsay Alexander, in the pastorate of the Church of St. Augustine, in Edinburgh. Dr. Alexander was one of the most eminent preachers and theologians of the present century in the Scottish capital. He was a man of wonderful power, both as a thinker and as an orator. Perhaps no theologian among the Independent churches of the past generation has more strongly impressed himself upon the thought and life of that country. That our author was called to succeed such a man in the pastorate of the leading Congregational Church in the great university city, is testimony enough to his intellectual strength and spiritual earnestness. He retained that pastorate for about fifteen years. He is a man of large ability, wide reading, and is greatly loved by his friends. As chairman of the Congregational Union of Scotland, in 1890, he gave an address from the Chair on "The Church and Social Problems," which attracted much attention. For years Mr. Gregory has been a student of Puritan times, and this book has been eagerly awaited by the friends who have known that it was in process of preparation.

Such works as this help greatly to clear the way for what many of us believe must come sooner or later—some kind of unity in the Christian Church. Before there can be unity either of spirit or of organization there must be first an accurate and sympathetic understanding of the principles for which the various denominations stand. Until recently there has been little attempt on the part of Puritans to understand those who put emphasis upon the doctrine of the church, and on the part of Anglicans and Episcopalians little honest effort to understand the principles and motives of Puritanism. The latter have studied the doctrine of the Church, and the former have very generally ignored it. The revival of interest in the subject has led, of late, to a more candid examination of the doctrine. The result in all parts of the world has been a conviction that somehow the scandal of a divided Christendom ought to be removed. But there are practical difficulties in the way, and little progress has as yet been made. In the meantime, we are gradually learning that unity can not be realized by the sacrifice of principles, but only as all Christians come to estimate at their true value those phases of truth to which each denomination has been chosen to give prominence.

Such works as those of the late Dr. Dexter, Dr. John Brown, of Bedford, and that which I am now commending to American readers, have performed a real service in showing that Puritanism is more than a protest. It represents at least one hemisphere of the doctrine of the church—that doctrine is a sphere with two poles, namely, the independence of the individual and the local church, and the union of all Christians and all local churches in one undivided body. It has been difficult for most thinkers to realize that while these truths are opposed to each other, they are not antagonistic. Books like this of Mr. Gregory ought to be widely read, especially by those who differ from the positions which he takes. From it they will learn that Puritanism had its origin in a profound religious experience, and that it has a continuity, reaching not only to apostolic times, but even to the days of the prophets. They will also better appreciate the truth that before the church can be one a broad and large place must be made for those whose fundamental belief is that each individual soul may come into direct contact with the Infinite Spirit, and that the Church of Christ is composed of all who from Jesus Christ have received the Divine life. Not by shutting our eyes to the beliefs of those who differ from us, but rather by a reverent and careful study of their teachings shall we come to that appreciation of the grounds of difference which is a necessary condition of the ultimate unity of the Church. As a book well calculated to help in this preliminary but important work, I commend to American readers "Puritanism in the Old World and in the New."

AMORY H. BRADFORD.

First Congregational Church,
    Montclair, New Jersey.

PREFACE

"One wishes there were a history of English Puritanism, the last of all our heroisms, but sees small prospect of such a thing at present." So wrote Carlyle in the introduction of his *Letters and Speeches of Cromwell*. This wish will probably go unfulfilled till the task is taken in hand by some genius like Carlyle himself, but with more genuine religious insight and sympathy.

It seems superfluous, and yet perhaps it is necessary, to say, in view of possible misjudgment, that this work does not purport to be "a history of English Puritanism." It originated in the idea of bringing together, and presenting in a succinct and readable form, the best, or the substance of the best, which has been written concerning Puritanism and Independency—their genesis in England and New England, their growth and vicissitudes and struggles, till, at the close of the seventeenth century, Puritanism lost its distinctive name, and became incorporated in the life of the nation as a whole. I have not altogether departed from this intention, but have made it my business to consult the writings of authors of acknowledged eminence and repute, with a view of collecting the most weighty pronouncements and opinions touching the character of Puritanism, and the work which Puritanism did. I have found it necessary, however, to weave these opinions and judgments into a narrative or monograph of my own, so that in its present form this book may in some sense (a very slender and modified sense, I am well aware) fairly claim to be an independent and original work. I have endeavoured to cast it into the form of a handbook, so that to those wishing to form a general acquaintance with the history of the period to which it relates, and to those wishing to pursue their inquiries further it may serve as a useful and, it is hoped, trustworthy guide. With a view to the requirements of the latter, a somewhat lavish *apparatus critici*, in the shape of notes, has been introduced, but not more unsparingly, it is believed, than the importance of the subjects they are introduced to illustrate seems to justify.

The literature of Puritanism is sporadic and fragmentary, either buried in antiquated and unreadable tomes,—for even Neal's history is hard reading in these days,—or in more bright and vivacious books (happily not few), treating the subject in too piecemeal a fashion to present any adequate conception of what Puritanism was, or what it contributed to the making of the England of to-day. My aim has been to give as complete and comprehensive a view of the subject as possible, bringing into one conspectus what Puritanism accomplished in the Old World and in the New, and showing how in both it became the parent of free institutions, and the founder of modern democracy.

I am not solicitous to clear myself from the imputation of being biassed, nay, of being very strongly biassed, in favour of the Puritans, and that for which the Puritans contended. It can serve no good purpose to lay claim to the merit of impartiality. Indeed, the parade of impartiality is always suspicious, and the assertion of it on the part of writers and authors, I have generally found to be in inverse relation to its real existence and exhibition. I fear I must be content to incur the reproach of such writers as the author of *Religious Thought in England*. In the preface to that able work, a work to which I gladly record my indebtedness, Mr. Hunt says: "I am dissatisfied, and I suppose most men are, with the spirit in which the history of religion in England is generally written. If it is the work of a Churchman, it takes the form of a defence of the Church of England; if by a Nonconformist, it is a defence of Nonconformity. And thus a subject which, in proper hands, might be prolific for good, is sacrificed to the glorification of a sect or a party." I trust I am as fully alive to the peril here indicated as Mr. Hunt himself; but the remedy is not to be found, as he appears to think, in endeavouring to steer a middle course, and inclining neither to the one side nor to the other. For men of strong convictions and principles, and who do not hesitate to avow them, this is clearly impossible. Notwithstanding all that may be urged to the contrary, it is possible to take sides, and yet be scrupulously just and fair. One may believe in Puritanism intensely, and yet be keenly alive to its vices and shortcomings; and one may deal out even-handed justice to its enemies and oppressors, without shutting ones eyes to their redeeming virtues and qualities. It is for others to judge how far this aim has been realised in the presentment of Puritanism given in the following pages.

CONTENTS

PART I

PURITANISM IN THE OLD WORLD

CHAP.		PAGE
	INTRODUCTION	1
I.	THE CREATIVE CAUSES OF PURITANISM	11
II.	THE CHURCH OF ENGLAND	31
III.	THE RISE OF PURITANISM IN ENGLAND	43
IV.	THE CHASM WIDENING: RISE OF PRESBYTERIANISM IN ENGLAND	61
V.	PURITANISM: FURTHER DEVELOPMENTS, AND MEANS USED FOR THEIR REPRESSION	83
VI.	THE CONFLICT BETWEEN PURITANISM AND THE CHURCH	101
VII.	RISE OF INDEPENDENCY	119
VIII.	THE CORRUPT STATE OF THE CHURCH: THE MARTIN MARPRELATE CONTROVERSY	145
IX.	THE PURITAN MARTYRS	171
X.	HOLLAND AND THE EXILED INDEPENDENTS	201

PART II

PURITANISM IN THE NEW WORLD

I.	FOUNDING OF NEW PLYMOUTH	231
II.	THE FOUNDING OF MASSACHUSETTS	251

CONTENTS

CHAP.		PAGE
III.	ROGER WILLIAMS: THE BEGINNINGS OF RELIGIOUS CONTROVERSY IN NEW ENGLAND . .	269
IV.	GROWTH AND DEVELOPMENT OF NEW ENGLAND	289
V.	RELIGIOUS AND SOCIAL ASPECTS OF NEW ENGLAND	311
VI.	THE GROWTH OF INTOLERANCE IN NEW ENGLAND .	333
VII.	TOLERATION AND RELIGIOUS LIBERTY: GENERAL CONCLUSIONS	357
	CONCLUSION .	389

NOTES

MEANING AND USES OF THE NAME PURITAN	4
THE HISTORIAN NEAL .	6
SCHISM	36
CONTINUITY OF THE CHURCH .	38
HOOKER'S THEORY OF CHURCH AND STATE .	115
CORRUPT STATE OF THE CHURCH	150
WHO WAS MARTIN MARPRELATE? .	166
ROBINSON'S FAREWELL WORDS .	224
"PILGRIM FATHERS NEITHER PURITANS NOR PERSECUTORS"	257
DUTY OF PERSECUTION .	366
THE TOLERANCE OF INDIFFERENCE .	367
DOES CALVINISM PROMOTE INTOLERANCE? .	381
CALVINISM AND PURITANISM NOT IDENTICAL	383

INTRODUCTION

THE genius of Puritanism has been transmitted, and is capable of being expressed, in manifold forms. The name is not much more than three hundred years old, but that which it describes is older than Christianity itself. As there were reformers before the Reformation, so there were Puritans before that which we call Puritanism had sprung into existence. To their influence in the Jewish Church must be traced all that was noblest, all that was best worth preserving. Samuel was a Puritan, so was Ezra, so was Nehemiah, so was John the Baptist. It was the zeal of Puritanism that moved the Divine Son to expel the traffickers from the Temple, and so vindicate the honour of His Father's house. The Prophets of Israel, in their insistence upon righteousness, in their exaltation of the moral above the legal and ceremonial, were anticipating the very gist of the Puritan contention.

It was the spirit of Puritanism that flamed up in the breast of Ambrose when he required the Emperor Theodosius, before entering the church at Milan, to make reparation for the slaughter of the citizens of Thessalonica. When Savonarola made the proud citizens of Florence to cower under his invective, and unsparingly assailed their sins and their corruptions, the weapon which he wielded was of the true Puritan temper. Nor is this using the word Puritan in a loose, inexact sense. All that is originally connoted by it is zeal for purity—purity of faith, worship, and manners.[1]

Puritanism simply represents the spirit of revolt against the corruptions of the Church and of the State. True, it has become identified with certain sharply defined doctrines and peculiar practices, but these adhere to it as separable accidents rather than as part of its real contents and substance. As against Pope, Council, and Church, the Puritans contended for the authority of what they called the "pure word of God." The Reformers called them *Precisianists,* from their alleged habit of magnifying mere punctilios, or things "indifferent," into matters of prime importance.

In the following pages we shall endeavour to show that Puritanism was pre-eminently a moral and religious force, and that it allied itself with certain forms of faith and practice, only that it might thereby more effectually promote the ends and righteousness of the kingdom of God. That is to say, the significance of Puritanism is not doctrinal but ethical. It was not necessary that it should be permanently identified with the system of Calvinism.[2] There was no necessity why a Puritan should be a Roundhead and go about with his hair

---

[1] "This name Puritan is very aptly given to these men, not because they be pure, no more than were the heretics *Cathari*, but because they think themselves to be more pure than others, as Cathari did, and separate themselves."—Archbishop Whitgift.

[2] "It is a paradox to say that old Calvinism was not doctrinal in the face of the *Institute*; but it is astonishing to find how little in

cropped, or speak with a nasal twang, or affect a preternaturally solemn and sanctimonious expression, any more than it was necessary for the old Hebrew prophet to appear in the bravery of unkempt hair, and wear a rough garment to deceive. We shall try to show that this was the mere outward skin intended to be sloughed, and that underneath was the permanent and imperishable force and virtue to which, by common consent, the name Puritanism is given.

ordinary life they talked or wrote about doctrine. The doctrine was never more than the dress. The living creature was wholly moral and political,—so, at least, I think myself." J. A. Froude, "Reminiscences," *Blackwood's Magazine*, Dec. 1894.

NOTES

The Spanish ambassador De Silva, writing to his sovereign Philip in 1568, says: "Those who call themselves of the *religio purissima* go on increasing. They are the same as Calvinists, and they are styled Puritans, because they allow no ceremonies nor any forms save those which are authorised by the bare letter of the gospel."—Froude's *History*, ix. 327.

"It is difficult to describe the party which about this time or soon after got the name of Puritans. The name was generic, and included men of widely different views. Tyndale, Hooper, and Coverdale might be called Puritans, and, indeed, many of Elizabeth's first bishops. Historically the word came to mean those who never entirely conformed, or those who suffered for nonconformity."—Hunt's *Religious Thought in England*, vol. i. p. 48.

Fuller dates the use of the term Puritan as a nickname for the English Nonconformists generally, from the year 1564, shortly after Elizabeth ascended the throne.

"The name Puritan got a new meaning in the time of the Commonwealth. All who were not Royalists were called Puritans. This comprehended those who opposed the arbitrary measures of the King, and the innovations of Archbishop Laud, as well as the Presbyterians and the sectaries of all kinds. Another use of the word Puritan was to designate all clergymen who held the views of Calvin. In this sense Whitgift and Hooper came to be called Puritans. After the restoration of Charles II., many of the moderate Puritans conformed. Those who did not were called Nonconformists."—Hunt, vol. iii. pp. 368, 369.

"The number of Puritans increased prodigiously in his reign (that of James I.), which was owing to one or other of these causes[1]—

"First, to their standing firm by the constitution and laws of the country, which brought over to them all those gentlemen in the House of Commons, and in the several counties of England, who found it necessary for the preservation of their properties to oppose the Court, and to insist upon being governed according to law; these were called State Puritans.

"Secondly, to their steady adherence to the doctrine of Calvin and the Synod of Dort in the points of predestination and grace, against the modern interpretation of Arminius and his followers. The Court divines fell in with the latter, and were thought not only

---

[1] Preface to Neal's *History of the Puritans*. See note on Neal, p. 6.

to deviate from the principles of the first Reformers, but to attempt a coalition with the Church of Rome; while most of the country clergy, being still in their old opinions (though otherwise well enough affected to the discipline and circumstances of the Church), were in a manner shut out from all preferment, and branded with the name of Doctrinal Puritans.

"Thirdly, to their pious and severe manner of life, which was at this time very extraordinary. If a man kept the Sabbath and frequented sermons, if he maintained family religion, and would neither swear nor be drunk, nor comply with the fashionable vices of the times, he was called a Puritan. This by degrees procured them the compassion of the sober part of the nation, who began to think it very hard that a number of sober, industrious, and conscientious people should be harassed out of the land for scrupling to comply with a few indifferent ceremonies which had no relation to the favour of God or the practice of virtue."

The last description is the one which has survived. In this sense it is used by Shakespeare—

"She would make a Puritan of the devil."

"In my conscience it was a shame to be a Christian within these fifteen, sixteen, or seventeen years in this nation! Whether 'in Cæsar's house' or elsewhere! It was a shame, it was a reproach to a man; and the badge of 'Puritan' was put upon it" (*Cromwell's Speeches*).

"Richard Baxter belonged to what was known as a Puritan family, though they were Episcopalians and strict Conformists, and this solely on account of their religious habits and pious manner of life." —Calamy's *Life of Baxter*, p. 48.

"It is the artifice of the favourers of the Catholic and of the prelatical party to call all who are sticklers for the Constitution in Church or State, or would square their actions by any rule human or divine, Puritans."—Rushworth, vol. ii. 1355.

See the account of the Puritan party in *Memoirs of Colonel Hutchinson*, pp. 79–82 :—

"If any out of mere morality and civil honesty discountenanced the abominations of those days, he was a Puritan. . . . If any showed favour to any godly, honest persons, kept them company, relieved them in want, or protected them against violent or unjust oppression. . . . Whoever was zealous for God's glory or worship, could not endure blasphemous oaths, ribald conversation, profane scoffs, derision of the word of God, and the like—whoever could endure a sermon, modest habit or conversation, or anything good,—all these were Puritans; and if Puritans, then enemies to the King and his government, seditious, factious hypocrites, ambitious disturbers of the public peace, and, finally, the pest of the kingdom."

NOTE ON NEAL

As we shall have occasion to cite the testimony of Neal, the well-known historian of the Puritans, pretty frequently in the following pages, it may be well to state at the beginning that so far from "pinning our faith" to everything which Neal says, we have relied on his authority only in those instances where we had independent reasons for regarding it as in the main trustworthy. Mr. Green, speaking of the "inaccuracies" of Neal's *History*, says it contains little concerning the Puritan period which is not taken from the "more colourless Strype." "He (Neal) blanches them into a sweet and almond whiteness." We are bound to say that there is less persistent glorification of the Puritans in the pages of Neal than we expected to find; nor have we discovered that he is more inaccurate than other previous or contemporary writers. In this respect he certainly compares favourably with Strype, whom we have not found so "colourless" (unless the word is intended to describe, not his opinions but his style) as Mr. Green led us to expect.

PART I

PURITANISM IN THE OLD WORLD

The Creative Causes of Puritanism

Memorable Events and Dates

Henry VIII. reigned 1509-1547
Luther . . . . . . born 1501 [1483], died 1546
„   nailed Theses to door of Church in Wittenberg 1517
Tyndale's Edition of the New Testament published 1525
Great Bible published 1539
Genevan Bible published . . 1560

Contents of Chapter I

Four main causes of Puritanism—The Reformation—The Bible—Tyndale's New Testament—The Great Bible—The Geneva Version—Foxe's *Book of Martyrs*—The spirit of freedom—Democracy—Puritanism advances to Separatism.

CHAPTER I

THE CREATIVE CAUSES OF PURITANISM

FOUR causes mainly contributed to the rise and spread of Puritanism, and ultimately of Independency—

First, The influence of the Reformation.

Second, The influence of the Bible.

Third, The growth of the spirit of freedom—liberty of conscience.

Fourth, The necessity of separation from the Church as by law established.

The influence of the Reformation.—The Reformation was essentially a religious movement, a revival of apostolic Christianity. At its outset it shared the fate of all great movements, and became mixed up with mean and more inglorious issues,—civil, political, and ecclesiastical,—and these tended in some measure to obscure its real character. It was so notably in England, where at first it seemed nothing better than a battle of kites and crows, a struggle between King and Pope for power and supremacy. Still the forces that directed it and bore it onward in its victorious course were moral and religious. Both Henry and Elizabeth found that they had raised a spirit which to some extent they were able to guide and to use, but which they were powerless to arrest. "They builded better than they knew." No one understood less than Elizabeth herself the real meaning of the Reformation, or cherished a more undisguised contempt for the zeal of the Reformers and the religious temper of the nation,—a force which she failed completely to estimate,—nevertheless to this more than to any other cause she owed the stability of her throne and the splendid success of her administration. It was the spirit of Puritanism which answered to her appeal when she invoked the aid of her people against Philip and Spain. The defeat of the Armada was the triumph of Protestantism, and, unwilling as she was to assume the title, Elizabeth became henceforth its recognised head. Yet Elizabeth had not only no sympathy with the doctrines of the Reformation, she resisted their introduction as tending to create dispeace in the Church and nation. In her judgment they emanated from the brain of a number of noisy and impracticable zealots.

It is sometimes said that up to the time of Elizabeth the English people as a whole were indifferent to the Reformation, and the change that came over them during her reign was due rather to the revulsion inspired by the atrocities of the previous reign than to any change of conviction in its favour. But this is an opinion that appears to rest upon no trustworthy basis. It is a saying of Burke that he did not know of any method of drawing up an indictment against a whole people. It was peculiarly difficult in those days to estimate the prevalence or gauge the strength of public sentiment. The fact is, the Reformation in England languished, so far as it did languish, for want of leaders. The people had no leaders to stir up their sympathies on its behalf, still less to kindle their enthusiasm. Imagine what would have been the fate of the Reformation in Germany without Luther, in Switzerland without Calvin, in Bohemia without Huss, in Scotland without Knox. In England, however, the Reformation had no prophet, no preacher, no herald deserving of the name. If Wyclif had been alive he might have stirred England from end to end as Luther stirred Germany with his trumpet-blast. But no Wyclif was forthcoming. Such prophet as it had was found in the person of Cranmer. He may not have been the despicable poltroon that Macaulay describes him, but he certainly had not the stuff of which heroes and Reformers are made. Hooper and Ridley, and Latimer and Taylor, and Jewel and Fisher and More were men of infinitely more grit and principle, but it was as much as they could do to resist the tyranny and encroachments of the papal power without leading a popular crusade in favour of the Reformation. It is no small proof of the growth of popular feeling in its favour, that notwithstanding Elizabeth's dislike of Protestantising zeal, and her determination, if possible, to stamp it out, yet the Reformation continued to grow and strengthen its hold upon the nation.

Puritanism was its offspring, and soon Elizabeth discovered that she had to reckon, not only with Reformers, but with Puritans. She imagined that persecution would exert a salutary repressive influence upon these mutinous spirits. As might have been expected, it produced the opposite effect. It made them more unbending and formidable than ever. It enlisted the sympathy of the people on their side. In the words of Macaulay: "It found them a sect, it made them a faction." "The power of the discontented sectaries was great. They were found in every rank, but they were strongest among the mercantile classes in the towns, and among the small proprietors in the country. Early in the reign of Elizabeth they began to return a majority of the House of Commons." "The same impulse which had carried millions away from the Church of Rome, continued to carry them forward in the same direction. As Catholics had become Protestants, Protestants became Puritans."

It was a great disappointment to Elizabeth that even her bishops could not be depended on to give effect to her policy, and their Protestant convictions were continually thwarting her. The persecutions of the previous reign had sent not a few Protestants into exile, and they had come back affected by, if not actually inoculated with, the tenets of Calvin and the Genevan form of worship. The leaven of their influence had spread among all sections of the nation. "The English Reformers were eager to go as far as their brethren on the Continent. They unanimously condemned as antichristian numerous dogmas and practices to which Henry had stubbornly adhered, and which Elizabeth reluctantly abandoned."

The influence of the Bible.—It would be difficult to discover a more striking coincidence, one that answers more perfectly to the idea of special overruling providence, than the occurrence of the Reformation and the invention of printing. There is no reason in the nature of things why the latter should have been delayed to the end of the fifteenth century. The art of writing was in use among the Egyptians long anterior to the time of Abraham, and it would seem as if the transition from writing to printing ought to have been effected without much difficulty, yet written characters had been in the possession of the world for five or six thousand years before printing was ever heard of. It was in the year 1474 that the first printing-press was erected in Westminster by William Caxton, an event which "did more for England than all the battles of kings or the statutes of Parliaments." The time was indeed most opportune. The introduction of printing synchronised with the Renaissance, that wonderful intellectual awakening which has caused the fifteenth century to be styled the "age of discovery of the world and of man." As might have been expected, it gave to the New Learning a mighty impulse. It contributed to the spread of knowledge through all sections of society, and the clergy, who had hitherto kept the key of knowledge in their own hands, at the beginning of the fifteenth century found that the laity were in no wise inferior to them in this respect. At the same time it put into the hand of those who attacked the abuses and corruptions of the Church a most formidable weapon, which they were not slow to use. This helped the cause of the Reformation immensely. But undoubtedly the chief service which printing rendered to the cause of truth and liberty was the multiplying of copies of the Bible. Until the reign of Henry VIII. the Bible had existed only in manuscript form. This was the translation (a translation of a translation, be it remembered) of Wyclif. After the death of Wyclif and the plague of Lollardism had been stamped out, or supposed to have been stamped out, by the energy and vigilance of the Popish party, the use of the Bible was rigidly proscribed, and according to a statute of Henry v. it was enacted that all who read the Scriptures in their native tongue should forfeit land, cattle, life, goods, they and their heirs for ever.

It was in the year 1525 that William Tyndale brought out his edition of the New Testament. His version of the Scriptures and reprint of the tracts of Wyclif, though printed in Germany, soon found their way into England. The universities of Oxford and Cambridge, where the New Learning had established itself and been the means of producing a widespread intellectual and religious awakening, became the seed-plot of this new heresy, and here it found a congenial and fruitful nidus.

The dream of Erasmus was at last realised. A translation of the Bible had appeared which the weaver might repeat at his shuttle and the ploughman might intone at the plough. The edition of 1540 was called the Great Bible, and there was prefixed to it a preface by Archbishop Cranmer; and from this circumstance the Great Bible is often, but improperly, called Cranmer's Bible. "This is the Byble apoynted to the use of the churches." This Bible was sold at 13s. 4d., " unless Cromwell would give the printers exclusive privileges, when it might be sold for 10s." This would represent a much larger sum in those days than in ours—about the value of £6. "The story of the supremacy," says Mr. Green, " was graven in its very title-page. The new foundation of religious truth was to be regarded throughout England as a gift, not from the Church but from the King. It is Henry on his throne who gives the sacred volume to Cranmer, ere Cranmer and Cromwell can distribute it to the throng of priests and laymen below. The Bible was formally adopted as the basis of English faith." A copy of Coverdale's translation was chained to a desk or pillar in every cathedral and parish church. The joy of the common people knew no bounds. Ability to read was looked upon as the most enviable of acquisitions, and knots of people stood all day long to hear read to them in their own tongue the wonderful works of God.[1] The next stage in the history of the English Bible was the appearance, in 1550, of the celebrated Genevan version, which became the household Bible of the English middle classes for at least two generations. This was mainly the work of the refugees who were driven from the kingdom by the Marian persecution and settled at Geneva, where they adopted the faith of Calvin and the Genevan mode of worship. It contained a marginal commentary which proved a great attraction to the Puritans. For nearly a hundred years it held the field in the estimation of the

[1] "It was wonderful," says Foxe the Martyrologist, "to see with what joy this book of God was received, not only among the learneder sort, and those that were noted for lovers of the Reformation, but generally all England over, among all the vulgar and common people; and with what greediness God's word was read, and what resort to places where the reading of it was. Everybody that could bought the book, or busily read it, or got others to read it to them if they could not themselves, and divers more elderly people learned to read on purpose; and even little boys flocked among the rest to hear portions of the Holy Scripture read."

English people, and this notwithstanding the fact that the Puritan theology, or, speaking more strictly, the theology of Geneva, was most conspicuous in its anotations. "So earnestly," says Strype, "did the people of the nation thirst in those days after the knowledge of the Scriptures, that the first impression was soon sold off."

The influence of the Bible and the revolution it effected in the mind and character of the English people have been thus eloquently described by Mr. Green: "No greater moral change ever passed over the nation than passed over England during the years which parted the middle of the reign of Elizabeth from the meeting of the Long Parliament. England became the people of a book, and that book was the Bible. It was, as yet, the one English book which was familiar to every Englishman; it was read at churches and read at home, and everywhere its words, as they fell on ears which custom had not deadened to their force and beauty, kindled a startling enthusiasm."[1]

Foxe's Book of Martyrs.—Next only to the Bible, in the influence it exercised upon the minds of the English people, was that moving and picturesque narrative of the sufferings of the martyrs which, despite its errors and prejudices, has done more, perhaps, for the cause of Protestantism than any other book that ever was written. By Elizabeth's own order this book was elevated to the dignity of being placed along with the

[1] See whole of this eloquent passage in "Puritan England," Green's *Short History of the English People*, pp. 447–9.

Bible, Homilies, and Prayer-Book, in all the colleges and chapels throughout the kingdom. It passed naturally into every English household, and its popularity was such that no other book has been able to vie with it—with the exception of the *Pilgrim's Progress*. The circulation of this book, and the avidity with which it was read by all classes of the people, not only helped to create an intense Protestant sentiment, it did much also to lodge in their minds the Puritan conception of religion, and to erect this as the strongest of all bulwarks against the encroachments and pretensions of papal power. Foxe was himself a Puritan, and when required by Archbishop Parker to subscribe to the Canons of the Church of England, he evinced his Puritan loyalty to the Scriptures by holding up a Greek Testament and exclaiming: "To this will I subscribe."

Disfigured as his great work must be judged to be, both by errors and the spirit of intolerance, it is pleasant to remember that he intervened in the cause of the hated and despised Anabaptists, and petitioned the Queen, though unsuccessfully, to spare the lives of two of them. He hated impartially *all* religious persecution, in this respect rising far above his age and contemporary Protestant convictions.

The growth of the spirit of freedom — Liberty of conscience. — " The real value of the religious revolution of the sixteenth century to mankind," says Mr. Green, " lay not in its substitution of one creed for another, but in the new spirit of inquiry, the new freedom of thought and of discussion which was awakened during the process of change." The immediate effect of the Reformation in England, as Macaulay has pointed out, was by no means favourable to political liberty. It only deposed the papal system to set up its worst tyranny afresh in the person of King and Prelate. The yoke of Protestantism promised to be just as intolerable as that of the Church of Rome, nay, as being nearer the base of its operations, more galling and inimical to individual freedom. The system of Henry VIII. has been described as Popery without the Pope; and had the Reformation stopped at the point to which it was carried by means of the breach with Rome, it would have been, not a forward, but a retrograde movement. But it could not stop at that point. It is the inevitable result of any great disruption such as that which had taken place in England and Europe, that forces and influences are let loose and brought into play which those who are responsible for its initiation are unable to guide and powerless to control. It is like a landslip, the effects of which are seen, not only in the immediate dislodgment of a vast quantity of earth, but in a loosening of the soil which extends far beyond the scene of the primal catastrophe. The earthquake which releases Paul and Silas, throws down for others besides apostles the walls of the prison-house. Religious freedom is never long divorced from civil and political liberty.[1] It was the stirring of men's minds under the preaching of Wyclif that was the real if not the proximate cause of the peasants' outbreak in 1381 and the insurrection under Wat Tyler. Wyclif

---

[1] "Oh, if we could but exercise wisdom to gain civil liberty—religion would follow!"—*Cromwell's Letters and Speeches*.

himself was as guiltless of the revolt of the peasantry as was Luther of the Peasant War in Germany, or of the reign of the Anabaptists. Nevertheless, neither of these Reformers could screen themselves from the responsibility which, indirectly at least, attached to their own acts and teaching. They both of them raised a spirit they were not able to lay, and the people who imbibed their doctrines insisted on carrying them to their extreme, and, as they deemed, their only logical conclusion. The same thing is illustrated in the progress of the Reformation. The genius of liberty—if we may use the impersonation—outran the zeal of its defenders, even its most strenuous upholders, and chiding their lagging pace seemed to mock their timorous mistrust. Not even the most advanced and intrepid Reformers, in England at least, realised the full consequences of their own action. Terrified by their own boldness, they were ever harking back like men venturing on quicksands or skating on thin ice, and only by feeling their way gradually could they gain confidence to proceed. In our age, experience of the value of liberty has to a large extent conquered the instinct of conservatism, but in the age of the Reformation men had no such experience. It is not surprising, therefore, that even the most ardent lovers of liberty should sometimes falter in their testimony for it. In the course of our inquiry we shall see how far the Puritans themselves fell short of acting with perfect loyalty to their own principles, and how long it took them to learn the lesson of religious toleration. Like the disciples of old, "as they followed they were afraid"; but they followed nevertheless, and they came out at length into a wealthy land.

Democracy the outcome of Puritanism.—If the newly awakened spirit of freedom contributed, as undoubtedly it did, to the rise and growth of Puritanism, Puritanism in its turn led to the establishment of Democracy, and this not by a series of successive steps, but as it were, *per saltum*, by a single bound. "The principle of the sovereignty of the people," says Dr. Borgeaud in his admirable book, *The Rise of Modern Democracy in Old and New England*,[1] "inalienable and imprescriptible, and its realisation in the modern State, belong peculiarly to the Reformation." "Calvinism, in spite of the aristocratic character which it temporarily assumed, meant democracy in Church government. It meant more than that, for its aim was to make society in all its parts conform to a religious ideal."[2] This was inevitable on the part of men adopting the Bible as their statute-book, and rejecting all authority which threatened to come into collision with this.

"We believe the word of God contained in the Old and New Testaments to be a perfect rule of faith and manners; that it ought to be read and known by all people; and that the authority of it exceeds all authority, not of the Pope only, but of the Church also, and of Councils, Fathers, men, and angels.

"We condemn as a tyrannous yoke whatsoever men have set up of their own invention, to make articles of faith, and the binding of men's consciences by their laws and institutions."[3]

---

[1] P. 7.   [2] Preface of same work, ix.
[3] Confession of Faith signed by those taking part in the Prophesyings in 1571. See Neal's *History of the Puritans*, vol. i. p. 223.

It does not follow that either Reformers or Puritans bent their energies consciously and of set purpose to the setting up of Democracy. In respect of this they were at first blind and unconscious instruments. "The early Puritans had no political views; they were completely absorbed by religious feeling."[1] It was this religious feeling and principle which drove them into constitution-making on popular democratic lines. The Church covenant which they formed among themselves strictly for a religious purpose, became the basis of the political society which they founded. Hence, as Dr. Borgeaud has it—"Modern Democracy is the child of the Reformation, not of the Reformers." "Puritanism, believing itself quick with the seed of religious liberty, laid, without knowing it, the egg of Democracy."[2]

The necessity of separation from the Church as by law established.— The revolt against the papal power led naturally to revolt against popery in Priest or King, in other words, to the creation of what we now call Protestantism. Protestantism advanced to Puritanism, and Puritanism advanced to Separatism. The process by which this was brought about forms the subject of this work, and to a large extent constitutes its *raison d'être*; but it will not be inappropriate at this point just to indicate in a few words how these three things came into line, and became related as cause and effect. The Protestant refugees who

---

[1] *The Rise of Modern Democracy*, p. 12.
[2] J. Russell Lowell's *Among my Books: New England Two Centuries Ago*, p. 227.

had been driven from this country by the relentless cruelty of Mary had found a home in Germany and Switzerland, and there they had learnt to prize the simple worship and the free democratic polity which prevailed and found doughty champions and eloquent expounders in Geneva, Zurich, and Strasburg. They returned home after the accession of Elizabeth, to find their hopes in regard to the Reformation violently frustrated. The lump was still unleavened—the old leaven of papistical corruption still untaken away. The temper of Elizabeth, if not as violent as that of her sister, was as unyielding. She was determined to make her profit out of the Reformation by resisting all further changes, and by making it subordinate to her own views and her own personal authority. Like her father before her, her aim was to establish Popery without the Pope. She agreed with Henry IV. that a kingdom was well worth a Mass. Against the protests of her bishops she retained an altar, crucifix, and lighted candles in her own private chapel.[1] With the zeal of the Reformers she had no sympathy whatever, and never lost an opportunity of pouring cold water upon it. The bigotry of the Protestant as much as the superstition of the Romanist excited her ridicule and her scorn. She interrupted the preacher who spoke disparagingly of the sign of the cross, disapproved of the marriage of the clergy, and threatened to unfrock the prelates that dared to resist her imperious demands. Elizabeth did nothing to further the reformation of the

[1] It was owing to her influence that the words, "From the tyranny of the Bishop of Rome and all his detestable enormities," were struck out of the Litany.

English Church, rather did everything to retard it. It is not a little remarkable that that reformation reached its highest point, not during her reign, but at the close of the reign of Edward VI., and more remarkable still, *it has never since advanced beyond this point.* There is abundant evidence to show that it stopped at this point, not because in the judgment of the Reformers it had gone far enough, but because their efforts were unavailing in the face of the opposition which they provoked.

Of that opposition Elizabeth was the heart and soul.—Her attitude in regard to the warring religious factions, her determination to side neither with Catholics nor with Protestants (though her attitude in regard to the former can hardly be called neutral), and not to allow the peace of the nation to be broken up by either, this is often pointed to as a striking proof of her astuteness and far-sightedness. Mr. Gladstone[1] says: " Apart from any ritualistic and theological leanings of the Queen, she did what the national safety and unity evidently required. Elizabeth admitted the Protestant claim in the gross, but admitted it with serious discounts. Yet these discounts were adjusted with extraordinary skill."

Mr. Green[2] says she forced on the warring religions a sort of armed truce, and though " no woman ever lived who was so totally destitute of the sentiment of religion," this only qualified her the better—if we understand him

[1] *Contemporary Review*, November 1888, p. 767.
[2] Green's *History of the English People*, vol. ii. pp. 395, 397.

aright—for reducing and guarding against the ill effects and danger arising from the religious zeal of others. We confess we have no faith in this sinister explanation of the cleverness of Elizabeth. As an attempt to exalt her intellect at the expense of her principles, it is a failure. Her policy, we hold, was shaped partly by the exigencies of her position, but mainly by her ungovernable aversion to all forms of religious zeal, and by her determination to resist at all cost any further changes in the constitution and ritual of the Church. By putting down her foot firmly at this juncture, she found it possible to reduce all the warring religious elements to a more or less passive condition. It was a rough and ready way of " settling " without " healing " the differences of the nation, but it was effectual for the time, and the success which attended it (not at all surprising under the circumstances) has led historians to ascribe to the self-willed and irreligious Queen a judgment and sagacity far beyond her desert.[1]

Her policy towards the Puritans was from first to last a huge blunder, and for the future of the nation was rife with disastrous consequences. It created and aggravated the evil it was intended to arrest. "One thing was evident, that the Puritan malcontents were growing every day more numerous, more determined, and more likely to win over the generality of those who sincerely favoured the Protestant cause."[2] Any casual observer might have seen that between their growing numbers and strength,

---

[1] Not all historians, however. See Hallam's *Constitutional History* in loco.

[2] *Ibid.* vol. i. p. 242.

and the severities which were directed against them, there was no mere temporary or accidental connection; but Elizabeth was blinded, and her hatred of the Puritans made her their ruthless and uncompromising oppressor.

Mr. Green says Elizabeth was a persecutor, but she was the first English ruler who felt the charge of religious persecution to be a stigma on her rule. Perhaps so, but in her dealings with the Puritans there is not much evidence of that feeling. After the manner of her successor she was at no pains to dissemble her determination to "make them conform," or "harry" them by all the means which the High Commission and Star Chamber could place at her command.[1]

We cannot give Elizabeth credit for any enlightened broad-minded policy either towards Roman recusants or Puritan separatists. It was a policy shaped by her own personal idiosyncrasies and virulent antipathies, and though she herself rode triumphantly over the difficulties and dangers which grew out of it, she left these as a bitter legacy to her successors and to the nation.[2] Her policy had certainly the merit of being "thorough," anticipating in this respect the policy of Laud and Strafford, and it provoked a resistance as thorough and unbending. It soon became clear to the Puritans and to

---

[1] Elizabeth told the French ambassador "that she would maintain the religion she was crowned in; and would suppress the papistical religion, that it should not *grow*; but that she would *root out* Puritanism and the favourers thereof."—Strype's *Annals*.

[2] See Introduction, p. xxv, of *Select Statutes and other Constitutional Documents illustrative of the reigns of Elizabeth and James I.*, edited by Professor Prothero.

all who sympathised with them that no freedom was to be enjoyed inside the Church which had the Queen as its governor, and if their consciences were to find relief it must be by seceding and separating from it. "We must obey God rather than man," said these successors of the apostles, and from the hour that banner was unfurled the real struggle for religious liberty began.

The Church of England

Memorable Events and Dates

Augustine, first Archbishop of Canterbury, landed with band of monks in Kent 597
Henry declared Supreme Head of the Church of England 1534
Thomas Cranmer created Archbishop of Canterbury and Primate of all England 1533

Contents of Chapter II

The Church of Rome in England—Augustine—England the "Pope's farm"—The Church of England—Theory of Continuity—The right of separation implied in Reformation—Note on Schism—Notes on Continuity of the Church.

CHAPTER II

THE CHURCH OF ENGLAND

THE Church of England was such a prime constitutive factor in the making of Puritanism, that it is impossible to understand the genesis and character of the latter without some acquaintance with the position and attitude of the former.

Now we shall go wrong at the outset in pursuing this branch of inquiry unless we bear in mind a distinction which is often forgotten, but which is of the first importance—the distinction between the Church *of* England and the Church *in* England. There was no Church *of* England till the reign of Henry VIII. The Church *in* England existed from the time that Augustine, with his band of monks, landed, in 597, on the shore of Kent, and planted the Christian faith in the southern part of the kingdom. The northern part of the kingdom was converted by Scoto-Irish missionaries. Thus paganism was conquered by Christianity as represented by the Roman Catholic Church. But neither then, nor at any other period up to the time of the Reformation, could the Church thus constituted be called the Church *of* England. The only term that could justly describe it was **the Church of Rome in England**; for though both portions united and became one Church, they united by submitting to the Roman primacy, thus becoming an organic portion of the one great Western Church. The papal character of the pre-Reformation Church has been grudgingly admitted by Church historians, by some it has been called in question, but the evidence by which it is substantiated is irresistible.

Augustine, the first Primate of Canterbury, was a missionary sent from Rome by Pope Gregory the Great. Wilfrid, the leader of the Scoto-Irish converts in the north, obtained his episcopal authority from Rome. The same is true of Theodore, the next Primate of Canterbury, who may be regarded as the organiser of the parish system, the first to unify the sees that were already created, and group them round the common centre of Canterbury.

Notwithstanding assertions often made to the contrary, it is easily demonstrable that England was not less papal, but more papal, than any other part of Europe. According to Milman, it was a common saying in the reign of Henry III. that "England was the Pope's farm." And according to Bishop Stubbs, "liberal tribute" began to be paid to Rome from the end of the eighth century; and Peter's pence, of which this was probably the origin, continued to be paid to Rome to the time of Henry VIII.[1]

The Church of England, as distinguished from the Church of Rome, did not come into existence until the reign of Henry VIII. It originated in the quarrel of Henry with the Pope, who refused to sanction his divorce

[1] Stubbs' *Constitutional History of England*, vol. i. pp. 250, 251.

from Katherine of Arragon. This led to the final rupture with Rome, and the casting off of the Pope's authority. There seems no reason to doubt that if, instead of thwarting the King in his design, he had been favourable and accessory to it, there would have been no breach with Rome, or such breach would have been postponed till fresh provocation had made her yoke no longer able to be endured.

Theory of continuity.—Church historians are greatly enamoured of the theory of a national Church, which has existed in unbroken continuity from the time that Augustine, with his monks, landed upon the isle of Thanet. The theory has been broached again and again. As stated by a popular clergyman—the Rev. W. Page Roberts—in a volume of sermons, entitled, *Reasonable Service*, p. 151, it has at least the merit of clearness. "Historically," he says, "the Church of England is the very first Church which was set up in this country. . . . There have been changes in it, corruptions in it, reformations in it, but still it is the Church which was founded by Christian Missionaries twelve hundred years ago."

This fallacy of unbroken continuity is so demonstrably transparent, that the wonder is it should impose upon any student of history; yet it is continually cropping up, not only in histories written from an Episcopalian point of view, but in statements where one might reasonably suppose it would be jealously extruded. It crops up even in the sober annals of Presbyterianism. It would seem as if no "common denominator" could be discovered between the "Romanist priesthood" and the "Protestant ministry" as construed by the spirit of Presbyterianism.

The anxiety of the latter to free itself from "the tyranny of the Bishop of Rome and all his detestable enormities," would seem to be an effectual restraint on any disposition to identify them even in the initial period of their history. Yet in his excellent sketch of the Church of Scotland Dr. M'Adam Muir says: "Despite the convulsions with which it was accompanied, the continuity of the Church was not broken by the Reformation." The Reformers did not dream of setting up a "new Church." The "purification of the Temple" was their sole object.[1]

It would be difficult to imagine a more perfect *reductio ad absurdum* of the theory of continuity. It reminds us of the fabled ship of antiquity which, in the course of its voyage, was so often repaired, that at length no part of the original material remained. On this theory the boy who refused to part with his knife because it had been handed down to him by his great-grandfather, though the haft and the blades had been all of them renewed, had good reason for clinging to it. By this method of reasoning the Parsee, the Hindoo, and the Mohammedan, who has embraced Christianity, might try and persuade himself that he had not broken with the faith of his fathers— that, in fact, he has only taken the step that he has taken

---

[1] "The new Church which he (Henry VIII.) had created could as little pretend to be the continuation of, and identical with, the old English Church, as might a statue of Socrates, whereon a head of Alcibiades had been set, do duty as the statue of the philosopher." —*Addresses on Historical and Literary Subjects*, by J. Ignatius von Döllinger, *D.D.*, p. 65.

in order to become a better Parsee, a better Hindoo, a better Mohammedan.

"The Reformers did not dream of setting up a new Church"—whatever they dreamed, or aimed at doing, they certainly succeeded in setting up a Church as different from, and as diametrically opposed to, the Church which it supplanted, as Christianity is opposed to Hindooism. They vehemently denounced the old Church as representing the very spirit of Antichrist. The purification of the temple was attained in no other way than by setting up a new temple; and had not the glory of the latter eclipsed that of the former, the condition of both Scotland and England had been indeed dark and deplorable![1]

The right of separation or schism.—No true Protestant can pretend to doubt that in whatever way the breach with Rome was effected and the independence of the Church achieved, the gain which the Reformation brought to the Church and nation, as well as to the cause of truth and liberty, was beyond all computation. Darkness covered the earth and gross darkness the people, and to Luther chiefly—though others are associated with him in this proud distinction—it was given to speak the word—"Let there be light: and there was light." Luther's "doctrine of Christian liberty and of the common universal priesthood," as Dr. Döllinger

[1] Dr. Muir is apparently content to follow his authorities without exercising his independent judgment. He quotes Dr. Story: "The Baptism and Ordination of the unreformed Church were alike held as valid. The old order changeth, yielding place to new, but there is no absolute disruption between the two—*Out of the Romanist priesthood emerges the Protestant ministry.*"

calls it, was bound, wherever it was embraced, to break the yoke which Rome had forged for the enslavement of the mind and conscience of men. It was this doctrine which created the strength and justification of the Protestant revolt against the Papacy. But Protestantism was only able to embody it partially in its own system and formularies. It found sovereign expression in the Puritan contention, and to its insistence upon this doctrine, and its unshrinking application of it, must be traced the beginning of the cleft between Puritanism and the Church.

The Reformation carried with it implications and conclusions which, however objectionable they might seem to the ruling powers, were logically and morally necessitated—so the Puritans believed—by the breach which had been made with Rome, and on grounds by which this schism could alone be justified. The Reformation settlement was at best a compromise, the result of statecraft and political expediency, and could not be expected to satisfy the aspirations of men who had dreamed a dream of the fair City of God, and of the Church as the pure and spotless Bride of His Son.

NOTE ON SCHISM

The word schism has acquired a somewhat sinister meaning. The "*sin of schism*" is a very favourite expression among a certain class of ecclesiastics, and the opprobrium which is supposed to attach to schism in any form or shape is very terrible. The sin of schism is specially visited by Anglican writers upon those who separate from the Established Church of the nation; and their ingenuity has been strained not a little in order to show that there exists no parallel between the position of the Protestant Church of England in separating from the Church of Rome, and that of the Puritan Separatists in seceding from the Church of England.[1]

In "The Anglican Brief against the Roman Claims," by the Rev. Thomas Moore and the Rev. Arthur Brinckmann, the question is asked—Are there any grounds for the argument frequently used by Nonconformists to justify their separation from the Church, which is to the effect, that their separation from the Church of England is no more than the Church of England's separation from the Church of Rome?

To this the answer is given—

There are no grounds for it whatever. The statement is, in fact, untrue. There is no resemblance between the two cases. The Church of England in 1534 did not dissent nor separate herself from the historical Church of the country. She simply threw off a foreign thraldom, liberated herself from foreign tyranny, and asserted and resumed her historical freedom and her independence of the usurped supremacy of Rome. The Church of England did not, in so doing, create a new Church and a new ministry. But the case of the Nonconformists is a very different one. They dissent from, and separate themselves from, the historic Church of the kingdom. They form new religious bodies, create new ministries, and establish antagonistic centres of worship.

What these unsupported assertions come to as to the Church of England being the ancient historic Church of the kingdom we have already seen, and shall probably be able to see better by and by. It is obvious at a glance that this attempt to disprove the analogy between the two acts of separation is a mere juggling with words. Suppose we say—what is nothing but the literal truth—that the Nonconformists threw off the thraldom of the Church of England, liberated themselves from its tyranny, and resumed the ancient

---

[1] The shifts, indeed, to which Anglican writers are driven in order to get rid of the imputation of "schism" are strange and extreme. "The attitude of our Church at the Reformation cannot indeed be too clearly or too frequently called to mind. It was not a breach or a schism that was intended. It was simply *a protest*. . . . The former of these two courses (the course denoted by the word protest) was chosen by the Church of England in the sixteenth century; the latter (that denoted by the word schism) by the Anabaptists and other sectaries."—Curteis' Bampton Lecture on *Dissent in its Relation to the Church of England*, p. 188. Could anything be more inconsequential?

independence which had been bequeathed to them by our Lord and His apostles—what becomes of the alleged difference between them?

Certainly, if the Church of England did not create a new Church and a new ministry when she broke with the Church of Rome, then the Nonconformists did not create a new Church and a new ministry when they broke off from the Church of England.

The following words from the *Spectator* newspaper, in reply to a letter from a correspondent on "Schism and the English Reformation," should carry some weight upon this question. "The English Church broke off doctrinally from Rome as well as politically. We do not understand the dread felt of the word 'schism' where there is no fear of the thing. If Rome were wrong both politically and doctrinally, then the schism was right, but it was schism all the same. If Rome were right, then the schism was wrong; but whether right or wrong, the breaking off from Rome was schism."— ED. *Spectator*, Dec. 24, 1892.

NOTES ON CONTINUITY OF THE CHURCH

We are well aware that the theory of the identity of the post-Reformation and pre-Reformation Church can plead the sanction and authority of not a few eminent names—W. E. Gladstone, the historian Freeman, Dean Hook, J. A. Blunt, and a host of Anglican writers; but no authority and no consensus of authority can avail to establish what is so manifestly opposed to the logic of fact and evidence.

Most conclusively we think Mr. Child has shown, in his impartial and careful study of *Church and State under the Tudors*,[1] that there was not and could not, from the nature of the then existing circumstances, be anything that answered to the designation of a national Church up to the time of the breach with Rome under Henry VIII. The series of measures culminating in the Act of Appeals and the Act of Supremacy, which were passed at the instance of Henry,

---

[1] *Church and State under the Tudors*, by Gilbert W. Child, M.A., Exeter College, Oxford (Longmans, Green, & Co.). A most valuable work, based upon "State papers, ambassadors' letters, and other original documents which were formerly too little known"— altogether indispensable to the careful and impartial study of this period.

made the Church in England a national Church. But at the same time that it became national it became schismatical, for then and there it was cast off and excommunicated by the Church of Rome.

"It was just because the Church in England was not in truth the Church of England, but was an organic portion of the one great Western Church . . . that it was enabled to occupy the position of independence, and sometimes almost of supremacy, in which we find it. . . . Had the Church been in truth the Church of England, it would have been a mere *imperium in imperio*, and would never have been able to hold its own generation after generation and century after century against the State, often represented by powerful and able monarchs, such as Henry II. or Edward III. It was just because it was not the Church of England, but a mere extension into England of the powerful Western Church, having its rights and its interests and its officers in every nation, and its independent seat of empire at Rome, and thus enabled to enlist one nation against another, or a nation against its own rulers, that it became in a greater or less degree, and for periods varying in different countries, independent of the State and a rival of the State." [1]

"It is difficult to study the actual facts of sixteenth-century history, putting apart preconceived ecclesiastical theories, without arriving at the conclusion that the English National Church was as completely the creation of Henry VIII., Edward's Council, and Elizabeth, as Saxon Protestantism was of Luther, or Swiss of Calvin or of Zwingle.[2] . . . A fair consideration of the actual facts of the Tudor history serves further to show that a theory like that which prevails so widely at present—which represents the English Church in any other light than that of one (though it may, perhaps, be admitted, the greatest and the most dignified) of the many Protestant Churches which arose in the sixteenth century—is a novelty which took its very earliest rise some half-century or more after the separation from Rome, as a direct consequence of Elizabeth's determination to give no quarter to the earlier Puritans, and which made little or no progress for another half-century still." [3]

Thus we see that the Church in England was in every sense a daughter of the Church of Rome. And notwithstanding the great

---

[1] See pp. 10, 11.   [2] P. 272.   [3] Pp. 273, 274.

Those who wish to see how this view of the Church of England appears to the present accredited organs of the High Church party, will do well to consult an article in the *Contemporary Review*, November 1892, by Mr. Child.

change she underwent at the time of the Reformation, she continued to bear, and still bears, the marks of the lineage from which she sprang. Her orders, her offices, and her ritual are modelled upon those of the Romish Church, though the more objectionable, and what were deemed distinctively popish, elements have been drastically expunged. As Macaulay says, she copied the Roman Catholic forms of prayer. "Utterly rejecting the doctrine of transubstantiation, and condemning as idolatrous all adoration paid to the sacramental bread and wine, she yet, to the disgust of the Puritan, required her children to receive the memorials of divine love meekly kneeling upon their knees. Discarding many rich vestments which surrounded the altars of the ancient faith, she yet retained to the horror of weak minds a robe of white linen, typical of the purity which belonged to her as the mystical spouse of Christ. Discarding a crowd of pantomimic gestures, which in the Roman Catholic worship are substituted for intelligible words, she yet shocked many rigid Protestants by marking the infant just sprinkled from the font with the sign of the cross. . . . The Church of England, though she asked for the intercession of no created being, still set apart days for the commemoration of some who had done and suffered great things for the faith. She retained confirmation and ordination as edifying rites; but she degraded them from the rank of sacraments. Shrift was no part of her system. Yet she gently invited the dying penitent to confess his sins to a divine, and empowered her ministers to soothe the departing soul by an absolution which breathes the very spirit of the old religion."[1]

---

[1] Macaulay's *History of England*, vol. i. pp. 53-4; see *Zurich Letters* Laurence Humphrey and Thomas Sampson to Henry Bullinger, "Some blemishes which still attach to the Church of England." "After the Council of Trent had effected such considerable reforms in the Catholic discipline, it seemed a sort of reproach to the Protestant Church of England that she retained all the dispensations, the exemptions, the pluralities, which had been deemed the peculiar corruptions of the worst times of Popery."—Hallam's *Const. History*, vol. i. p. 194.

In his *Life of Grindal*, p. 542, Strype gives a list of dispensations and their prices.

The Rise of Puritanism in England

MEMORABLE EVENTS AND DATES

Edward VI. reigned 1547-1553
Mary reigned 1553-1558
Elizabeth reigned 1558-1603
Acts of Supremacy and Uniformity passed 1559
Puritan Party arose in England . . 1556

CONTENTS OF CHAPTER III

Puritanism originated not in England but in Holland—John Hooper, first Puritan Confessor—Made Bishop of Gloucester—Martyrdom of Hooper—Puritanism and Anglicanism—Jewel—Orders, non-Episcopal—Macaulay on Orders—Strype—Dr. Hammond — Cosin — Bacon — Bishop Barlow — Archbishop Parker — Elizabeth and the Puritans—Act of Supremacy—Act of Uniformity—Vestments Controversy—Sacerdotal and non-Sacerdotal conceptions—Resistance to Vestments Convocation—Suspension of Clergy—Hallam's Judgment—Parker's *Advertisements*.

CHAPTER III

THE RISE OF PURITANISM IN ENGLAND

IT is a common impression that Puritanism is a growth that first sprang upon British soil—that, from the seed sown by the early Protestant Reformers, it first pushed its way into the light of day during the reign of Elizabeth, or during the closing years of the reign of her sister Mary. This, however, is an error. Its origin must be sought at a much earlier period than this, and in a country relatively smaller and historically much less important. It was in HOLLAND or the NETHERLANDS that Puritanism first sprang and took root. But of this we shall have occasion to speak presently,[1] and mention it here only as a caveat to prevent any premature conclusion being drawn as to its British origin.

John Hooper, bishop of Gloucester, may be regarded as the father and founder of English Puritanism. Canon Perry speaks of him as the "first Puritan confessor." He was the first Nonconformist, though his nonconformity did not lead him to cross the Rubicon of separation from the Church of England. He had been a Cistercian monk, but, embracing the principles of the

[1] See p. 203.

Reformation, he advocated them with such zeal that it became unsafe for him to remain in his own country. This was in the closing years of the reign of Henry VIII. Hooper fled to Switzerland, and settled down in Zurich, where, under the influence of Bullinger, his Puritan leanings became developed and strongly confirmed. On the accession of Edward VI. he returned to England, and, with the exception of Latimer, became the most popular preacher of his day. He was the first champion of the cause of religious liberty after the Reformation, and stood alone amongst the English Protestants of his age in the clearness with which he grasped the doctrine of the independence of the Church and the spirituality of the kingdom of Christ. "As touching," he says, "the superior powers of earth, it is not unknown to all of them who have readen and marked the Scripture, that it appertaineth nothing unto their office to make any law to govern the conscience of their subjects in religion. . . . Christ's kingdom is a spiritual one. In this neither King nor Pope may govern. Christ alone is the Governor of His Church, and the only lawgiver."[1] Preaching before the King, he called for the restoration of the primitive Church, and demanded the abolition of all vestments, crosses, and altars.

King Edward conceived a great liking for this honest and brave man. He was offered the bishopric of Gloucester, and, though willing to accept the appointment, he "scrupled the vestments," and refused to take the oath— "So help me God and all the saints." A change in the wording of the latter relieved his conscience, but

[1] *Early Writings of Bishop Hooper*, p. 280 (Parker Society, 1843).

he still stood out against the "old symbolising popish garments." Persisting in his *nolo episcopari*, the King and his governing prelates sought to enforce his compliance, "a usage which the doctor," says Neal, "thought very severe. To miss his promotion was no disappointment, but to be persecuted about clothes by men of the same faith as himself, and to lose his liberty because he would not be a bishop — this was possibly more than he well understood." He consulted with the continental Reformers, who urged upon him to comply, but could not succeed in removing his scruples; and being still contumacious, he was committed to the Fleet Prison. At length, yielding to the remonstrance and entreaties of his friends, he consented to wear the vestments at his consecration, on condition that he might dispense with them at other times, and was accordingly made Bishop of Gloucester in March 1551. Here, for four years, preaching sometimes two or three times a day to crowds of people who hungered for the word of Life, he laboured in season and out of season "in the faithful discharge of every branch of his episcopal character, even beyond his strength, and was himself a pattern of what he taught to others."

When the reign of persecution commenced under Queen Mary, Hooper was one of its first victims. He was burnt at Gloucester on 9th February 1555, suffering torture of the most aggravated and horrible description. With the prayer on his lips, "Lord Jesus, receive my spirit," died the first martyr of the Reformation in England, the forerunner and champion of English Puritanism.

Puritanism and Anglicanism.—But Hooper was by no means singular in his Puritanism. Many of Elizabeth's first bishops were Puritans—Tyndale, Coverdale, Jewel, Barlow, and Grindal; while Cranmer, Latimer, and Ridley became more and more Puritan as their Protestant sympathies and convictions became more pronounced. A large number of them would gladly have dispensed with Episcopacy; they disliked exceedingly the ceremonies which were associated with it, and which reminded them only too forcibly of the ceremonies of the Church of Rome. Jewel, bishop of Salisbury, in a letter to Peter Martyr, describes the worship which the Queen was establishing as such as had often moved their ridicule:[1] "The scenic apparatus of divine worship is now under agitation, and those very things which you and I have so often laughed at are now seriously and solemnly entertained by certain persons (for we are not consulted), as if the Christian religion could not exist without something tawdry." The only excuse Jewel can find for it was the extreme ignorance of the clergy, who were "no better than mere logs of wood, without talent, learning, or morality." They were of no use as ministers of a Protestant Church, and to cast them out would have been to convert them into enemies, so they resolved, says Jewel, "to commend them to the people by a comical dress. . . . Since they cannot obtain influence in a proper way, they seek to occupy the eyes of the multitude with these ridiculous trifles."

---

[1] Jewel's *Letters* are well worth reading for their outspokenness, and for the light which they shed upon this period.

Orders—Non-Episcopal valid.—None of the prelates of the Church appear to have had at first any decided leanings to Episcopacy; it was only after a time that these leanings became very manifest, and when their alliance with the Court made it highly useful and expedient. "The founders of the Anglican Church," says Macaulay, "had retained Episcopacy as an ancient, a decent, and a convenient ecclesiastical polity, but had not declared that form of church government to be of divine institution. We have already seen how low an estimate Cranmer had formed of the office of a bishop. In the reign of Elizabeth, Jewel, Cooper, Whitgift, and other eminent doctors defended prelacy as innocent, as useful, as what the State might lawfully establish; as what, when established by the State, was entitled to the respect of every citizen. But they never denied that a Christian community without a bishop might be a pure Church.[1] On the con-

---

[1] Whitgift was not likely to gratuitously disparage his own order; yet in a letter to Sir Francis Knollys, which Strype has printed in the Appendix to his *Life of Whitgift* (bk. iii. No. xlii.), he says: "For if it had pleased Her Majesty, with the wisdom of the realm, to have used no bishops at all, we could not have complained justly of any defect in our Church." And again: "If it had pleased Her Majesty to have assigned the imposition of hands to the deans of every cathedral church, or to some other number of ministers which in no sort were bishops, but as they be pastors, there had been no wrong done to their persons that I can conceive."

In the weighty and valuable note (note vi. p. 293) on "Orders in the Church of England," which Mr. Child has appended to his work on *Church and State under the Tudors*, he quotes from a letter addressed by Dr. Hammond to Lord Burleigh, Nov. 4, 1588: "The bishops of our realm do not (so far as I ever yet heard), nor may not, claim to themselves any other authority than is given them by the statute of the 25th of King Henry the Eighth, recited in the first year of

trary, they regarded the Protestants of the Continent as of the same household of faith with themselves. . . . An English Churchman, nay, even an English prelate, if he went to Holland, conformed, without scruple, to the established religion of Holland. Abroad, the ambassadors of Elizabeth and James went in state to the very worship which Elizabeth and James persecuted at home, and carefully abstained from decorating their private chapels after the Anglican fashion, lest scandal should be given to weaker brethren. An instrument is still extant by which the Primate of England, in the year 1582, authorised a Scotch minister, ordained according to the laudable forms of the Scotch Church by the Synod of East Lothian, to preach and administer the sacraments in any part of the province of Canterbury. . . . In the year 1603 the Convocation solemnly recognised the Church of Scotland, a Church in which episcopal control and episcopal ordination were then unknown, as a branch of the Holy Catholic Church of Christ. It was even held that Presbyterian ministers were entitled to place and voice in Œcumenical Councils. . . . Nay, many English benefices were held by divines who had been

Her Majesty's reign, or by other statutes of this land; neither is it reasonable they should make other claims, for if it had pleased Her Majesty, with the wisdom of the realm [the similarity between these and Whitgift's words is not a little striking], to have used no bishops at all, we could not have complained justly of any defect in our Church; or if it had liked them to limit the authority of bishops to shorter terms, they might not have said they had any wrong. But sith it hath pleased Her Majesty to use the ministry of bishops, and to assign them this authority, it must be to me, that am a subject, as God's ordinance, and therefore to be obeyed according to St. Paul's rule."

admitted to the ministry in the Calvinistic form used on the Continent; nor was reordination by a bishop in such cases thought necessary or even lawful."[1]

Bishop Cosin says: "We had many ministers from Scotland . . . ordained by presbyters only, and they were initiated into benefices, and were never reordained."

"There is no difference in any essential matter betwixt the Church of England and her sisters of the Reformation," is the statement of Bishop Hall; and Bishop Hall wrote *Episcopacy by Divine Right Asserted,* in which, while expressly excluding the Presbyterian Church of Scotland, he manages, by some unaccountable dexterity, to bring the Churches of Geneva and Zurich within the charmed and sacred circle.[2]

In his *Advertisement touching the Controversies of the Church of England,* Lord Bacon censures the indiscretion of those persons who called in question the orders of foreign Protestant Churches: "Yea, and some indiscreet persons have been bold in open preaching to use dishonourable and derogative speech and censure of the Churches abroad; and that so far as some of our men (as I have heard), ordained in foreign parts, have been pronounced to be no lawful ministers."

This was fifty years after the separation from the Church of Rome.

Bishop Barlow.—The oldest Protestant bishop was Barlow; yet of the fact of his consecration there is no extant evidence. All we know is that he was made

[1] Macaulay's *History of England,* vol. i. pp. 75-7.
[2] Hunt's *Religious Thought in England,* vol. i. pp. 175-6.

4

Bishop of St. Asaph's in 1535. The slight importance Barlow was disposed to attach to ordination, episcopal or otherwise, may be gathered from his own words—

"If the King's grace, being supreme head of the Church of England, did choose, denominate, and elect any layman (being learned) to be a bishop, that he so chosen (without mention being made of any orders) should be as good a bishop as he is, or the best in England. Wheresoever two or three simple persons, as cobblers or weavers, are in company and elected in the name of God, there is the true Church of God." We may imagine, indeed, Barlow's hearty approval of Lacordaire's great saying: "Where there is the love of God, there is Jesus Christ; and where Jesus Christ is, there is the Church with Him." All probable sources of information as to the consecration of Barlow have been searched, but searched in vain. Now, it was through Barlow, in point of law, that Parker received his consecration, and through him it passed to the succeeding line of bishops in the Church of England. Here, then, is a missing link in the chain of apostolical succession—missing, at anyrate, so far as the absence of documentary evidence can show it.

The Queen selected **Matthew Parker**, who had been her mother's chaplain, to be head of the new Establishment; but as none of the bishops in any of the existing sees would take part in consecrating the new Protestant primate, recourse had to be had to four deprived bishops of Edward VI.'s time, and accordingly Parker was inducted by William Barlow, John Scory, John Hodgkins, and Miles Coverdale, the last of whom had been an elder

THE RISE OF PURITANISM IN ENGLAND 51

in Knox's church in Geneva, and is said to have officiated on this occasion in his Genevan gown.

Elizabeth and the Puritans.—It was about the year 1556 the Puritans[1] rose into power and became recognised as a separate party in the State. Long prior to this, the leaven of Puritan influence had been silently working in the heart of the best part of the nation,—conspicuously so since the days of Wyclif, who was himself a Puritan of the Puritans,—but as yet it had found no concerted, no organised, expression. It was driven to find this at length by the relentless fury of persecution. Mary was on the throne, and her reign was signalised by that series of unparalleled atrocities, so vividly depicted in Foxe's *Book of Martyrs*, which has loaded her memory with execration, and gained for her the soubriquet of Bloody Mary.

Only by flight could the obnoxious Protestants (and of these the Puritan section was the most obnoxious) escape the violence of the storm which now burst upon them. It is estimated that the refugees numbered about eight hundred. Some found an asylum in France, some in Switzerland, some in Holland, some in Germany. They were most numerous in Frankfort; and here, after con-

---

[1] Fuller dates the use of the term Puritan, as a nickname for the English Nonconformists generally, from the year 1564. Mr. Froude, however, does not find any mention of the name before the year 1585. He quotes from a document drawn up by a "distinguished Jesuit" three years before the Armada, as follows:—"The only party that would fight to death for the Queen, the only real friends she had, were the *Puritans* (*it is the first mention of the name which I have found*), the Puritans of London, the Puritans of the sea towns."—*English Seamen in the Sixteenth Century*, p. 6.

siderable discussion as to what form of service they should adopt, it was agreed to use the service book of Edward VI., subject to certain changes and modifications. This was no sooner agreed to than it was departed from at the instance of a Dr. Cox, who refused to dispense with the portions which had been objected to. This led to a secession, and part of the congregation withdrew to Geneva, where they discarded the service book entirely, and substituted in its place the Genevan form of worship and discipline. The two parties became known as **Conformists and Puritans.** The death of Mary, the accession of Elizabeth, and her supposed sympathy with the work of the Reformation, induced the exiles to return to their native land. "They came home threadbare," says Strype, "bringing nothing with them, but much experience as well as learning."

Elizabeth was not slow to take advantage of her position by asserting her absolute authority. The ecclesiastical edifice reared by Elizabeth rested mainly upon two pillars, the Act of Supremacy and the Act of Uniformity. These continued in force for more than a century, and the system built upon them, setting aside the period of the Long Parliament and that of the Commonwealth, existed unchanged till the passing of the Toleration Act in 1689.

The Act of Supremacy was entitled, *An Act restoring to the Crown the ancient jurisdiction over the State, ecclesiastical and spiritual, and abolishing all foreign power repugnant to the same.*

All jurisdiction was to be vested in the Queen and her successors. This simply meant the transference of authority from the Pope to the Crown, and just as little secured the rights of conscience and the liberty of the people. Elizabeth was the supreme head, or, as she preferred to style herself, the supreme governor, of the Church. The extent of the authority of the Crown may be gathered from the following terms of the Act of Supremacy:—"That the King has power to redress and amend all errors and heresies; he might enjoin what doctrines he would should be preached, not repugnant to the laws of the land. And if any should preach contrary, he was for the third offence to be judged a heretic, and suffer death." His Majesty claimed a right to forbid all preaching for the time, as did Henry VIII., Edward VI., Mary, and Elizabeth,[1] or, as did Charles I., to limit the clergy's preaching to certain of the Thirty-nine Articles.

The Act of Uniformity was entitled, *An Act for the uniformity of Common Prayer and Divine Service in the Church, and the Administration of the Sacraments.*

This forbade the use of any but the second Prayer-Book of Edward VI. A fine of one shilling, nearly equal to ten shillings at the present time, was imposed on all who absented themselves from divine worship, "having no lawful or reasonable excuse to be absent." This was the beginning of sorrows. "Upon the fatal rock of uniformity was the peace of the Church of England split. The rigorous pressing of this Act was the occasion of all the mischiefs that befell the Church

---

[1] *Zurich Letters.* Jewel, in letter to Peter Martyr, January 26, 1559, says: "The Queen has forbidden any person, whether Papist or Gospeller, to preach to the people."

for above eighty years." "What good," asks Neal pertinently, " could it answer to press men's bodies into the public service without convincing their minds ? " Let those who wish to see how complete the absolutism of the Crown was, and the power which they put into the hands of the bishops and their officers, read the provisions of these two Acts, the Act of Supremacy and the Act of Uniformity.[1]

The Vestments Controversy.—We have seen how Hooper " scrupled the vestments," and consented to wear them at his consecration to the see of Gloucester, only on condition that he might dispense with them on other occasions. This was really the beginning of the " Vestiarian Controversy,"—" a dispute which raged apparently round outward symbols, but which really turned on grave differences of opinion." It is no uncommon thing to hear the Puritans sneered at on account of their scrupulosity in regard to the wearing of vestments prescribed and commanded to be worn. Hume's contemptuous reference to their hatred of " surplices and tippets and church millinery " is well known. Canon Curteis speaks of it as a prejudice due to their " morbid want of imagination," magnifying mere " trifling matters . . . into matters of morbid scruple and obstinate antipathy." [2]

[1] They may be conveniently consulted in Professor Prothero's work, *Statutes and Constitutional Documents illustrative of the Reigns of Elizabeth and James I.*, edited by G. W. Prothero, Fellow of King's College, Cambridge, in which they are printed in full.

[2] Curteis' Bampton Lecture on *Dissent in its Relation to the Church of England*, p. 54.

This is a very superficial judgment, and no more explains the dislike which the enforced wearing of the habits inspired in the Puritans than it explains the tenacity with which modern Ritualists cling to their distinctive habits and ceremonies. If alb and stole, and chasuble and cope and rochet had no underlying meaning and symbolism, they would soon cease to be things to wrangle about, and would neither find favour on the one hand nor stir up opposition on the other.

Sacerdotal and non-sacerdotal conceptions of the Christian ministry were struggling for supremacy in the English Establishment. No one can look into the *Zurich Letters* and read carefully the correspondence between Sampson, dean of Christ Church; Humphreys, president of Magdalen; and Bullinger, Peter Martyr, and Gualter, at Zurich,[1] without realising, not only the unfairness, but the absurdity of describing the Puritan revolt against the vestments as arising from mere faddiness or narrow bigotry—mere hatred of "surplices and tippets and church millinery." Rightly or wrongly, the Protestant Puritans saw in them only a relic of the Babylonish garments which pertained to the Church of Rome; and because they symbolised, and were, as they held, intended to symbolise,

---

[1] It is true that the continental Reformers counselled a less hostile attitude than their friends in England were disposed to take up. Bullinger thought it would not be "unlawful to use, in common with Papists, a vestment not superstitious." Peter Martyr wrote to Sampson: "You may therefore use those habits either in preaching or in the administration of the Lord's Supper, provided, however, you persist in speaking and teaching against the use of them."—See *Zurich Letters*; Hallam's *Const. Hist.* vol. i. pp. 237-8.

that in which they did not believe, they refused to wear them. Many of the bishops sympathised with them, and did their utmost to prevent the use of the prescribed vestments being made compulsory; and, indeed, "the number of the clergy who participated in the scruples of Sampson and Humphreys must have been considerable. When Parker summoned to Lambeth a hundred clergymen, and exhibited one Thomas Cole canonically robed, with 'a square cap, a scholar's gown priestlike, tippet, and, in the church, a linen surplice,' only sixty-one out of the hundred were willing to be robed after the fashion of Thomas Cole.[1] They wrote their names with a *Nolo*, and preferred losing their benefices to wearing a surplice."

Speaking of the ferment which the vestments controversy produced in Cambridge, Strype relates how "the fellows and scholars in St. John's College there, chiefly the younger sort (to the number of nearly three hundred, some said), about the beginning of December 1565, or sooner, threw off the surplice with one consent, however they had worn it before in the chapel; as in Trinity College about the same time, all except three, by T. Cartwright's instigation."[2]

The Queen was highly incensed on hearing of this contumacious behaviour. In reply to a communication from Cecil, who was at that time Chancellor of the university, it was averred by the heads of colleges "that a great many persons in the university, of piety and learning, were fully persuaded of the unlawfulness of the habits; and therefore, if conformity were urged, they would be

---

[1] Hunt's *Religious Thought in England*, vol. i. pp. 47, 48.
[2] Strype's *Annals of the Reformation*, vol. i. part ii. pp. 153, 154.

forced to desert their stations, and thus the university would be stripped of its ornaments. They therefore gave it as their humble opinion that indulgence in this matter would be attended with no inconveniences; but, on the other hand, they were afraid religion and learning would suffer very much by rigour and imposition."[1] Incredible as it may appear, among the signatories attached to this statement was the name of *John Whitgift*, Master of Trinity, afterwards Archbishop of Canterbury, and in that position the relentless oppressor of the Puritans.

How divided opinion and feeling were, may be gathered from what took place in the Convocation of 1563. The Puritan demands that the habits, all but the surplice, should be done away, also the use of organs, the sign of the cross in baptism, enforced kneeling at the communion, were defeated by a majority of one (fifty-eight for, fifty-nine against). "It would have been interesting to see how such proposals would have been received by Elizabeth had this trifling majority been reversed." It is clear that at that time no appeal in favour of the habits on the ground of order and comeliness could avail in the face of their dubious origin and their Romish associations. Everything that savoured of Rome was, for that reason, specially repugnant to Protestant feeling. "I wish," said Jewel, "that all, even the slightest, vestiges of Popery might be removed from our churches, and, above all, from our minds. But the Queen at this time is unable to endure the least alteration in matters of religion." Elizabeth had fully made up her mind that no latitude was to be allowed the clergy in regard to the

[1] Strype's *Life of Parker*, bk. iii. p. 125, and also Appendix.

wearing of the prescribed vestments. In this, as in all other respects, the requirements of the Act of Uniformity must be rigorously carried out. In Parker, archbishop of Canterbury, the Queen found an ally and supporter after her own mind, and, needless to say, the power which they wielded bore down all opposition. Humphrey, president of Magdalen, was admonished, and Sampson was deprived of his deanery. Out of ninety-eight ministers in London, thirty-seven refused to comply with the prescribed ceremonies, and were, in consequence, suspended from their ministry, and their livings sequestrated.[1]

Many will concur in the very moderate judgment of Hallam: "I am far from being convinced that it would not have been practicable, by receding a little from that uniformity which governors delight to prescribe, to have palliated in a great measure, if not put an end for a time to, the discontent that so soon endangered the new Establishment. The frivolous usages, to which so many frivolous objections were raised, such as the tippet and surplice, the sign of the cross in baptism, the ring in matrimony, the posture of kneeling at the communion, might have been left to private discretion, not possibly without some inconvenience, but with less, as I conceive, than resulted from rendering their observance indispensable."[2]

---

[1] The Advertisements, as the articles drawn up by Archbishop Parker were called, may be consulted in Professor Prothero's work, pp. 191–4. They are styled *Parker's Advertisements*, 1565, and prescribe the conditions to be observed in connection with doctrine and preaching, the administration of prayers and sacraments, certain orders in ecclesiastical policy, and the kind of apparel to be worn by all ecclesiastical persons.

[2] Hallam's *Constitutional History of England*, vol. i. p. 241.

The Chasm Widening: Rise of Presbyterianism in England

MEMORABLE EVENTS AND DATES

Archbishops of Canterbury during reign of Elizabeth :—

Matthew Parker	. 1553-1575
Edmund Grindal	. 1575-1583
John Whitgift .	1583-1604

Thomas Cartwright appointed Lady Margaret
Professor of Divinity in 1569 . . . died 1603
John Calvin . . . . born 1509, died 1564

CONTENTS OF CHAPTER IV

Rise of Separatism—The Puritans and the Church—Points of divergence—Early and later Puritans—All early Puritans desired uniformity—Rise of Presbyterianism—Return of Refugees—Cartwright—His positions stated—Founder of Presbyterianism in England—Cartwright and Whitgift—Puritan and Anglican antitheses—Walter Travers—Presbyterianised State Church—Book of Discipline—Five hundred signatories—Presbyterians not Separatists—Not friendly to religious liberty—Impermanence of Presbyterianism in England.

CHAPTER IV

THE CHASM WIDENING—RISE OF PRESBYTERIANISM IN ENGLAND

Rise of Separatism.—In this "vestiarian controversy"—the resistance which the enforcement of the habits provoked—Separatism originated. "A most unhappy event," says Strype, "whereby people of the same country, of the same religion, and of the same judgment in doctrine, parted communion; one part being obliged to go aside into secret houses and chambers to serve God by themselves, which begat strangeness between neighbours, Christians, and Protestants." This was the beginning of the breach between the Church and the people,—the breach in which Dissent and Nonconformity took its rise, and which has gone on widening ever since, till it has divided the nation into two rival religious camps, and run a line of cleavage throughout the entire strata of English society.

The Puritans and the Church.—The Puritans were not sorry to see the authority of the Queen substituted for that of the Pope, but they could not bring themselves to submit to her assumption of headship over the Church. "The Christian sovereign," said Cartwright in "An

Admonition to the Parliament," composed by himself and others, " ought not to be called head under Christ of the particular and visible churches within his dominions. It is a title not fit for any mortal man; for, when the apostle says that Christ is the Head, it is as much as if he had said, Christ and no other is Head of the Church."

"They were no enemies," says Neal, "to the name or function of a bishop, provided he was no more than stated president of the college of presbyters in his diocese, and managed the affairs of it with their concurrence and assistance.[1] They did not object against prescribed forms of prayer, provided a latitude was indulged the minister to alter or vary some expressions, and to make use of a prayer of his own conception before and after sermon. Nor had they an aversion to any decent and distinct habits for the clergy that were not derived from Popery. But, upon the whole, they were the most resolved Protestants in the nation, zealous Calvinists, warm and affectionate preachers, and determined enemies to Popery and to everything that had a tendency towards it."

The main points of divergence between the Puritans and their opponents may be thus summarised—

The ruling powers contended that every prince had authority to correct all abuses of doctrine and worship within his own territories. This the Puritans resisted as an invasion of the rights of conscience.

The rulers contended that, in spite of all apostasy and

---

[1] Neal, vol. i. p. 398. But, as Hallam observes, this was in effect to demand everything. "For," he adds, "if the office could be so far lowered in eminence, there were many waiting to clip the temporal revenues and dignity in proportion."

corruption, the Church of Rome was a true Church, and the Pope held his title as Bishop of the Church by an indefeasible right; for, without admitting this, it was held that the Church of England could not establish the validity of her own orders. It is needless to say that the Puritans could not approve this contention. To them the Pope was Antichrist, the Church of Rome an idolatrous and corrupt Church.

The Court reformers held that while the Scriptures are supreme as the standard and rule of faith, their authority did not extend to questions of Church government and discipline. These were to be determined by Church rulers with sole reference to considerations of wisdom and expediency. This the Puritans of that age could not admit, holding as they did to the authority of the Scriptures, not only in matters of doctrine, but also in questions of discipline.

The rulers maintained " that things indifferent in their own nature, which are neither commanded nor forbidden in the Scriptures, such as rites and ceremonies, habits, etc., might be settled, determined, and made necessary by the command of the civil magistrate; and that in such cases it was the indispensable duty of all subjects to observe them." It was upon this principle the bishops justified their severities against the Puritans. The unyielding attitude of the latter was due to nothing but selfwilled perversity (this was the charge commonly brought against them), and of this they must be cured by chastisement and condign punishment. To the Puritans, on the other hand, the path of duty seemed plain. Christ, they said, is the sole lawgiver of His Church, and has enjoined all things necessary to be observed in it to the end of the world; consequently, where He has indulged a liberty to His followers, it is as much their duty to maintain it as to observe any other of His precepts. Besides, if the magistrate has a power to impose things indifferent, and make them necessary in the service of God, he may dress up religion in any shape, and instead of one ceremony, may load it with a hundred.[1]

Early and later Puritans.—It may be well to note at this point, though we shall have occasion to advert to it afterwards, that there was a very marked discrepancy between the views held by the early, and those held and promulgated by the later Puritans, more especially in regard to the functions and power of the civil magistrate, and in regard to the necessity of uniformity in doctrine and worship. In regard to both these, the views and sentiments of the Puritans underwent considerable modification, and this change naturally influenced their beliefs and opinions in other directions.

The two pillars on which, as we have said, the ecclesiastical system of Elizabeth rested, could not have been set up, or, at any rate, could not have proved so stable as they did, had they not been based more or less on the will and convictions of all sections of her Protestant subjects. The Act of Supremacy was welcomed by all alike, and the Prayer-Book was regarded with favour, as substituting a purer form of worship for the Breviary and the Mass. In like manner, the Act of Uniformity would have been hailed with satisfaction by the Puritans,

[1] Neal, vol. i. p. 98.

had it not demanded compliance with a number of needlessly offensive and, as they thought, Popish ceremonies, such as the sign of the cross in baptism, bowing at the name of Jesus, the compelled wearing of the cap and surplice, etc.

Errors afterwards abandoned, clung to by the Puritans.—Neal deplores the widespread misconception which at that time prevailed as to the nature of true religion, and the powers and jurisdiction of the Church. "Why must we believe as the King believes, any more than as the clergy or Pope? If every man could believe as he would, or if all men's understandings were exactly of a size, or if God would accept of a mere outward profession when commanded by law, then it might be reasonable there should be only one religion, and one uniform manner of worship. . . . The jurisdiction of the Church is purely spiritual. No man ought to be compelled, by rewards or punishments, to become a member of any Christian society, or to continue in it any longer than he apprehends it to be his duty."[1] But Neal is here speaking the language of the nineteenth century, at all events, the language of seventeenth century Puritanism. Such opinions would have staggered most of the Elizabethan Puritans.

"*The Reformers, as well Puritans as others, had different notions.* They were all for *one* religion, *one* uniform mode of worship, *one* form of discipline or Church government for the whole nation, with which all must comply, whatever were their inward sentiments; it was therefore

[1] Vol. i. p. 89.

resolved to have an Act of Parliament to establish an uniformity of public worship, without any indulgence to tender consciences, neither party having the wisdom or courage to oppose such a law, but both endeavouring to be included in it." [1]

It is not the least service which Mr. S. R. Gardiner has rendered to the cause of historic truth to exhibit as he has the gradual growth and development of Puritanism, both within and without the Established Church. He shows most clearly what a different thing the Puritanism of Elizabeth's time was from the Puritanism of the time of Charles I., not to speak of the Puritanism of the Commonwealth.[2] This is a view still too commonly disregarded by writers upon this subject, and forgetfulness of it has been the source of much error and confusion.

The rise of Presbyterianism.—Germinal ideas of the Church system to which the name of Presbyterianism is given may be detected in England within a few years of the Reformation, but it was not till the reign of Elizabeth, when many of those who had been driven to Germany and Switzerland by the Marian persecution returned to their native land, that they began to grow in numbers and strength. These came to Eng-

---

[1] Neal, vol. i. p. 90.
[2] "Neither a knowledge of human nature nor of history justifies us in confounding, as is commonly done, the Puritans of Old and New England, or the English Puritans of the third and those of the fifth decade of the seventeenth century" (J. Russell Lowell's *Among My Books: New England Two Centuries Ago*, p. 222). We may add, neither does it justify us in confounding the Puritans of the sixteenth century with those of the seventeenth century.

land filled with Calvinistic ideas regarding Church and State, only to find the royal supremacy absolute, and uniformly enforced under crushing penalties.

About the year 1568 there arose a storm of persecution in France and Holland, and this had the effect of driving a large number of Protestants (chiefly Calvinistic Presbyterians) to take refuge in England. The rapid growth of Presbyterian ideas is attested by the fact that by an Act of Parliament in 1571, ordination by presbyters, without a bishop, is declared to be valid.[1] The distinctive features of Presbyterianism are, however, as might be expected at this period, merged for the most part in those of Puritanism as a whole. Purity in Church government, as well as purity in doctrine, this was the aim of all Protestant Reformers, and to this they directed their united strength.

Thomas Cartwright.—In Thomas Cartwright, English Puritanism found a most able exponent and a courageous and stalwart leader. He was the first to crystallise its contention and raise it to the dignity of a developed system. He was a fellow of Trinity College, Cambridge, and Lady Margaret Professor of Divinity. His great

[1] This was entitled an *Act for the Ministers of the Church to be of sound Religion*, which, though a disabling Act, aimed at the surviving Catholic clergy, and requiring them to give security for their loyalty to the Queen and the Church, did, as a matter of fact, recognise the validity of non-episcopal orders; in other words, the validity of Presbyterian ordination. *Called to the ministry by the imposition of hands, according to the laudable form and rite of the Reformed Church of Scotland*, are the words of Archbishop Grindal.—Strype's *Grindal*, book vi. chap. xiii. See also Bishop Cosin's Works, vol. iv. pp. 403-7, 449-50.

learning (Beza says he thought there was not a more learned man under the sun), and his argumentative acumen and power of popular address, drew a crowd of scholars to listen to his prelections. When he preached at St. Mary's it is said that the windows had to be taken out, so that the large numbers outside the church might be able to hear him. Cartwright was a Puritan of the most thoroughgoing and, according to his enemies, the most dangerous type. He attacked the hierarchy of the Church with unsparing and trenchant vigour.

Cartwright's position, which was probably that of the majority of the Puritan party at that time, may be summed up in the following propositions, drawn up by his own hand:—

(1) That the names and functions of archbishops and archdeacons ought to be abolished.

(2) That the apostolic order and offices should be revived, namely, bishops and deacons; the former to preach and to conduct worship, the latter to attend to the ministration of the poor.

(3) That the Church should be governed by its own ministers and presbyters, and not by bishops, chancellors, and nominees of archdeacons.

(4) That each minister should have charge of a particular congregation, and not exercise supervision over others.

(5) That no minister should put himself forward as a candidate for the ministry.

(6) That ministers ought not to be created by the authority of the bishop, but to be openly and fairly chosen by the people.

Needless to say, Cartwright's leanings were towards

Presbyterianism, and he may be regarded as the founder of that system in England. Some of his positions have been departed from, but in the main the Presbyterian Churches of Great Britain and America still stand by his principles.[1] He opposed, as did all the Puritans, the use of the cross and sponsorship in baptism, the observance of religious festivals, and the practice of kneeling at the Lord's table. The adoption and advocacy of these views soon brought him into collision with the authorities, and they proceeded to use their power in order to punish his heresies, and if possible to crush him. He was forbidden to lecture or preach, deprived of his degree of Doctor and of his fellowship, and expelled from the university. He went abroad, and was induced to minister for two years to a number of English merchants, first at Antwerp, and then at Middelburg for three years. Then, at the earnest solicitation of his friends in England, he was prevailed upon to return. Meanwhile the struggle between the Puritans and the ecclesiastical hierarchy had reached a most acute stage. Finding that the Queen took no notice of their remonstrances, the Puritans consulted together to address an admonition to Parliament. "We have used," they said, "gentle words too long, which have done no good. The wound grows desperate, and wants a corrosive." But Parliament was too much under the influence of the Queen and the bishops to pay much heed to this petition, and they retaliated by putting the presenters of it in prison. "This admonition finding small entertainment (the authors or chief preferrers

[1] Professor C. A. Briggs in *Religious Encyclopædia*, edited by Dr. Schaff.

thereof being imprisoned), out cometh the second admonition towards the end of the same Parliament. . . . In the second admonition the first is wholly justified."[1] This second petition was drawn up by Cartwright, who had just returned from over the sea. Bancroft, afterwards Archbishop of Canterbury, describes it as "great lightning and thunder, as though heaven and earth should have met together."

The controversy between Cartwright and Whitgift.—Whitgift, then Master of Trinity College and Vice-Chancellor of Cambridge, was instructed to answer this petition, and he did so with great elaboration and show of completeness. This drew from Cartwright a vigorous rejoinder, to which Whitgift again replied.

It is not necessary to give any extended account of this passage of arms between these two redoubtable antagonists.[2] Their divergences were radical at the outset. They each took their stand upon different grounds, and it was as impossible that a common conclusion should be reached as that two parallel lines should meet, however far they may be produced. Cartwright took his stand upon the Protestant principle—what in those days was the recognised Protestant principle—that the authority of Scripture is final, both in regard to matters of faith and matters of Church government. Entrenching himself upon this ground, he had no difficulty in showing

[1] Bancroft's *Dangerous Positions*.
[2] Hooker took up the controversy twenty years after, and it must have been not a little flattering to Cartwright in his old age to see his own initials (T. C.) figuring so prominently in the pages of the *Ecclesiastical Polity*.

"that ministers ought not to be created by the sole authority of the bishop, but to be openly and fairly chosen by the people," etc. On the other hand, Whitgift maintained that "no form of Church government is by the Scriptures permitted to us, or commanded by the word of God." "I do not deny," he said, "but in the apostles' time, and after, even to Cyprian's time, the people's consent was in many places required in the appointment of ministers, but I say there is no commandment that it should be; and I add that, however in the apostles' time that kind of electing and calling ministers was convenient and profiteth, now, in this state of the Church, it were pernicious and hurtful. In the apostles' time all or most that were Christians were virtuous and godly, and such as did sincerely profess the word, and therefore the election might be safely committed to them. Now, the Church is full of hypocrites, dissemblers, drunkards, whoremongers, so that, if any election were committed to them, they would be sure to take one like to themselves. Now the Church is full of Papists and Atheists."

To attempt to bring a Church of this order to a condition of apostolical purity, in the judgment of Whitgift, was utterly out of the question, and the pretence of such renovation mere hypocrisy. He showed himself Cartwright's inferior in dialectical skill, but the balance was redressed by the exercise of arbitrary power; or, as Fuller puts it, "if Cartwright had the better of his adversary in learning, Whitgift had more power to back his arguments, and by this he not only kept the field, but gained the victory."

Puritan and Anglican antitheses.—The Puritan and Anglican positions have been admirably summed up by Dr. Fairbairn in his work, *The Place of Christ in Modern Theology*. " Cartwright maintained that ' the Commonwealth must be made to agree with the Church '; but Whitgift, that ' the Church must be framed according to the Commonwealth.' Cartwright, that ' although the godly magistrate be the head of the Commonwealth, and a great ornament unto the Church, yet he is but a member of the same '; but Whitgift, that this was to ' overthrow monarchies,' since it made the prince 'a servant, no master, a subject, no prince; under government, no governor, in matters pertaining to the Church '; Cartwright, that ' infidels under a Christian magistrate are members of the Commonwealth, but not of the Church,' nor are known ' drunkards or whoremongers,' and the excommunicated, ' though sundered from the Church, may yet retain his burgeship or freedom in the city '; but Whitgift, that while ' in the apostles' time all or most that were Christians were virtuous and godly,' yet ' now the Church is full of hypocrites, dissemblers, drunkards, whoremongers.' It is this latter that gives its religious significance to the controversy, and makes apparent the moral passion that was at its heart. On the Puritan side, what they wanted, and were by their theological idea bound to want, was a Church in which the moral will of God should be supreme."[1]

Walter Travers.—The name which falls to be

[1] See the whole of this valuable note in *The Place of Christ in Modern Theology*, pp. 188-190.

bracketed with Cartwright in upholding what Mr. Soames calls "Disciplinarian Puritanism"—*i.e.* Presbyterianism— is that of Walter Travers. The two were, as Fuller describes them, the "head and neck" of the Presbyterian party. Travers was the afternoon lecturer at the Temple, and when the Mastership of the Temple became vacant through the death of Alvey, Lord Burghley used his influence to secure the appointment for Travers, who was his chaplain, and stood high in his regard. Whitgift, however, with whom the appointment rested, gave the preference to Hooker. Travers retained his lectureship for some time, refuting in the afternoon what Hooker had advanced in the morning, Hooker again replying on the succeeding Sunday morning; so that it became a current saying that the forenoon sermon spake Canterbury, the afternoon Geneva. Travers was at length silenced by Whitgift, on the ground that he had not received episcopal ordination, but had been ordained abroad by presbyters. He did not go the length of saying that his ordination was invalid, only that it unfitted him for exercising his ministry in England. Travers was the author of a work composed in Latin in 1574, and translated into English by Cartwright under the title, *A Full and Plain Declaration of Ecclesiastical Discipline out of the Word of God, and of the Declining of the Church of England from the same.*

The goal to which Cartwright and Travers directed their efforts was the establishment of a **Presbyterianised State Church**,—in other words, the transplanting to England of the Genevan rule of faith and discipline,— whereby the consistorial theories of John Calvin should receive concrete embodiment and national recognition.

The first presbytery was organised at Wandsworth in 1572. This was the first tentative experiment "for the better bringing in of the said holy discipline," "and by little and little, as well as possibly they might," to "draw the same into practice." This was a movement,[1] not outside, but inside, the Church of England—"an *Ecclesiosola in Ecclesia*, or a Church within the Church, consisting of those who desired a purer communion, and who combined together for higher fellowship and discipline than what the ordinary Church regulations required." The Wandsworth Presbytery became the model of numerous presbyteries set up in parish after parish throughout the whole country. In 1582 the consistorial system was in full working order. In his *Dangerous Positions*, etc., Bancroft quotes from a letter written in Latin to Mr. Field by one Cholmsley, resident in Antwerp, in 1583: "I am rejoiced with all my heart for the better success of your affairs, not only in that I hear of your assemblies, but most delightfully of all, in respect of your so effectually practising of the ecclesiastical discipline in all its parts."

---

[1] It is greatly to be deplored that the only contemporary record of this movement is that given in a work written by Bancroft, then bishop of London, and entitled, *Dangerous Positions and Proceedings published and practised within this Island of Britain under pretence of Reformation and for the Presbyterial Discipline.* Extracts from this work are given in Professor Prothero's *Statutes and Constitutional Documents*, p. 247. But the work bears upon its face that it is "written for the express purpose of discrediting and defacing the movement" it professes to describe.

The Book of Discipline.—A Directory or Book of Discipline was, contemporaneously with the growth of this movement, in course of construction. This took shape about the year 1583, and was in its completed form the joint work of Cartwright and Travers.[1] It was revised at a national synod in London in 1584, and put into the hands of Travers "to be corrected and ordered by him." This Book of Discipline was a handbook or Directory of worship and government framed on Presbyterian lines, according to the Genevan model, and has been called "the palladium of English Presbyterianism."

But the fact of chief interest and importance in connection with the Book of Discipline is this, that in the year 1590 it had spread all over England, and was subscribed by as many as **five hundred ministers**. It is hardly possible to exaggerate the significance of this fact. Five hundred clergymen of the Church of England prayed Parliament that this book "might be from henceforth authorised, put in use, and practised throughout all Her Majesty's dominions." How large this proportion was we may gather from the statement of Neal, endorsed by Hallam, that there were only about two thousand preaching clergymen in the whole kingdom. So that it need not excite surprise when, in 1589, we find Cooper, bishop of Winchester, declaring "that the most part of men" and "all inferior subjects" were averse to Episcopacy, and proclaimed their aversion "at every table, in sermons, and in the face of the whole world."

[1] This Directory must not be confounded, as it often has been, with the earlier work of Travers, which was not a Directory at all, but a treatise and vindication of Presbyterian order.

Presbyterians not Separatists.—It must not be supposed, however, that those who subscribed the Book of Discipline had any intention of separating from the Established Church. Their position was probably that of Cartwright, who, although he found much that was objectionable in the Church, did not separate from it himself, nor approved of separation on the part of others. "Though deformed," he said, "the Church of England is still the 'body of Christ'; without walls, it may be, nevertheless it is a 'city' and a 'vineyard,' though without a 'fence.'" He opposed the contention of Robert Browne, and disavowed all sympathy with his aims and followers. "We are not for an unspotted Church on earth, and therefore, though the Church of England has many faults, we would not willingly withdraw from it." Such was the language employed by those who framed the first Admonition to Parliament.

Though they disapproved of bishops, and believed in the popular election of ministers, they went no further than to urge that the system they favoured should be adopted "by public authority of the magistrate and of our Church," they promising obedience "so far as it may be lawful for us so to do by the publique lawes of this kingdom and by the peace of our Church."

The doctrine of religious liberty not avowed by Cartwright and his party.—Considering the part which the Presbyterian party played afterwards in the day of their ascendency, it is probably not an unjust or un-

charitable judgment to say, as one[1] does, that their
object "was to work in obedience to the Church system
already established, by treating it as a mere legal
appendage, until the time came when, undermined
from below, it might be successfully and entirely over-
thrown."

A party which had Cartwright as its leader and in-
forming spirit was not likely to err upon the side of
moderation, or to grasp at the shadow so long as the
substance of power was within its reach. "The disciples
of Cartwright now learned," says Hallam, "to claim
an ecclesiastical independence, as unconstrained as the
Romish priesthood in the darkest ages had usurped."[2]
"No leader of a religious party," says Mr. Green, "ever
deserved less of after sympathy than Cartwright. He
was unquestionably learned and devout, but his bigotry
was that of a mediaeval inquisitor. The relics of the
old ritual—the cross in baptism, the surplice, the giving
of a ring in marriage—were to him not merely distasteful, as they were to the Puritans at large, they
were idolatrous, and the mark of the beast. . . . The
absolute rule of bishops, indeed, he denounced as be-
gotten of the devil, but the absolute rule of Presbyters
he held to be established by the word of God. For the
Church modelled after the fashion of Geneva he claimed
an authority which surpassed the wildest dreams of the

---

[1] H. O. Wakeman, M.A., in *The Church and the Puritans*, p. 47.
[2] In his strictures upon Cartwright, Hallam adds the needful
caveat: "We are not, however, to conclude that every one, or even
the majority, of those who might be counted on the Puritan side in
Elizabeth's reign would have subscribed to the extravagant opinions
of Cartwright."

masters of the Vatican. All spiritual power and jurisdiction, the decreeing of doctrine, the ordering of ceremonies, lay wholly, according to his Calvinistic creed, in the hands of the ministers of the Church. To them, too, belonged the supervision of public morals. In an ordered arrangement of classes and synods they were to govern their flocks, to regulate their own order, to decide in matters of faith, to administer 'discipline.' Their weapon was excommunication, and they were responsible for its use to none but Christ. The province of the civil ruler was simply 'to see their decrees executed, and to punish the contemners of them,' for the spirit of such a system as this naturally excluded all toleration of practice or belief. With the despotism of a Hildebrand, Cartwright combined the cruelty of a Torquemada. Not only was Presbyterianism to be established as the one legal form of Church government, but all other forms, Episcopalian and Separatist, were to be ruthlessly put down. For heresy there was the punishment of death. Never had the doctrine of persecution been urged with such a blind and reckless ferocity. 'I deny,' wrote Cartwright, 'that upon repentance there ought to follow any pardon of death. . . . Heretics ought to be put to death now. If this be bloody and extreme, I am content to be so counted with the Holy Ghost.'"

The strictures both of Hallam and Green upon Cartwright err, in our judgment, in excess of severity, and the passages from his writings upon which they rely as evidence are susceptible of a much milder construction when read in the light of their context. But there can be no doubt that Cartwright was a man of uncompromis-

ing temper, of an unyielding, not to say intolerant, spirit,
and that he succeeded in communicating to his followers
much of the infection of this temper and spirit. The
prevalence of his opinions and the victory of his party
would have been a blow to the cause of religious liberty,
hardly less severe than that which it suffered at the
hands of Whitgift and the dominant hierarchy of the
Church, and it is not without reason (though he may
seem to be speaking from prejudice) that Mr. Soames[1]
says that Whitgift saved England from a *democratical
pontificate*.

Impermanence of Presbyterianism in England.—
It is, indeed, curious, and not a little striking, to contrast
the claims made on behalf of the Holy Discipline with
its shortlived lease of power, its abruptly ended career,
so far as England was concerned. In 1588, John Udall
wrote his famous demonstration of discipline, which he
entitled, *A Demonstration of the Truth of that Discipline
which Christ hath prescribed in His Word for the government of His Church in all times and places, until the end
of the world.* "Here comes," says Mr. Arber, "the irony
of history in regard to such confident dogmatising. As
a matter of fact, the Holy Discipline, in its integrity, and
as here defined by Udall, did not last two generations in
England."[2] The Presbyterian system took deep roothold
in Scotland; but in England it never had more than a
struggling, precarious, sporadic existence. It was a

[1] *Elizabethan Religious History*, by Rev. H. Soames, M.A., p. 557.
[2] See introduction to (Rev. John Udall) *A Demonstration of Discipline*, by Edward Arber, in English Scholars' Library.

clerical rather than a national creed, and, even when under the Commonwealth, it seemed to have won its way to power and ascendency, it had its stronghold only in London and Lancashire, and was rejected by every other part of England.[1]

[1] Green's *Short History of the English People*, p. 457.

Puritanism: Further Developments, and Means used for their Repression

Memorable Events and Dates

The Court of Star Chamber constituted in . . 1487
The Court of High Commission established in . 1559
Both Courts abolished by Long Parliament in . . 1641

Contents of Chapter V

Prophesyings—Confession of faith by those taking part in—Profitableness of these exercises—Bacon—Strype—Liberty of Prophesying—Benefits of—Queen's hostility to—Remonstrance vain—Grindal refuses to suppress—Suspended—Grindal a true Puritan—Whitgift—Test articles—Enforcement of—Interrogatories—Court of High Commission—Its tyranny and use by Whitgift—Lord Burghley disgusted.

CHAPTER V

Puritanism: Further Developments, and Means used for their Repression

Prophesyings.—In 1571 a number of the clergy, zealous for the increase and propagation of true religion, mainly Puritans, and including several of the bishops of the Church, commenced the religious exercises to which the name Prophesyings was given. This movement was intended to supply an antidote and corrective to the widespread ignorance of the clergy, and to rescue the people from the state of torpor and religious indifference into which large numbers had sunk through the incompetence or neglect of their supposed spiritual guides. These prophesyings were an attempt to revive the practice of the primitive Church to call forth the varied gifts of the clergy and laity, with a view to their mutual edification and the practice of spiritual religion. They were nothing more than religious conferences,—ministerial associations, they might be called, with a large infusion of the lay element. Briefly stated, this was the course of procedure: A discourse was delivered on a portion of Scripture appointed for the day, then the subject was thrown open to discussion, and, after a free and wide expression of opinion, then the moderator or presiding elder would review what had been advanced; and, after summing up the various points, the exercises would be concluded with prayer. The first of these prophesyings was set up in Northampton in 1571, and is "a remarkable specimen of what English Protestantism could become under favourable conditions."[1]

The propositions subscribed by those taking part in these prophesyings, as already stated,[2] were as follows: "We believe the word of God contained in the Old and New Testaments to be a perfect rule of faith and manners; that it ought to be read and known by all people; and that the authority of it exceeds all authority, not of the Pope only, but of the Church also, and of councils, fathers, men, and angels. We condemn, as a tyrannous yoke, whatsoever men have set up of their own invention to make articles of faith, and the binding of men's consciences by their laws and institutions."[3]

Large audiences gathered together at these conferences, and among the intelligent and religiously disposed part of the community the prophesyings or preachings became immensely popular. "The word of the Lord was precious in those days; there was no open vision."

---

[1] Froude's interesting and appreciative description of these exercises in connection with the Church at Northampton deserves to be carefully read.—*History of England*, vol. x. p 113.

[2] See *ante*, p. 22.

[3] For Bishop Parkhurst's permission of exercises in the diocese of Norwich, 1572, see Strype's *Annals*, ii. p. 494. For regulations in the diocese of Peterborough, 1571, also the order of procedure and confession of common faith, see Strype's *Annals*, iii., or as given by Professor Prothero in his *Statutes and Constitutional Documents*, pp. 202-204.

For the clergy themselves, such as had any mind to profit by them, they became an invaluable means of self-training and discipline, so much so, that we find Bacon, even while admitting their liability to abuse, expressing a distinctly favourable opinion: "Is there no means to nurse and train up ministers, . . . to train them, I say, not to preach, . . . but to preach soundly, and handle the Scriptures with wisdom and judgment? I know prophesying was subject to great abuses. . . . But I say the only reason of the abuse was because there were admitted to it a popular auditory, and it was contained with a private conference of ministers."[1]

Strype speaks of these prophesyings as "a very commendable reformation"; and when we reflect upon the dearth of preaching, and the blight and wintry barrenness which religiously covered all parts of the land, we can imagine the springtide of grace and blessing they must have brought to numbers of spiritually starved and hungry men and women. Truly, those were days in which the hungry sheep looked up and were not fed. Thus, in Cornwall, about the year 1578, out of one hundred and forty clergymen not one was capable of preaching, only two in the whole diocese of Bangor. In

[1] In the section, "Touching a preaching Ministry," in his *Essay on the Pacification of the Church*, Bacon asks "whether it were not requisite to renew that good exercise which was practised in this Church some years, and afterwards put down by order, indeed, from the Church, in regard of some abuse thereof inconvenient for those times, and yet against the advice and opinion of one of the greatest and gravest prelates of this land, and was commonly called prophesying," etc. "And this was, in my opinion, the best way to frame and train up preachers to handle the word of God as it ought to be handled that hath been practised."

the course of a sermon preached before the Queen, Sandys, bishop of Worcester, says: "Many there are that hear not a sermon in seven years; I might say in seventeen."

Liberty of prophesying.—Naturally, as we may easily conceive, these prophesyings would come to take a wider range than what was at first contemplated, and would embrace a wider variety of themes. The liberty of prophesying in those days resembled the liberty of the press, and was, indeed, the substitute for it, preachers not confining themselves to the mere exposition of Scripture, but enlarging the scope of their preaching, and handling and discussing public questions, and thus gradually assuming the position of leaders and tribunes of the people. That opinions would be broached and doctrines disseminated that would not exactly square with the views of the Queen, nor encourage docile submission to her authority and that of her bishops, is only what might have been expected. These prophesyings, no doubt, afforded excellent opportunities for the spread of puritanical and Presbyterian doctrines; but this is only saying that the air of free thought and speech and discussion was eminently congenial to these doctrines, and favourable to their growth.

Probably Mr. Marsden does not go too far in saying that "the future character of the Church of England was the real question at issue. Should the reformed Church of England expand itself; . . . cast itself on the affections of the people, etc. etc. ? Or should it risk all hazards, resist every innovation, and subdue by authority, rather than conciliate by gentleness and love? In a word, should the Church be made more popular or more imperious?"[1]

The benefits of these prophesyings outweighed all risks and drawbacks that could possibly accrue from them. Had Elizabeth been as wise and far-sighted as she is sometimes assumed to have been, she would have shown towards these innovations a less stiff and more relenting attitute than she did. She would have done as she did in Lancashire, where the disturbances and the state of ferment into which that part of the kingdom was thrown obliged her to connive at these exercises and to encourage their continuance, as furnishing the most efficacious means of resisting the invasion and growth of Popery. More than all other causes, these prophesyings were helping to create an atmosphere, a tone of thinking and feeling in the minds of the soberer part of the nation, which was the best security against all seditious influence and Romanising tendencies; and if Elizabeth had thrown the weight of her authority into this scale, would have made her more supreme, more invincible than ever. As it was, they rendered signal service to the cause of Protestantism in England. No doubt there were excesses and possible dangers connected with them which showed the necessity of wise and sympathetic guidance. The new wine was in danger of bursting the old bottles, yet the fermentation was needful and salutary. As Mr. Froude observes: "It would have fared ill with England had there been no hotter blood there than filtered in the

[1] Marsden's *Early Puritans*, p. 109.

sluggish veins of the officials of the Establishment. There needed an enthusiasm fiercer to encounter the revival of Catholic fanaticism, and if the young Puritans, in the heat and glow of their convictions, snapped their traces and flung off their harness, it was they after all who saved the Church which attempted to disown them."[1]

Suppression of the prophesyings.—Some of Elizabeth's bishops were favourable to the prophesyings, and encouraged them both as a means of benefit to the clergy and as a means of promoting and spreading what John Wesley would have called "scriptural holiness." The Queen herself, however, had an intense dislike to them. Her maxim was Talleyrand's, "*Non trop de zèle.*" She would have sympathised, at least, with part of the advice said to have been given by Archbishop Sutton to Bishop Heber on his consecration to the see of Calcutta: "Place before your eyes two precepts, and two only. One is, Preach the gospel; and the other is, *Put down enthusiasm.*" With characteristic promptitude and decision the Queen had made up her mind that the prophesyings must be put down. She was told by the archbishop that they were no better than seminaries of Puritanism; that the more averse the people were to Popery, the more they were in danger of Nonconformity.

Archbishop Parker received the royal mandate to "repress immediately these vain prophesyings," and wrote at once to Parkhurst, bishop of Norwich, directing him to take steps for their immediate suppression. The

[1] *History*, vol. x. p. 114.

latter, unwilling to do what was so against his own conscience and judgment, addressed a plea to the archbishop urging their profitableness and freeness from abuse. His remonstrance was supported by Sandys, bishop of London, Sir Francis Knollys, Sir Thomas Smith, and Sir Walter Mildmay, who, in a letter to the Privy Council, said: "Some, not well-minded towards true religion and the knowledge of God, speak evil and slanderously of these Exercises as commonly they do against the sincere preaching of God's holy word," etc. But the imperious Queen was not to be moved, and, armed with her authority, the archbishop reduced the recalcitrant bishop to submission. Thus the prophesyings were stamped out in the diocese of Norwich. It is worth noticing, that though put an end to in this diocese, when the bishopric fell vacant, a number of the clergy seized the opportunity of resuming the forbidden exercises. It shows how in the soil of Norwich, prepared as it had been by the doctrine of Lollardism, the influence of the Walloon settlers, and, may we not add, the labours of Robert Browne (though this was some years afterwards), the tree of liberty continued to grow, and put forth its spreading branches.

Archbishop Grindal was raised to the see of Canterbury on the death of Parker, in 1574. He was a man of a very different temper from his predecessor. He had been in exile, had learned to look with indulgence upon the Puritans and their doctrines, and maintained an active correspondence with the Reformers on the Continent. He did not dissemble his sympathy with the prophesyings; on the contrary, he did everything he could to encourage and uphold them, taking care, however, to guard against their abuse, and to remove as far as possible all that made them obnoxious to the ruling powers.[1] But his zeal in the latter respect could not mollify the spirit of the Queen. She had fully made up her mind to have none of them. In an interview with the archbishop, she rated him soundly for his dilatoriness in carrying out her behests, told him plainly that there were far too many preachers, that three or four for a county were quite enough, and all that was needful was that they should be able to read the Homilies. This greatly scandalised the grave man, as Strype calls him, and he was so moved that he wrote to the Queen in the following terms:[2]—"I cannot marvel enough how this strange opinion should once enter your mind, that it should be good for the Church to have few preachers. Alas! Madam, is the Scripture more plain in any one thing than that the gospel of Christ should be plentifully preached?" After showing the superiority of preaching over the reading of the Homilies, he goes on to say— "I cannot, with a safe conscience, and without the offence of the majesty of God, give my assent to the suppressing of the said Exercises: much less, send out any injunction for the utter and universal subversion of the same. If it be your Majesty's pleasure for this or any other cause to remove me out of this place, I will,

---

[1] See Grindal's *Regulations*, 1576. *Orders for Reformation of Abuses about the Learned Exercises and Conferences among the Ministers of the Church.*—Strype's *Grindal*, pp. 327, 328.

[2] See Appendix to Strype's *Grindal*, p. 558.

with all humility, yield thereto, and render again to your Majesty what I received. . . . "Bear with me, I beseech you, Madam, if I choose rather to offend your earthly Majesty than to offend the heavenly majesty of God."

This courageous and noble letter had no effect upon the Queen, save to rouse her Tudor spirit, and call forth all her unbending determination. It was only through the intervention of her counsellors that she was prevented from carrying out a sentence of deprivation. This was commuted into a sentence of suspension and sequestration. Meanwhile, the Queen took upon herself the authority of the degraded prelate, and wrote[1] to every bishop in England, telling him "to see these dishonours against the honour of God and the quietness of the Church reformed," etc. With characteristic obsequiousness (though not without considerable reluctance and hesitation on the part of one or two) the bishops made their submission to the Queen. Aylmer, bishop of London, who had formerly been a favourer of the Puritans, specially signalising himself for his zeal against the prophesyings. Grindal alone stood firm, and for this contumacious conduct he continued to lie under sentence of suspension and sequestration till within a few months of his death, in 1583. In "The Epistle Dedicatory" of his *Life of Grindal*, Strype says, "Nothing to this day sticks upon our archbishop but the matter of the Exercises and his suspension." But it sticks not in the way of opprobrium, but in way of glory and deathless

---

[1] The Queen's letter against Prophesyings, 1577, is given in Professor Prothero's *Statutes*, etc., pp. 205, 206.

renown in the pages of the illustrious Puritan poet, Edmund Spenser—

"Ah! good Algrind,[1] his hap was ill."

Grindal, like Hooper was a true Puritan. If any doubt could exist in regard to that, it would surely be removed by the truculent description of him in the sermon preached by Sacheverell at St. Paul's, on the 5th of November 1709. In that sermon, Archbishop Grindal was denounced as a false son of the Church, because he was the first that tolerated the Puritans,— those "miscreants begot in rebellion, born in sedition, and nursed in faction."[2]

Archbishop Whitgift.—On the death of Grindal, Whitgift, bishop of Worcester, was appointed to succeed him in the primacy. His relation to the Puritans, and the series of oppressive measures which he put in execution against them, cause him to figure more prominently in these pages than any of his predecessors in the see of Canterbury.

Whitgift's administration "embodied the worst passions of an intolerant State priest. It knew no mercy; it exercised no compassion. It is vain to defend the administration of Whitgift on the ground of the excesses of the Puritans. Those excesses were provoked by his cruelty. Neither can the archbishop be justified on the plea that he acted on the commands of the Queen.

---

[1] Algrind is simply a transposing of the syllables of Grindal's name.
[2] Hunt's *Religious Thought in England*, vol. iii. p. 12.

He was the Queen's adviser, to whose judgment she deferred, and of whose hearty concurrence in every measure of severity and intolerance she was fully assured." Macaulay speaks of him as "a narrow-minded man, mean, tyrannical, who gained power by servility and adulation, and employed it in persecuting both those who agreed with Calvin about Church government and those who differed from Calvin touching the doctrine of reprobation."[1] To say that he was conscientious in what he did, is only what might be said of Spanish inquisitors and the whole brood of religious persecutors. He is said to have been "personally pious, liberal, and free from harshness,"—qualities by no means incompatible with a depraved mind and the absence of high principle. The calm and judicious Hallam is hardly less severe than Macaulay in his animadversions upon Whitgift, and the rigour and ruthlessness of his rule.

Whitgift had not been primate three months before he showed the temper he was of, by promulgating the Test Articles, generally described as the **Whitgift Articles**.[2] These were six in number, and their rigour may be anticipated in the initial words, "That the laws made against the recusants be put in more due execution. That all preaching, reading, catechising, and other such like exercises in private places and families whereunto others do resort, being not of the same family, be utterly inhibited."

"That none be permitted to preach or interpret the Scriptures unless it be a priest or deacon at the least, admitted thereto according to the laws of this realm.

---

[1] Macaulay's *Essay on Lord Bacon*.
[2] Strype's *Life of Whitgift*, vol. i. pp. 229-232.

That none be permitted to preach, read, catechise, minister the sacraments, or to execute any other ecclesiastical function . . . unless he first consent and subscribe to these articles following . . . *videlicet* :—

"(*a*) That Her Majesty, under God, hath, and ought to have, the sovereignty and rule over all manner of persons born within her realms, dominions, and countries; of what estate, ecclesiastical or temporal, soever they be;

"(*b*) That the Book of Common Prayer, and of ordering bishops, priests, and deacons, containeth nothing contrary to the word of God, and that the same may be lawfully used, and that he himself will use the form of the said book prescribed in public prayer and administration of the sacraments, and none other."

Whitgift was determined that the Articles should not only be imposed, but be resolutely enforced; and in order that objectors and waverers should have no loophole of escape, he drew up a series of interrogations, "so comprehensive as to embrace the whole scope of clerical uniformity, yet so precise and minute as to leave no room for evasion." These interrogations, twenty-four in number, were submitted by what was technically styled the oath *ex officio* "to such of the clergy as were surmised to harbour a spirit of puritanical disaffection."

These interrogations, among other things, obliged the examinee to state whether he had refused to wear the surplice, or to use the sign of the cross in baptism, the ring in marriage, and the form of words prescribed in burial; and whether he had adhered strictly and in every respect to the order and services of the Prayer-Book, etc.

The form in which the interrogatories were put was—

"*Item objicimus, ponimus, et articulamur.* That for the space of these three years, two years, one year, half a year, three, two, or one month last past, you, ... have used and worn only your ordinary apparel, and not the surplice, as is required. Declare how long, how often, and for what cause, consideration, or intent you have so done, or refused so to do.

"*Item objicimus,* etc.—That within the time aforesaid you have baptized divers, or at least one infant, and have refused to use, or not used, the sign of the cross in the forehead with the words in the said Book of Common Prayer, there prescribed to be used. Declare how many you have so baptized, and for what cause, consideration, and intent."

This is a fair specimen of the whole series of interrogatories.[1]

The Court of High Commission. — The special machinery relied upon for the enforcement of these Test Articles was that set in motion by that terrible engine of oppression known as the Court of High Commission, which was created under the Act of Supremacy, and specially designed to deal with all offences against this Act and the Act of Uniformity. It was armed with powers so absolute and inquisitorial, that no obnoxious opinion could be professed, no non-attendance at church could be indulged, no service be conducted in chapel or private house, without bringing down upon delinquents fine and imprisonment, and even death. It had power to "visit, reform, redress, order, correct, and amend all

[1] See Appendix to Strype's *Whitgift,* vol. iii. p. 81.

errors, heresies, schisms, abuses, offences, contempts, and enormities whatsoever."[1]

"By the mere establishment of such a court half the work of the Reformation was undone." It made the primate for the time being—for the powers of the Commission fell practically into his hands—absolute dictator, and master of the lives and liberties of the Queen's subjects. "No Archbishop of Canterbury," says Mr. Green, "had wielded an authority so vast, so utterly despotic, as that of Parker and Whitgift, and Bancroft and Abbot and Laud." The most terrible feature of this tyranny on the part of the bishops was its personal character. No fireside was safe from the intrusion of his officers and pursuivants. No act, no word, was so innocent but it could be construed into a crime. The primates created their own tests of doctrine with an utter indifference to those created by law. In one instance, Parker deprived a vicar of his benefice for the denial of the verbal inspiration of the Bible. This is but a sample of the charge of heresy which was liable to be brought home to anyone who expressed an opinion upon religious subjects. This and the mode of taking evidence in the court, which was contrary to the "most simple ideas of justice and equity," made it a terrible engine of oppression, and, according to Hume, its jurisdiction was more terrible than that of the **Star Chamber**.[2]

[1] See *Statutes and Constitutional Documents illustrative of the Reigns of Elizabeth and James I.*, edited by G. W. Prothero, Fellow of King's College, Cambridge, p. 227.

[2] The Court of Star Chamber was a court where "great riots and contempts" were punished. Its jurisdiction was civil rather than ecclesiastical, and extended to everything that might be supposed to

No wonder that the Ecclesiastical Commission "stank in the nostrils of the English clergy." It was even more detestable to the English laity; to them it remained, as Froude says, "an inexpressible detestation and scorn. All sides united in dread and hatred of those ecclesiastical tribunals, whose yoke had been broken by Henry, and which had so fearfully abused their recovered power."

In the Court of High Commission, Whitgift had all the machinery he required made ready to his hand for carrying out his Test Articles. In 1583, on Whitgift's accession to the primacy, a new Commission was appointed. It is generally believed that this Commission was invested with greatly expanded powers, and became, for this reason, a more terrible instrument of oppression; but this belief, though resting on the authority of Hallam (in this following Neal), does not seem to be substantiated.[1]

The power which the Court put at Whitgift's command was practically absolute and unlimited, and he proceeded to use it without mercy in the case of all persons known to be incriminated by the Test Articles,—a species of ecclesiastical tyranny utterly at variance alike with our English laws and all principles of natural equity.[2]

Lord Burghley, who, though at first rather friendly to

disturb or endanger the government, and to misdemeanours, such as libels. Hence it regulated and controlled the censorship of the press. The court consisted of all the members of the Privy Council, together with two Chief Justices.

[1] "It is true that under Whitgift the Commission was more active and efficient than before; but this change was apparently due, not to any additional powers, but to the energetic and uncompromising character of its new head."—Introduction to *Select Statutes and other Constitutional Documents*, by Professor Prothero, p. xlii.

[2] See Hallam, *in loco*.

Whitgift, was soon disgusted by his intolerant and arbitrary behaviour, wrote in strong terms of remonstrance against these articles of examination, " which I have read, and find so curiously penned, so full of branches and circumstances, as I think the inquisitors of Spain use not so many questions to comprehend and to trap their preys. . . . According to my simple judgment, this kind of proceeding is too much savouring of the Romish Inquisition, and is rather a device to seek for offenders than to reform any." [1] Burghley was no Puritan, but, like Bacon, his " calm and sagacious mind " was affronted and scandalised by such high-handed proceeding. Whitgift, however, was as little inclined as his royal mistress to resile from a position which he had once taken up. With him it was war to the knife and to the bitter end.

[1] See Appendix to Strype's *Whitgift*, vol. iii. pp. 104-107.

The Conflict between Puritanism and the Church

Memorable Events and Dates

Richard Hooker	. . . . born 1553, died 1600
Francis Bacon	„ 1561 „ 1626

Contents of Chapter VI

Oppression of the Puritans — Result of — Sympathisers with Puritans — Popular sympathy — Queen inexorable — Predominance of Puritans — Growth of Puritanism — Hooker and his Ecclesiastical Polity — Law or Reason — Hooker and Puritanism — Misconceptions as to Puritanism — Not opposed to reason — Lord Bacon — Note on Hooker's theory of Church and State.

CHAPTER VI

THE CONFLICT BETWEEN PURITANISM AND THE CHURCH

WHEN, during the primacy and rule of Parker, the Act for enforcing subscription to the Articles in 1572 was put into execution, a hundred clergymen, according to Strype's estimate, resigned their benefices rather than subscribe. But if Parker chastised the refractory Puritans with whips, Whitgift chastised them with scorpions. The Test Articles were an instrument of torture that was to be remorselessly applied. And applied it was, regardless of consequences. The archbishop's "peremptory requisition encountered the resistance of men pertinaciously attached to their own tenets, and ready to suffer the privations of poverty rather than yield a simulated obedience."[1]

Result of the enforced severities.—Two hundred and thirty-three ministers were suspended, of whom forty-nine were deprived absolutely and at once, without time to consider whether they would or would not comply with the obnoxious Articles. Sixty-four ministers were suspended in Norfolk alone, sixty in Suffolk, thirty-eight in Essex by Bishop Aylmer, thirty in Sussex,

[1] Hallam.

twenty in Kent, and twenty-one in Lincolnshire. This was a small number compared with the two thousand ministers ejected in 1662, but it must be remembered that at that time there were not more than two thousand clergymen in the whole country. In 1586, "after twenty-eight years establishment of the Church of England, there were only two thousand preachers to serve near ten thousand parishes, so that there were almost eight thousand parishes without preaching ministers." And, in general, the number of those who could not preach, but only read the service, was to the others nearly as four to one, the preachers being a majority only in London. "The Puritans," says Hallam, "formed so much the more learned and diligent part of the clergy, that a great scarcity of preachers was experienced throughout this reign, in consequence of silencing so many of the former." "Thus in Cornwall," says Neal, "about the year 1578, out of one hundred and forty clergymen, not one was capable of preaching."[1]

Puritans not without friends and sympathisers even in high places.—It must not be supposed that

[1] "This may be deemed by some an instance of Neal's prejudice," adds Hallam. "But that historian is not so ill-informed as they suppose; and the fact is highly probable. Let it be remembered that there existed few books of divinity in English; that all books were comparatively, to the value of money, far dearer than at present; that the majority of the clergy were nearly illiterate, and many of them addicted to drunkenness and low vices; above all, that they had no means of supplying their deficiencies by preaching the discourses of others,—and we shall see little cause for doubting Neal's statement, though founded on a Puritan document."—Hallam's *History*, vol. i. p. 270, note.

Archbishop Whitgift had upon his side all who were socially influential in Church and State. The Queen's most eminent ministers of State—Lord Burghley, the Earl of Leicester, the Earl of Bedford, Sir Francis Walsingham, Sir Francis Knollys, and Sir Nicholas Bacon—disapproved strongly of the archbishop's measures, and the rigour with which they were carried out by him and his suffragans. The Lords of the Council wrote to the archbishop and the Bishop of London, " That they had heard of a great number of zealous and learned preachers suspended from their cures ; the vacancy of the places for the most part without any ministry or preaching, prayer, and sacraments, and in some places of certain appointed to those void rooms being persons neither of learning nor of good name ; and in other places of that county (Essex) a great number of persons occupying the cures being notoriously unfit, most for lack of learning, many charged or chargeable with great and enormous faults, as drunkenness, filthiness of life, gaming at cards, haunting of alehouses, and such like ; against whom they (the Council) heard not of any proceedings, but that they were quietly suffered to the slander of the Church, to the offence of good people, yea, to the famishing of them for the lack of good teaching. . . .

" That there was a third sort, being a number having double livings with cure, and not resident upon their cures. That against all these sorts of lewd, evil, unprofitable, and corrupt members they (the Council) heard of no inquisition, nor of any kind of proceeding to the reformation of those horrible offences in the Church ; but yet of great diligence, yea, and extreme usage, against those that were known diligent preachers. . . . That the people of the realm might not be deprived of their pastors being diligent, learned, and zealous, though in some points of ceremonial they might seem doubtful only in conscience, and not of wilfulness," etc.

This letter of expostulation, signed by Lord Burghley, the Earls of Warwick, Shrewsbury, and Leicester, the Lord Charles Howard, Sir James Croft, Sir Christopher Hatton, and Sir Francis Walsingham, Secretary of State,[1] might as well never have been written. Convinced in his own way, and secure of Elizabeth's support, the archbishop nailed his colours to the mast, and went on his determined course.

Popular sympathy on the Puritan side.—The high-handed proceedings of Whitgift and the bishops, armed with the powers of the High Commission, and the truculence of the officials to whom the carrying out of their measures was entrusted, outraged the humanity and right feeling of all sections of the community, and the result was a marked and notable reaction in favour of the Puritans and their doctrines. A body of public opinion, growing every day in strength, declared against the legality of these proceedings, of the use of excommunication, and of the oath "*ex officio*."[2] This found expression in a petition presented to the House of Lords by the House of Commons in 1584, in which it was

---

[1] Strype's *Whitgift*, vol. i. pp. 328–330.

[2] "The oath *ex officio*, binding the taker to answer all questions that should be put to him, inasmuch as it contravened the generous maxim of English law, that no one is obliged to criminate himself, provoked very just animadversion."—Hallam.

prayed that certain reforms should be made and certain abuses removed,—among others, that ministers diligent in their calling, and of good conversation and life, should not be "molested . . . for omitting small portions of some ceremony prescribed in the Book of Common Prayer," that the scandal of such ministers being "openly disgraced by officials and commissaries, who daily call them to their courts to answer complaints of their doctrine and life, or breach of orders prescribed by the ecclesiastical laws and statutes of this realm," should be removed, and that all alleged offences of this description should be brought before the bishops themselves.

"That for the better increase of knowledge, it might be permitted to the ministers of every archdeaconry . . . to have some common exercises and conferences among themselves, to be limited and prescribed by their ordinaries." Perhaps the most significant of all the reforms pressed upon the attention of the "Lords spiritual and temporal" was that part of the petition which prayed that a certain number of the clergy might be associated with the bishops in performing the rite of ordination. This, however, is much more strongly emphasised in another petition [1] presented about the same time to the Queen, and which is said to have been endorsed by Lord Burghley, openly proposing that the authority with which the bishops had hitherto been invested should be transferred to provincial synods and national and general councils. The Presbyterian drift of this latter petition is

[1] The two petitions—that of the House of Commons and that of private individuals to the Queen—are given in Strype's *Whitgift*, vol. iii. pp. 118–124.

unmistakable; but it shows the strong sympathy there was with it, even among the ruling classes, that the Privy Council was itself divided in regard to it; while in the House of Commons the feeling was so strong, that had its will prevailed, Whitgift would have been deposed and his Articles abolished, and the whole system of Church and State as it then existed would have been profoundly modified.

But the presenters of these petitions might as well have whistled to the wind. Whitgift remained firm, and the Queen was inexorable. She gave one more proof of her unyielding temper in the speech she made on proroguing Parliament in 1585, in which she declared that the Church and herself, "whose over-ruler God hath made me," would be guilty of a "negligence" which "cannot be excused, if any schisms or errors heretical were suffered." She had made up her mind to "tolerate no new-fangledness." This quelled for the time at least all hope of reform. Elizabeth and her archbishop were masters of the situation. It may be interesting to note in this connection what Hallam says about the

Predominance of Puritan influence in Parliament. —" I conceive," he says, " the Church of England party, that is, the party adverse to any species of ecclesiastical change, to have been the least numerous of the three— *i.e.* those who were neutral, those attached to the ancient Church, and those who wished for further alterations in the new. The Puritans, or at least those who rather favoured them, had a majority among the Protestant gentry in the Queen's days. It is agreed on all hands, and is quite manifest, that they predominated in the House of Commons. But that House was composed, as it has ever been, of the principal landed proprietors, and as much represented the general wish of the community when it demanded a further reform in religious matters as on any other subject. One would imagine by the manner in which some express themselves, that the discontented were a small faction who, by some unaccountable means, in despite of the government and the nation, formed a majority of all Parliaments under Elizabeth and her two successors. . . . The Puritan party acquired strength by the prevailing hatred and dread of Popery, and by the disgust which the bishops had been unfortunate enough to excite. This contributed with the prevalent tone of public opinion, to throw such a weight into the puritanical scale in the Commons, as it required all the Queen's energy to counterbalance."[1]

Growth of Puritanism.—Puritanism went on steadily increasing and strengthening its hold upon the nation. "At the opening of the Queen's reign, Oxford was a nest of Papists, and sent its best scholars to feed the Catholic seminaries. At its close the university was a hotbed of Puritanism, where the fiercest tenets of Calvin reigned supreme. The University of Cambridge was at a far earlier period impregnated with the Puritan spirit, and this continued to grow in spite of all the efforts of Whitgift, the Vice-Chancellor, to exorcise it.[2] The

---

[1] Hallam, vol. i. p. 257.
[2] "It was in Cambridge that the Reformation first commenced; and though that great movement had its foundation laid much

progress which Puritanism had made, in spite of all the repressive measures which were directed against it, was indeed amazing. It may be said without exaggeration that the best part of the religion of England, as nearly all the virtue and serious-mindedness of the nation, were on the side of Puritanism. The purest and noblest of Elizabethan heroes were Puritans. The most typical poet of the Elizabethan age was a Puritan. The blending of religion and chivalry in the *Faerie Queen* reveals the spring at which Spenser had drunk, while the *Shepheard's Calender* and the satire of *Mother Hubbard's Tale* reflect only too faithfully the corruption into which religion had sunk, both among the clergy and the large body of the people.[1]

There is one figure, however, upon the opposite side which stands out in noble proportions, and to this dutiful and loyal son of the Church and defender of her institutions it is a relief to turn from defenders of a different temper and type.

Richard Hooker.—The genius of Hooker has in-

more in nationalism than in theology, yet latent energies of a religious character were at work; and of their influence, on the Reforming side, not the greater part, but almost the whole, belonged to Cambridge. Oxford devoted herself [that is, at the opening of the Queen's reign] to make recusants, and Cambridge to the formation of Zwinglians and Calvinists."—Right Hon. W. E. Gladstone, M.P., Speech at Oxford, October 24, 1892.

[1] "The highest expression of the Puritan view of English religion in the latter half of the reign of Elizabeth is to be found in the First Book of Spenser's *Faerie Queen*. The highest expression of the opposite view is in the *Ecclesiastical Polity* of Richard Hooker."—Henry Morley's *History of English Literature*, p. 190.

vested his writings with an adventitious importance,— an importance which they owe less to the relevance and conclusiveness of his reasoning, than to his majestic style and prose. His *Ecclesiastical Polity* is the earliest specimen of English prose, in which the preserving salt of literary excellence is such as to recommend it to the taste of modern readers. Its massive eloquence, its vigour and grasp of thought, its wealth of learning and illustration, as well as its amplitude of style, have given to Hooker's great work a permanent position in English literature. Its abiding interest, however, is philosophical and political; as a theological polemic, time has reduced it to a condition of irrelevance.

The fundamental principle of the *Ecclesiastical Polity* is the supremacy, unity, and all-embracing character of **Law**,—"Law whose seat is the bosom of God, whose voice the harmony of the world." Law is that which binds the whole creation in all its ranks and subordinations to the perfect goodness and reason of God. Every law of God is a law of reason, and every law of reason is a law of God. There is a divine order, Hooker argues, not only in written revelation, but also in the course and constitution of nature, in the moral order and government of the world. It pertains to human reason to discover and to apply the laws of this order, and even within the province of Scripture itself to distinguish between those elements which are accidental and temporary and those which are essential and immutable. The authority of the Church Hooker finds in the authority of Reason or Law, in other words, in the historical, ordered, and continuous progression of the Church herself, an authority enshrined for Hooker as truly as for Augustine, in the famous words, *Securus judicat orbis terrarum*. The first four books of the *Ecclesiastical Polity* were published in 1594, and in them Hooker set himself to undermine the position of Cartwright and Travers, that for the individual Christian the maxim is, "Scripture is the only rule of all things which may be done of man"; while for the Church the maxim is, "There must be in Scripture a form of Church Polity, the laws of which may not be altered."

Did Hooker refute Puritanism?—It is sometimes affirmed that the argument of Hooker is directed against *the Puritan position*,[1] and that by it the Puritan contention was disproved and disposed of for all time to come. A more preposterous statement was never made. Its absurdity is manifest at a glance, when we remember that both the Puritan position and the Puritan party were only in their nascent beginning, and Puritanism—which never was a reasoned system of belief—was at that time an inchoate principle, struggling, at tremendous odds, to make itself felt.

Dean Church[2] says that while the Reformation was, in one sense, an appeal to reason, it was an appeal also to authority, the authority of Scripture against reason; and of this appeal to authority against reason, Puritanism was the most extreme and absolute form, and showed the

[1] The Anglican and Presbyterian positions are briefly but conveniently exhibited in extracts from the *Ecclesiastical Polity*, by Professor Prothero, in his *Select Statutes*, etc. pp. 245-247.

[2] Dean Church's Introduction to book i. of Hooker's *Laws of Ecclesiastical Polity* (Clarendon Press Series).

consequences of sacrificing fact to theory. We venture to think that from such insufficient data as we have, as to what Puritanism really was at this time, this is much too large a generalisation. It proceeds on the precarious assumption that Puritanism is to be identified with the opinions of Cartwright and Travers. Hallam warns us against concluding that everyone, or even the majority, of those who might be counted on the Puritan side in Elizabeth's reign, would have subscribed to the extravagant opinions of Cartwright. But this loose, undiscriminating use of the term "Puritanism," as we have already pointed out, quite ignores the change and development which Puritanism itself underwent during the succeeding century.

Misconceptions as to the true meaning of Puritanism.—There is no error which is more widespread than that Puritanism is bound up with certain theories and doctrines, such as those put forth by Cartwright. Canon Curteis speaks of the Puritan delusion that the Scriptures are the *sole* organ of the Holy Ghost, and says that this, and the Calvinistic system in general, " belong to the very *essence* of Puritanism."[1] " For whereas God hath left sundry kinds of laws unto men, and by all these laws the actions of men are in some sort directed, they [Cartwright and his disciples] held that one only law, the Scripture, must be the rule to direct in all things, even so far as to the taking up of a rush or straw."[2]

[1] Curteis' *Bampton Lecture*, p. 271.
[2] Hooker's *Ecclesiastical Polity*, book ii. chap. ii.
Readers of Mr. Matthew Arnold—those who have read his paper on

In the course of our inquiry we shall probably find good reason for doubting whether such notions as these did belong to the very essence of Puritanism. Even among the Elizabethan Puritans it would have been difficult to extract a perfect consensus of opinion that "Scripture is the only rule of all things which may be done of man"; and certainly as regards the rule and order of the Church, their notion was far from being exhausted in the thesis, "The apostolic polity is the authoritative and normative polity for all time."[1]

Is it so very certain that the Puritans did appeal to the authority of Scripture *against* reason? It seems to be taken for granted, that because the Puritans appealed to the authority of Scripture as against the authority of the Church of Rome and that claimed by the Anglican Church, *therefore* they did not appeal to reason.[2] Surely,

"Puritanism and the Church of England"—are familiar with his wild unsupported assertions that the Puritans staked their existence on the "assumption that there is a divinely-appointed Church order fixed once for all in the Bible, and that they have adopted it"; also that "*the Puritan Churches found their very existence* on the doctrines of predestination, imputed righteous, etc., but *the historic Churches do not*."—*St. Paul and Protestantism*, popular edition, pp. 115, 85.

[1] *Jubilee Lectures.* Introductory chapter on "Ecclesiastical Polity and the Religion of Christ," li.

[2] "Puritan theocracy, though strict, and sure to melt away when the sun of freedom had mounted higher in the heaven, was not reactionary or obscurantist. It had for its rule the Bible, but *the Bible interpreted by reason*. It owed paramount allegiance, not to authority, but to truth."—*The United States: An Outline of Political History*, by Goldwin Smith, D.C.L., p. 10.

Chillingworth is regarded as a very liberal theologian, but it may be doubted whether many of the later Puritans would not have had serious doubts regarding a position like this: "Propose me anything out of this book, and require whether I believe it or not, and

with equal force, the same objection may be brought against their opponents, because they appealed to antiquity—to the authority of the Fathers and of councils. Even Hooker was not content to find in reason the sole basis and justification of Church authority. "It may be justly objected," says Hallam, "to some passages [in the *Ecclesiastical Polity*] that they elevate ecclesiastical authority, even in matters of belief, with an exaggeration not easily reconciled to the Protestant right of private judgment, and even of dangerous consequence in those times, as when he inclines to give a decisive voice in theological controversies to general councils, not, indeed, on the principles of the Church of Rome, but on such as must end in the same conclusion, the high probability that the aggregate judgment of many grave and learned men should be well founded. It is well known that the Preface to the *Ecclesiastical Polity* was one of the two books to which James II. ascribed his return into the field of Rome; and it is not difficult to perceive by what course of reasoning, on the position it contains, this was effected."[1]

"It cannot be said that Hooker added anything to the answers that were made to the Puritans. He carried the question up to a higher region, where the atmosphere was purer. The Puritan was not without a sense of that order of which Hooker discoursed. He believed, however, that it was not furthered, but hindered, by the retention of the order and ceremonies that had been in the Church

---

seem it never so incomprehensible to human reason, I will subscribe it with hand and heart, as knowing no demonstration can be stronger than this: God hath said so, and therefore it is true."

[1] Hallam, vol. i. p. 296, note.

of Rome. Why, it was asked, are we to conclude that what is retained is any more the expression of a divine order than that which has been rejected."[1] The Puritans could not see the force of the long disquisition about law as urged against them, nor can we. It may have been relevant to some of the reasoning employed by Cartwright and Travers, but so far from turning the flank of the Puritan position, Hooker's great work has become an armoury from which Puritanism has drawn its most fit and effective weapons.[2]

Lord Bacon was one with Hooker in counselling unity in the Church, and deploring the unhappy controversies which were dividing the Church and nation; but to the acuteness of the philosopher, Bacon added the practical sagacity of the statesman. Hooker would have the Puritan comply with the laws and regulations of the Church; while Bacon would have these sufficiently elastic to accommodate his views and prejudices.[3] "Therefore it is good we return to the ancient bands of unity in the Church of God, which was one faith, one baptism, and not one hierarchy, one discipline, and that we observe the league of Christians as it is penned by our Saviour Christ, which is in substance of doctrine this: All that is not with us is against us; but in things indifferent, and but of circumstance, this: He that is not against us is with us; . . . as it is excellently alluded

---

[1] Hunt's *Religious Thought in England*, vol. i. p. 60.
[2] In his admirable little handbook on *Church and State*, Mr. Taylor Innes (p. 175) acutely points out how Hooker's views of the original source of Church authority are parallel and in accordance with those of his Presbyterian and Puritan opponents.
[3] *The Puritan Revolution*, 1603-1660, by S. R. Gardiner.

by the father that noted that Christ's garment was without seam, and yet the Church's garment was of divers colours, and thereupon set down for a rule, Let there be variety in the vesture, but not a rent."[1]

NOTE ON HOOKER'S THEORY OF CHURCH AND STATE

The *Ecclesiastical Polity* contains Hooker's peculiar theory of Church and State, the false and mischievous position that the Church and commonwealth are but different denominations of the same society. "A Church and a commonwealth, we grant, are things in nature the one distinguished from the other. A Church is one way, and a commonwealth another way, defined." "We hold that, seeing there is not any man of the Church of England but the same man is also a member of the commonwealth, nor any member of the commonwealth which is not also of the Church of England ; therefore, as in a figure triangle, the base doth differ from the sides thereof, and yet one and the self-same line is both a base and also a side,—a side simply, a base if it chance to be the bottom, and underlie the same,—so albeit propositions and actions of one do cause the name of a commonwealth, qualities and functions of another sort the name of the Church, to be given to a multitude, yet one and the self-same multitude may in such sort be both."—Book viii. chap. i. section 2.

It is obvious at a glance that such identity as this never existed in point of fact, and the comment which history writes upon the attempts which, at different times and in various ways, have been made to bring it about is instructive and tragical. Such union of Church and State is a chimera ; the fact that religion and politics belong to two totally distinct and dissimilar spheres it entirely ignores. His deftly constructed theory should have dissolved under the touchstone of his own words : "A commonwealth we name it simply in regard of some regiment or policy under which men live ; a Church, for the truth of that religion which they profess."—Book viii. chap. i. section 5.

"To profess a religion is a personal act ; must be voluntarily and

---

[1] *Advertisement touching the Controversies of the Church of England.*

consciously done to be done at all." But this was precisely what could not happen, or be allowed to happen, in Hooker's theory of the Church. To him "one society is both the Church and commonwealth," and, as a necessary result, "our Church hath dependence from the chief in our commonwealth." But this was to transform the profession of religion into a matter of loyalty, and to identify Nonconformity with rebellion. Responsibility to the King supplanted responsibility to God, godliness became a species of political obedience, and the Church was emptied of its transcendental and ethical ideals that it might be organised into a system which was all the more civil that it was so intensely sacerdotal."[1]

---

[1] Dr. Fairbairn on *Ecclesiastical Polity and the Religion of Christ*. Introductory chapter to *Jubilee Lectures*. See whole of Dr. Fairbairn's criticism on Hooker's "splendid idea of a Church," and the comparison between this and the ideal of Independency and the religion of Christ.

Rise of Independency

MEMORABLE EVENTS AND DATES

Robert Browne, born 1550, died between 1631 and 1633
Church of Richard Fitz met in London . . . 1567
Church in Norwich gathered by Robert Browne . 1580

CONTENTS OF CHAPTER VII

Puritanism not a Church System—Independency at first not a polity—Harbingers of Independency—Puritans libelled—Beginnings of Separatism—Church of Richard Fitz—Robert Browne—His relation to Independency — Browne and the Brownists — Raleigh's estimate of number of Brownists—Dissenters and Separatists—What Separatism originally implied—Separatists through force of circumstances.

CHAPTER VII

Rise of Independency

It should always be remembered that Puritanism at the beginning had nothing to do with any question of Church government. Neither Presbyterianism nor Independency were involved in it, and Episcopacy only because it had possession of the field, and appeared, even to the majority of the Puritans of that age, the only possible and practicable polity. What they supremely desired and vehemently contended for was to get Luther's "doctrine of Christian liberty, and of the common universal priesthood," embodied in visible form, so as to become the corner-stone of a temple in which men could worship God without the intervention of priest, altar, and sacrifice. Contemned and rejected by the Church of Rome, it was in their eyes the condemnation of the Reformed Protestant Church, that this was the stone also which the builders rejected.

Independency at first not a polity.—The rise of Independency must not be confounded with the rise of Separatism. This confusion is a common one, but no one who reads the history of that period with any degree of care should fall into it. Separatism led, no doubt, to the assertion of Independency, and eventually to its setting up as an organised sytem, but in the beginning it had no connection with it whatever, for the simple reason that Independency proper had not then come into existence. Moreover, it came into existence at first, not as a system at all, but as the vehicle and natural expression of the religious life, and of the fellowship which that life seeks and creates. A shipwrecked crew of religious men and women, united by no tie but that of a deep spiritual faith, and cast upon a desert island, would be at first compelled to form themselves into an independent Church or fellowship, though they might afterwards graft upon it a system utterly at variance with the principles of Independency. Independency is thus seen to be the form towards which the religious life at first spontaneously gravitates, the mould into which it immediately and naturally runs. Of this we shall find subsequent and striking illustrations.

The harbingers of Independency.—The first heralds of religious freedom in England, those who were Reformers before the Reformation, became, less by choice than of necessity, the harbingers of Independency Among them must be included such names as Grosseteste, bishop of Lincoln in 1248; Wyclif, Colet, Erasmus, Hooper, Latimer, Ridley, Tyndale, and More. The most notable of all is **Wyclif**. It is in his writings that we find the first explicit statement of the principle that lies at the root of Independency. "The Temple of God is the congregation, living religiously, of just men, for whom Jesus shed His blood." "Looking at the present state of the Church, we find it would be better, and of greater use to the Church, if it were governed purely by the law of Scripture, than by human traditions, mixed up with evangelical." "For Christ, our Lawgiver, has given us a law which is itself sufficient for the whole Church militant." When Wyclif's poor priests went about the country preaching, they gathered assemblies of like-minded religious people, and by them the foregleams of Reformation light were kindled and kept burning. As early as the commencement of the reign of Henry IV. a law was passed, the preamble of which ran—" Some had a new faith about the sacraments of the Church, and the authority of the same; and did preach without authority, gathered conventicles, taught schools, wrote books against the Catholic faith, with many other heinous aggravations."[1] The preamble of an Act for the burning of heretics, passed in 1401, that is, seventeen years after the death of Wyclif, states that "divers false and perverse people of a certain new sect, usurping the office of preaching, do perversely and maliciously, in divers places within the realm, preach and teach divers new doctrines and wicked, erroneous opinions; and of such sect and wicked doctrines they make unlawful conventicles."

Misstatements and prejudice regarding the Puritans. —The story of the early Separatists is with difficulty disentangled from the allegations and aspersions which prejudice and rancour have woven round it, or substituted for the final and sober judgment of history itself. "Much as the Puritans have been vilified in history, their treatment

[1] Burnet's *History of the Reformation* (1841), vol. i. p. 20.

has been mild compared with that which has been accorded to the Separatists." It should never be forgotten that we are dependent upon their adversaries for the main part of our information regarding both Puritans and Separatists, and consequently this information needs, as far as possible, to be subjected to the most careful investigation and sifting.[1] What Carlyle says about " the old narratives " in respect of Cromwell is applicable to not a little of the " rumour " regarding the Puritans in general, which passes muster for history. " How many grave historical statements still circulate in the world, accredited by Bishop Burnet and the like, which, on examination, you will find melt away into after-dinner rumours. . . . I have examined most of them; found not one of them fairly believable: wondered to see how already in one generation, earnest Puritanism being hung on the gallows or thrown out in St. Margaret's Churchyard, the whole History of it had grown *mythical*, and men were ready to swallow all manner of nonsense concerning it. Ask for dates, ask for proofs: Who saw it, heard it; when was it, where?"[2]

The temper in which this subject is approached by a

---

[1] The restrictions upon printing in these days were so great, and the search made for books or pamphlets supposed to be tainted with schism, sedition, and heresy was so jealous and unremitting, that the literature of this description which did get into circulation was, with the exception of the Martin-Marprelate tracts, of the scantiest description. " This has probably," says Hallam (*History*, vol. i. p. 323, note), " been one cause of the extreme scarcity of the puritanical pamphlets." The censorship of the entire literature of the time was practically in the hands of the Primate and the Bishop of London. See p. 158.

[2] Carlyle's *Letters and Speeches of Cromwell*, vol. i. p. 239.

certain class of writers may be gathered from a remark by Mr. Maskell in his *History of the Martin-Marprelate Controversy*. " I do not think that we must listen to objections from the Elizabethan Puritans in the same temper as we would to other men's; neither can we allow them to have the same weight." [1]

The beginnings of Separatism and Independency. —" The martyrs of the primitive Churches of old," says John Owen, " lost more of their blood and lives for their meetings and assemblies than for personal profession of the faith; and so also have others done under the Roman apostasy." We have evidence as to the prevalence of secret meetings and assemblies long before the beginning of the Reformation in England. " There were secret multitudes," says Foxe, " who tasted and followed the sweetness of God's holy word, and whose fervent zeal may appear by their sitting up all night in reading and hearing." The number of these appears to have increased during the Marian persecution; and even with the fires of Smithfield blazing, as it were, before their very eyes, they forsook not the assembling of themselves

[1] *A History of the Martin-Marprelate Controversy*, by the Rev. William Maskell, M.A., p. 116. The extent to which unconscious prejudice may influence the minds of writers who make the "epitomised synopsis of rumour," to use Carlyle's phrase, do duty for history, is well illustrated in the two short articles on " Robert Browne," and " The Brownists," which appears in the last (ninth) edition of the *Encyclopædia Britannica*. A statement like this, "The occasion of the Brownists' separatism was not any fault they found with the faith, but only with the discipline and forms of government of the other Churches in England," should either have been omitted, or it should have been amplified and explained.

together. On New Year's Day 1555, we hear of certain honest men and women of the city (of London), to the number of thirty, taken, as they were at the communion in a house in Bow Churchyard, and carried off to prison. On the death of Mary and the accession of Elizabeth these secret meetings continued to be held less or more openly. Thomas Lever, one of the returned exiles, writing to his friend Bullinger in 1559, says: "There had been a congregation of faithful persons concealed in London during the time of Mary, among whom the gospel was always preached, with the pure administration of the sacraments; but during the rigour of the persecution of that Queen they carefully concealed themselves, and on the cessation of it under Elizabeth they openly continued in the same congregation. . . . Large numbers flocked to them, not in churches, but in private houses."

The Church of Richard Fitz.—In the year 1567 a number of people—about two hundred—were in the habit of meeting in London, in what was known as Plumbers' Hall. They had chosen as their pastor one Richard Fitz. "Some London citizens have openly separated from us," says Bishop Grindal, writing to Bullinger, "and sometimes in private houses, sometimes in fields, and occasionally even in ships, they have held meetings and administered the sacraments. Besides this, they have ordained ministers, elders, and deacons, after their own way. The Privy Council have lately committed the heads of this faction to prison." The latter refers to a meeting at Plumbers' Hall, held in connection with some marriage festivity, which was surprised by the vigilance of the authorities, broken up, and the incriminated persons hailed off to Bridewell Prison. This little company, with Richard Fitz as their pastor, is sometimes, but incorrectly, described as the first Independent Congregational Church, if, indeed, it could be called, in any strict historical sense, an Independent Church at all. It seems more probable that it was a resumption or continuation of the previously existing band of Separatists already mentioned as composed of "certain honest men and women of the city, to the number of thirty."[1] "These humble men really believed that Jesus Christ established His empire upon the consent, not the fears, of men, and trusted Himself defenceless among mankind,"[2] and, so far, the little Church was founded upon the Congregational idea; but much more is needed to show that it was modelled upon the Congregational system. In his

---

[1] The claim of this little Church, which had Richard Fitz as its pastor, to be considered an Independent or Congregational Church, and also (for both claims have been made for it) the *first* Independent or Congregational Church in England, has been very much debated. The opinion to which the present writer inclines will be gathered from what follows in the text. A careful and interesting statement of the case will be found in a paper entitled, "Congregationalism: Old and New," in a little work on the *Early Independents*, by Rev. John Brown, D.D.; also in *The Story of the English Separatists*, pp. 41–45, by Rev. A. Mackennal, D.D. Both these works were published in 1893 by the Congregational Union of England and Wales, and present in the smallest compass—and far more effectively than many bulky works—a clear, concise, and altogether admirable history of the period to which they relate.

[2] Dr. Stoughton's *History of Religion in England*, vol. i. p. 343, new and revised edition. Dr. Stoughton's statement, that "a Congregational Church existed in London *so early as* 1568," calls for some revision in the light of what has been already advanced.

work on *The Congregationalism of the last Three Hundred Years*, p. 115, we think Dr. Dexter very forcibly deals with this contention, and shows that while the little company of Separatists held some good Congregational principles, yet these " scarcely more touched the question of pure polity than the pile, driven deep below the foundations of a building, suggests whether it is to be Gothic, Grecian, or pure Yankee in its façade." His figure implies a much less complete approximation to Independent polity than that actually made by the little company; but certainly to speak of them as being the founders of Independency is, we must hold, historically inaccurate. That honour, however the necessity may be regretted, has to be accorded to one of a very different temper from Richard Fitz or any of his little flock.

Robert Browne.[1]—No account of Independency would be complete which did not embrace extended and due reference to Robert Browne, the founder of the Brownists, the name which has since been given to the

[1] "While they (the English Independents) seek the original warrant for their views in the New Testament and in the practice of the primitive Church, and while they maintain, also, that the essence of these views was rightly revived in old English Wyclifism, and perhaps in some of the speculations which accompanied Luther's Reformation on the Continent, they admit that the theory of Independency had to be worked out afresh by a new process of the English mind in the sixteenth and seventeenth centuries, and they are content, I believe, that the crude immediate beginning of that process should be sought in the opinions propagated between 1580 and 1590 by the erratic Robert Browne, a Rutlandshire man, bred at Cambridge, who had become a preacher at Norwich."—Professor Masson's *Life of Milton*, vol. iv. p. 536.

followers of Independency. This remarkable man, extraordinary both for the force of his personality and character, was the son of Anthony Browne of Tolthorp, in Rutlandshire, and was born in 1550. His grandfather, by a charter of Henry VIII., had acquired the singular distinction of being allowed to wear his cap in the King's presence. After he had taken his degree at Cambridge, he became, according to Strype, private chaplain to the Duke of Norfolk. He was cited to appear before the Ecclesiastical Commissioners on a charge of disseminating seditious doctrines; and had not that nobleman befriended him and taken his part, he would doubtless have become acquainted with the inside of a prison much earlier than he did.[1] At the age of twenty-two he became a schoolmaster, and afterwards a lecturer and preacher, though without a licence; and it would appear that about this time he adopted the opinions with which his name has been since identified. Neal says he was "a fiery, hot-headed young man, and went about the countries inveighing against the discipline and ceremonies of the Church, and exhorted the people by no means to comply with them." In 1580 he removed to Norwich, where his preaching was the means of attracting a numerous congregation, which comprised, probably, a considerable number of Dutch refugees, who at that time formed more than half the population of Norwich. Among these were doubtless not a few Anabaptists and other sufferers in the cause of liberty

[1] This intervention, however, on the part of the Duke of Norfolk, and the statement that Browne was chaplain to that nobleman, appears to be an error on the part of Strype. See note appended to Dr. Dale's "Lecture on the Early Independents" in *Jubilee Lectures*, p. 55.

and conscience.[1] In the year 1582 he published a book entitled, *The Life and Manners of True Christians*, to which is prefixed "A Treatise of Reformation without tarrying for any, and of the wickedness of those preachers which will not reform themselves and their charge, because they will tarry till the magistrate command and compel them."

Browne seems to have been the first to protest against multitudinism in the Church, or what is better known by the term, promiscuous communion. "The kingdom of God," he says, "was not to be begun by whole parishes, but rather of the worthiest, be they never so few." The Church must be constituted of sincere God-fearing Christian men and women. This is his definition of a Church: "The Church planted or gathered in a company or number of Christians or believers, which, by a willing covenant made with their God, are under the government of God and Christ, and keep His laws in one holy communion. The Church government is the lordship of Christ in the communion of His offices, whereby His people obey His will, and have mutual use of their graces and callings to further their godliness and welfare."

"For Browne, as before for Cartwright, the voice of the people was literally the voice of God. Christ was the King. As His will was revealed equally to all, all had an equal right to interpret it. He reigns; the community governs in His name. *Thus the Puritans, by*

---

[1] "The Independents of England and the Congregationalists of America are to-day in lineal descent from that little Norwich church of two hundred and ninety-six years ago."—Dexter's *Congregationalism as seen in its Literature*, p. 114, published in 1879.

means of their idea of monarchy itself, arrived practically at democracy. They proclaimed a kind of Divine Right Democracy." [1]

Holding the views he did, he could have no communion with the Church of England, nor could he acknowledge her " to be a true Church, or her ministers true ministers." He exhorted his hearers to separate from the parish churches, and "seek the Church of God wheresoever." [2] Such extreme views, and the endeavour to embody them by the formation of a separate congregation, naturally exposed Browne and his followers to the severity of the Queen and her bishops, and he was obliged to leave the kingdom. He and several of his friends found in Holland the freedom which was denied them in their own country, and, by permission of the authorities, a Church, which may properly be described as an Independent Church, was formed in Middelburg, in Zealand. This Church at Middelburg included not a few who afterwards became eminent for their zeal and piety and learning. The unanimity that at first prevailed was, however, soon broken, and the Church split up into two sections, the one insisting with Browne upon the duty of absolute separation from the Church of England, and the other favouring a more modified nonconformity. This latter section, under Robinson, took the name Independents. These became growingly strong and influential, and the Brownists soon

---

[1] "Puritanism and the English Revolution," p. 34, chap. i. of the *Rise of Modern Democracy in Old and New England*, by Charles Borgeaud, Member of the Faculty of Law, Geneva. Translated by Mrs. Birkbeck Hill, with a preface by C. H. Firth, M.A., Balliol College, Oxford.

[2] See, however, pp. 185-6.

faded out of view, and gave place to the Independents. As the breach between his associates and himself became wider, and troubles increased, Browne found his position intolerable. He determined to try Scotland, to see if that would furnish more congenial and fruitful soil for the growth of his free Church principles. But if he had little to hope for from Episcopacy, he soon found that he had still less to expect from Presbyterianism. King James said: "They" (meaning Browne and Penry) "have come to Scotland to sow their popple amongst us." The next thing we find is that Browne was cited to appear before the Archbishop of Canterbury to answer for one of his publications. He was delivered from this dilemma by the friendly interposition of his kinsman, Lord Burghley. After this, Browne found an asylum under his father's roof, and here apparently everything was done that parental solicitude could suggest to induce him to change his opinions and conform to the established religion. But, says Fuller, "it seems Browne's errors were so inlaid in him, no conferences with divines would convince him to the contrary, whose incorrigibleness made his own father weary of his company. Men may wish, God only can work, children to be good. The old gentleman would own him for his son no longer than his son owned the Church of England for his mother, desiring to rid his hands of him."

Concerning the closing period of Browne's life, it is very difficult to ascertain correctly what the facts are. We have only the testimony of men like Fuller, who was intensely prejudiced against the man and his views, and whose statements therefore must be received with the utmost caution. It seems, however, impossible to acquit him of gross inconsistency and tergiversation. Weary of enduring " the slings and arrows of outrageous fortune," he accepted a living in Northamptonshire, and found rest, or such rest as was possible to so turbulent a spirit, in the bosom of the Church which he had so unsparingly assailed and denounced. For this act no apology can be offered but his ungovernable temper, and the fact that he was an old man soured by disappointment and broken by reverses. " One may justly wonder," says Fuller, " when many meaner accessories in this schism were arraigned, condemned, and executed, how this Browne, the principal, made so fair an escape, yea, enjoyed such preferment. Yet he came off at last both with saving his life and keeping his living (and that none of the meanest—Achurch in Northamptonshire) until the day of his death."

" More probable it is that the promise of his general compliance with the Church of England (so far forth as not to make future disturbance therein) met with the archbishop's courteous acceptance thereof, both which effectually improved by the countenance of Thomas Cecil, Earl of Exeter (Browne's near kinsman and patron), procured this extraordinary favour to be indulged unto him."

But though Browne consented to eat the bread of the Church of which he had been so unsparing an assailant, it is quite clear that his compliance was merely outward and formal, and represented no change of principle or conviction. Strype says of him: " He continued still very freakish"; while Fuller says: " I will never believe that he ever formally recanted his opinions, either by word or writing, as to the main of what he maintained."[1]

Browne, in what sense the founder of Independency.—It is assumed by adverse critics of Independency that the relation between it and Browne is like that which exists between the stream and its source, and, consequently, if they can show the impurity of the one, they can demonstrate the impurity of the other. This assumption is, however, unfounded and gratuitous.

Browne was the founder of Independency only in the sense that he was the first (so far as we know) to grasp its fundamental contention and principle, and give it practical and visible embodiment. He saw clearly enough that the primitive Church was very different from the Church of England, that its most characteristic features had been obliterated, its simplicity superseded and overlaid by an elaborate ritual, by a graded hierarchy, by ceremonies and customs which had no existence, and could have had no sanction in the apostolic age. Now as then, it was within the right of any number of Christians to form themselves into a separate congregation, elect their own officers, arrange for the conduct of worship, the observance of ordinances, and the maintenance of discipline, free from all external authority and control; and acting upon this conviction, he took steps to gather a Church founded upon these principles. Browne's part in the movement was simply that of the discoverer who gives to some new fruitful idea its initial impulse and shape, leaving it to others to expand

[1] See Fuller's *Church History*, vol. v. p. 68.

and develop. But as the worth of a discovery, either in science or morals, is not affected by the discoverer's personal character or manner of life, so it is no derogation to Independency to say that his reputation for piety and consistency was decidedly damaged. But if Browne had been a much worse man than he was, it would not invalidate or impugn his claim to have originated and struck out a most fruitful idea, nor yet to have demonstrated its practicability as the basis of a free democratic Church system. In gathering the first separate congregation, Browne had, at least, the courage of his convictions. This quality was certainly not lacking in one who boasted that for preaching against bishops, ceremonies, etc., "he had been committed to thirty-two prisons, in some of which he could not see his hand at noonday."

It is no part of our brief to defend the character of Robert Browne, and we confess that if it were, we should shrink from essaying the task. Let those, however, who are desirous to see what apology can be constructed for his later errors, turn to Dr. Dexter's account of him.[1] Dr. Dexter is a convinced and ardent believer in the genuineness of his character and the honesty of his religious convictions. Whatever be thought of his final judgment in regard to him, no one can consider the evidence he brings forward, and examine carefully what he has to say regarding it, without admitting the groundlessness of the charge that Robert Browne was "an ambitious bigot in his earlier, and a contemptible sneak in his later years ; with the easy, if not inevitable, inference

[1] Dexter's *Congregationalism as seen in its Literature*, Robert Browne and his Co-workers, pp. 116-128.

that he must have been a hypocrite through all." Dr. Dexter's deliverance is summed up in the words, that he was "a long maligned, eccentric, infirm, and probably insane, yet, I must think, a mainly good and singularly clever man."

Browne and the Brownists.—In his admirable lecture on the early Independents, Dr. Dale says: "I have never been able, however, to satisfy myself as to the ground on which the Congregationalists of the latter years of Elizabeth's reign so bitterly resented identification with the Brownists."[1] But we submit that this is sufficiently explained by the suspicion and odium which Browne naturally incurred by his tergiversation, and also by the reputation he had previously acquired by his imperious and fiery temper. If Browne's personal character had been such as to command unhesitating confidence and respect, there is no reason to suppose that the later Independents would have shown any indisposition to bear his name, or have shrunk from avowing themselves his followers. The Brownists—the name afterwards given to his followers—carried his principles to a most extreme length. They denied the Church of England to be a true Church, and maintained that its rites and discipline were popish, antichristian, and corrupt. The constitution of the existing ecclesiastical hierarchy seemed to them too bad to be mended, the very pillars of it were rotten, and the only hope of reforming it lay in razing it to the ground and beginning to build anew.

[1] "No Independent will take it well at any man's hand to be called a *Brownist*."—Hanbury's *Historical Memorials relating to the Independents*, vol. iii. p. 132.

Neal the historian, and, as some aver (we think on insufficient grounds), the unsparing panegyrist of the Puritans and all their doings, admits that the Brownists were involved in frequent quarrels and divisions. "Their chief crime," he said, "was their uncharitableness in unchurching the whole Christian world, and breaking off all manner of communion in hearing the word, in public prayer, and in the administration of the sacraments, not only with the Church of England, but with all foreign reformed churches, which, though less pure, ought certainly to be owned as Churches of Christ." John Cotton, one of the organising minds of New England, and to whom the credit specially belongs of reducing Independency to a working system, energetically repelled the imputation of Brownism, or, as he expressed it, the "disclaiming the Churches in England to be no Churches, but as limbs of the devil"; adding, that for using such violent language as this, Roger Williams was censured and condemned.[1]

Twenty thousand Brownists in England.—Obnoxious as Brownism was, not less, perhaps, to Cartwright and the Puritans at large than to the ruling powers, it is clear from contemporary evidence it had grown even under

[1] Dr. Dexter says Brownism has been misunderstood by the great mass of Congregationalists, who have been wont to associate with this term the thought of narrowness and exclusion. Thus he says Cotton calls Brownism the "way of rigid separation." But by Brownism, Dr. Dexter evidently means the opinions of Browne himself. We suspect that Cotton is here speaking, not of Browne, but of his followers, who certainly went further in the way of narrowness and exclusion.

the primacy of Whitgift to considerable dimensions, and become a force that had to be reckoned with. "In my conceit," said Sir Walter Raleigh, in a speech he delivered in Parliament in 1580, "the Brownists are worthy to be rooted out of the Commonwealth; but what danger may grow to ourselves if this law pass, it were fit to be considered. For it is to be feared that men not guilty will be involved in it. . . . If two or three thousand Brownists meet at the sea, at whose charge shall they be transported, or whither will you send them? I am sorry for it. *I am afraid there are near twenty thousand of them in England,* and when they be gone who shall maintain their wives and children?"[1]

Dissenters and Separatists.—A certain degree of confusion on the part of those who have treated of the germinal upspringings of Independency would, we think, have been avoided if they had kept more clearly before their minds the fact that during and after the Reformation (and to some extent, as we have seen, even before) there were *three* classes of Dissenters or Separatists.

1st. Those who dissented from the Established Church because of its corruptions, but still clung to it in the hope that the leaven of its apostasy might be purged away.

2nd. Those who dissented from the Church for the same reason, but had abandoned all hope of possible reformation, and so justified their secession from it.

3rd. Those who dissented from the principle of an Established Church as being opposed to the whole spirit

[1] D'Ewes' *Journal*, p. 517.

as well as the express teaching of the New Testament, and as violating the constitution and contravening the very nature of Christ's kingdom. All these three classes were Puritans, but Puritans with a difference, which, as between the first and the last, was most broadly marked. The first may be described as Nonconformists inside the Church, or nonconforming members of the Church of England; the second and third as Nonconformists outside the Church, that is, Nonconformists proper, Nonconformists in the real and historical sense of the word.

The Brownists belonged to the second class, and the distinction between them and the "Conforming Puritans," *i.e.* the Puritans belonging to the first class, is very clearly drawn by Neal: "Most of the Puritans were for keeping within the pale of the Church, apprehending it to be a true Church in its doctrines and sacraments, though defective in discipline and corrupt in ceremonies; but being a true Church, they thought it not lawful to separate, though they could hardly continue in it with a good conscience. They submitted to suspensions and deprivations; and when they were driven out of one diocese, took sanctuary in another, being afraid of incurring the guilt of schism by forming themselves into separate communions. Whereas the Brownists maintained that the Church of England, in its present constitution, was no true Church of Christ, but a limb of Antichrist, or, at best, a mere creature of the State; that their ministers were not rightly called or ordained, nor the sacraments duly administered, or, supposing it to be a true Church, yet, as it was owned by their adversaries (the conforming Puritans) to be a very corrupt one, it must be as lawful to separate from it as for the Church of England to separate from Rome."[1]

The distinction is brought out again very clearly by Knight regarding some ministers who, about the year 1607, took what he calls a middle course.[2] These were called brethren of the second separation, by way of distinction from those who had preceded them in a more open and decided dissent, and their principles may be best gathered from their own words in a published defence of their conduct, in which they say: "We protest before the Almighty God that we acknowledge the Churches of England, as they be established by public authority, to be true visible Churches of Christ; that we desire the continuance of our ministry in them above all earthly things, as that without which our whole life would be wearisome and bitter to us; that we dislike not a set form of prayer to be used in our churches; nor do we write with an evil mind to deprave the Book of Common Prayer, ordination, or homilies, but to show our reasons why we cannot subscribe to all things contained in them."

With this accords in the main the more general statement of Fuller.[3] He distinguishes between three classes of Nonconformists, the earlier, the middle and the later; the earlier were those in King Edward's days, " who desired only to shake down the leaves of Episcopacy, misliking only some garments about them," the middle were those in the end of Queen Elizabeth's and beginning

---

[1] Neal, vol. i. p. 438.
[2] Knight's *Pictorial History of England*, vol. iii. p. 461.; Neal, vol. i. p. 446.
[3] *Church History*, vol. iv. p. 72.

of James' reign, "who struck at the branches thereof," etc., and the later were those "who did *lay the axe to the root of the tree*, to cut down the function itself as unlawful and anti-Christian."

Separatism, and what it originally implied. — It ought to be remembered that under the peculiar circumstances in which dissenters from the established religion were then placed, isolation and separate assembly became really an outward necessity, and did not necessarily imply anything like inward Congregational convictions on their part.[1] Thus, in Queen Mary's reign, we read of "a congregation of godly men at London," who met together for religious worship "in the very mouth of danger," and among them was Scambler, afterwards bishop of Peterborough, and Bentham, afterwards bishop of Coventry and Lichfield.[2] Hooper was no Separatist, and no adviser of Separatism. Yet, as early as 1553, Hooper wrote from the Fleet Prison "to certain godly persons, professors and lovers of the truth, instructing them how they should behave themselves at the beginning of the change of religion," as follows: "There is no better way to be used in this troublesome time for your consolation than many times to have assemblies together of such men and women as be of your religion in Christ, and then to talk and renew among yourselves the truth of your religion," etc.[3] Archdeacon Philpot uses language to the same effect, but still stronger. "Our God is a jealous God, and

---

[1] Dexter's *Congregationalism*, p. 632.
[2] See *Zurich Letters*, and Strype's *Memorials*, cf. III, ii. 147.
[3] *Later Writings of Bishop Hooper*, Parker Society (1852), p. 589.

cannot be content that we should be of any other body than of that unspotted Church whereof He is the Head only, and wherein He hath planted us by baptism."[1] Yet Philpot was a loyal son of the Church of England. It is thus clearly implied that under certain circumstances separation is not only defensible, but may become the highest duty. It is then perfectly obvious that the term Separatist can only be used strictly to describe those who belonged to the second and third class of Dissenters from the Established Church. The second class is represented, as has been pointed out, by Browne and his followers. It would appear from the six propositions laid down by Cartwright that his position was similar to Browne's, but we have his explicit testimony that he disapproved of separation. "We are not for an unspotted Church on earth, therefore though the Church of England has many faults we would not willingly leave it."

The third class, up to the period of the Commonwealth, was very sparsely represented,—represented, it may be said, by a mere handful of people, the Anabaptists of Holland and some of the more extreme sectaries.

An American author, Mr. Douglas Campbell, says in his recently published and elaborate work:[2] "To the Puritan and Separatist alike the Church as established was obnoxious on account of its abuses. But the one sought its reformation by Act of Parliament, looking forward to the time when his form of worship and dis-

[1] *Writings of Archdeacon Philpot*, Parker Society (1852), pp. 220–223.

[2] *The Puritan in Holland, England, and America*, an Introduction to American History, by Douglas Campbell, A.M., LL.B., Member of the American Historical Association, vol. ii. p. 181.

cipline should be established for the nation. The other thought that a reformation would never come, *that the whole system of a State Church was inherently wrong*, and that the only duty before the new believers was to leave the Church to its abuses, and set up independent congregations." The words italicised have a meaning which is somewhat doubtful. If Mr. Campbell means that the Separatist thought that the whole *then existing* system of the Church was inherently wrong, he is quite right: not so, however, if the statement be taken as referring to the system of State Churchism broadly and generally. To that, with the exception of a few Anabaptists, they had no conscientious objection. Mr. Douglas Campbell seems to be aware of this, for he says, in a previous part of his work, "at that time no one, except the members of the poor despised sect of Dutch Anabaptists, thought of such a thing as a separation of Church and State."[1]

The foregoing classification is sufficiently complete; but to make it exhaustive, another class of Dissenters would need to be included: those who became such through pressure of circumstances more than through force of original conviction. An apposite illustration of that class is furnished in connection with the founding of the colony of Massachusetts under Winthrop. These were not origin-

[1] Vol. ii. p. 9.

Mr. Green's statement—"The Separatists who were beginning to withdraw from attendance at public worship, on the ground that the *very existence of a national Church was contrary to the word of God*, grew quickly from a few scattered zealots to twenty thousand souls" (Green's *Short History*, p. 459)—is open to the same exception. The number of those who, in that age, objected to the very existence of a national Church as being contrary to the word of God, must have been very small indeed.

ally Separatists, like the Pilgrim Fathers at Plymouth. "We separate," they said, "not from the Church of England, but from its corruptions. We came away from the Common Prayer and ceremonies in our native land where we suffered much for Nonconformity. In this place of liberty we cannot and will not use them." The result was, they became free Churchmen and zealous Independents. Certainly the establishment of such a system as Independency was a great advance upon the idea of reforming the Church of England; yet, as a well-known American writer says, the mere change of surrounding conditions made it seem not a revolution in Church government, but the only natural and possible thing to do.[1]

[1] *Historic Towns: Boston*, by Henry Cabot Lodge, pp. 25, 26.
"How Puritanism glided into a state of separation, and the Nonconformist in the Church became a Dissenter outside its pale, is curiously illustrated in the records of the Church assembling in Broadmead, Bristol." See Dr. Stoughton's *History of Religion in England*, vol. i. (new and revised edition) pp. 99, 100.

The Corrupt State of the Church: the Martin Marprelate Controversy.

Memorable Events and Dates

The Spanish Armada defeated . . 1588
Publication of Martin Marprelate Tracts. . 1588-1590

Contents of Chapter VIII

Corrupt state of the Church—Illiteracy of the Clergy—Character of the Bishops—Notes on Latimer's Sermon of the Plough—Child's answer to Canon Dixon—Arber on corruption of Clergy—Martin Marprelate Controversy—Interest of this Controversy—Note on works dealing with—The Epistle—Style of—Assumption of—Conditions of Peace—Effect of Epistle—Restrictions on printing—The Epitome — The four Bishops attacked — On their defence — Hay any worke for Cooper—Press seized—Martin renounced by Puritans—Defended—Conclusion of Epistle—Notes on authorship—Who was Martin Marprelate?

CHAPTER VIII

THE CORRUPT STATE OF THE CHURCH : THE MARTIN MARPRELATE CONTROVERSY

I

THE CORRUPT STATE OF THE CHURCH

WE have seen how Archbishop Whitgift objected to the contention of Cartwright, that ministers ought to be openly and fairly chosen by the people, on the ground that "in this state of the Church such practice were pernicious and hurtful. In the apostles' time all, or most that were Christians, were virtuous and godly, and such as did sincerely profess the word, and therefore the election might be safely committed to them; now, the Church is full of hypocrites, dissemblers, drunkards, and whoremongers, so that if any election were committed to them, they would be sure to take one like to themselves. Now, the Church is full of Papists and atheists."

This description of the then existing condition of the Church was only too true. Among the clergy there was ignorance and licentiousness; among the bishops, sordid greed, sycophancy, and truckling to power. That "lying, cheating, theft, perjury, and whoredom were the complaints of the times,"[1] is abundantly testified by such Churchmen as Bucer and Sanday. The picture which the latter draws of patrons gaping for gain, and hungry fellows, destitute of all good learning and godly zeal, yea, scarcely clothed with common honesty, who found ready entrance to the Church, is surpassed even by Bishop Jewel:[2] "The poor flock is given over to the wolf; the poor children cry out for bread, the bread of life, and here is no man to break it unto them. . . . View your universities, view your schools, which have ever been nurseries to this purpose. Alas! how many shall you find in both the universities and in all the schools throughout England, not only that are already able, but also that are minded to the ministry? If they be not found there, alas! where think you to have them? Where think you they will be found? Think you they will spring out of the ground or drop down from the heavens? No, no, they be of you, and must be bred and reared amongst you. . . . I speak not of the curates, but of the parsonages and the vicarages; that is, of the places which are the castles and towers of defence for the Lord's temple. They seldom pass nowadays from a patron, if he be no better than a gentleman, but either for the lease or for present money. Such merchants are broken into the Church of God, a great deal more intolerable than were they whom Christ chased and whipped out of the temple. Young men that are toward and learned see this. They see that he which feedeth the

---

[1] Collier's *Ecclesiastical History*, vol. ii. p. 294.
[2] Hunt's *Religious Thought in England*, vol. i. p. 77, note. See *Zurich Letters* (1588–79) p. 33, 85.

flock hath least part of the milk; he which goeth a warfare hath not half his wages. Therefore they are wearied and discouraged; they change their studies; some become aprentices, some turn to physic, some to law: all shun and flee the ministry." "Sad was the state of religion at these times," says Strype; "the substantials being lost in contending for externals; the Churchmen heaped benefices upon themselves, and resided upon none, neglecting their cures. Many of them alienated their lands, made unreasonable leases and waste of woods, and granted reversions and advowsons to their wives and children, or to others, for their use. Churches ran greatly into dilapidations and decays, and were kept nasty and filthy and indecent for God's worship. Among the laity there was little devotion, the Lord's day greatly profaned and little observed, the common prayer not frequented. Some lived without any service of God at all; many were heathens and atheists; the Queen's own court a harbour for epicures and atheists, and a kind of lawless place, because it stood in no parish; which things made good men fear some sad judgments impending over the nation."[1]

Illiteracy of the Clergy.—The mass of the clergy were so illiterate that, even had they been pure of life, they could have done little to elevate the people, or reflect honour upon the Church. In 1530, Tyndale declared that there were 20,000 priests in England who could not translate the Lord's Prayer into English (*Answer to Sir Thomas More*, p. 75); and Bishop Hooper found scores of the clergy in Gloucestershire who were unable

[1] Strype's *Parker*, p. 395.

to tell who was the author of the Lord's Prayer, or where it was to be read.¹ Such a deficiency of Protestant clergy had been experienced at the Queen's accession that for several years it was a common practice to appoint laymen, usually mechanics, to read the service in vacant churches.²

Reference has been already made to the statement of Neal, that there were only two thousand preachers to serve near ten thousand parish churches, so that there were almost eight thousand parishes without preaching ministers; also that in 1578, out of one hundred and forty clergymen in Cornwall, not one was capable of preaching; and throughout the kingdom those who could preach were in the proportion of about one to four,—a statement that Hallam regards as highly probable, seeing that "the majority of the clergy were nearly illiterate, and many of them addicted to drunkenness and low vices." Bakers, butchers, cooks, and stablemen, men wholly illiterate, and not a few utterly licentious (and these were the class of which the clergy were to a large part composed), could not be expected to add dignity to the ministry or shed lustre upon the Church.³

---

[1] Rev. R. Demaus, *Life of Tyndale*, p. 28.

[2] Strype's *Annals*, pp. 138, 177.

[3] "It pierces our hearts with grief to hear the cries of the country people for the word of God. The bishops either preach not at all or very seldom. . . . And whereas the Scriptures say that ministers of the gospel should be such as are able to teach sound doctrine, and convince gainsayers, yet the bishops have made priests of the basest of the people, not only for their occupations and trades whence they have taken them, as shoemakers, barbers, tailors, water-bearers, shepherds, and horse-keepers, but also for their want of good learning and honesty."—*Supplication of Puritan Ministers to Parliament in* 1586, Neal, vol. i. p. 317.

Character of the Bishops. — "The bishops of this reign," says Hallam, "do not appear, with some distinguished exceptions, to have reflected so much honour on the Established Church as those who attach a superstitious reverence to the age of the Reformation are apt to conceive. In the plunder that went forward they took good care of themselves. Charges against them of simony, corruption, covetousness, and especially destruction of their Church estates for the benefit of their families are very common, sometimes, no doubt, unjust, but too frequent to be absolutely without foundation." The peculation of the bishops almost passes belief.[1] They were guilty of the grossest malversation, sold the livings in their gift in order to enrich themselves, and made long and dishonest leases of the ecclesiastical lands, not hesitating even to plunder their own dioceses, cut down the timber, and dispose of the brick and the lead which were used in the buildings. Aylmer, bishop of London, cut down and sold the timber in his diocese until prevented by an injunction. When he grew old and reflected that a large sum of money would be due from his family for dilapidations of the palace of Fulham, etc., he actually proposed to *sell his bishopric* to Bancroft.[2] The Bishop of Lichfield is said to have made seventy "lewd and unlearned ministers for money" in the course of a single day. Archbishop Parker disposed of the benefices in his gift according to a fixed tariff, regulated according to the age and money power of

---

[1] See Strype's *Annals*, vol. iii. pp. 331, 463, 467.
[2] Strype's *Aylmer*, p. 169. See Hunt's *Religious Thought*, p. 74, note; Froude's *History*, vol. xii. pp. 4–7 and p. 543.

the applicant. They were disposed of to boys under fourteen, provided they could raise the necessary sum of money.[1]

NOTES

Who that knows anything of Bishop Latimer does not know his famous *Sermon of the Plough*, preached in St. Paul's, London, in 1548, in which he thus attacked his own order: "But this much I dare say, that since lording and loitering hath come up, preaching hath come down, contrary to the apostles' times; for they preached and lorded not, and now they lord and preach not.... For ever since the prelates were made lords and nobles, the plough standeth; there is no work done, the people starve. They hawk, they hunt, they card, they dice; they pastime in their prelacies with gallant gentlemen, with their dancing minions, and with their fresh companions, so that ploughing is set aside; and by their lording and loitering, preaching and ploughing is clean gone." It is in this sermon that the famous passage, which has become classical in pulpit literature, occurs: "And now I would ask a strange question: Who is the most diligentest bishop and prelate in all England?... There is one that passeth all the others, and is the most diligent prelate and preacher in all England. And will ye know who it is? I will tell you. It is the devil. He is the most diligent preacher of all others; he is never out of his diocese," etc.

The order which Latimer thus so trenchantly assailed were the Protestant bishops of King Edward VI.'s reign.

In the Appendix to his work on *Church and State under the Tudors*, Mr. Child has introduced a somewhat lengthy note on *the alleged corruption of the clergy in the sixteenth century*. Canon Dixon, in his *History of the Church of England*, vol. i. p. 23, had alleged that "no general charge of corruption has ever been made good against the English clergy." Mr. Child subjects this statement to a searching examination, and reaches the conclusion that "to say, as Canon Dixon does, that no proof of deep corruption has been made good against the English clergy, is simply to fly in the face of the evidence, not only of satirists and lampooners, but of annalists and historians, of records and law reports." It is true that the evidence

---

[1] Froude's *History*, vol. xi. p. 82.

he adduces is mainly directed to prove the deep corruption of the "*late pre-Reformation clergy*," but he indicates very plainly how it was not confined to the Catholic clergy, but extended to their Protestant successors.

"'Three times in modern English history have the bulk of the clergy, as a class, been corrupt and rotten. In Henry VIII.'s reign, when the remedy came by the Reformation and the dissolution of the monasteries. In Whitgift's primacy, when it came through the rise of the Puritans. In Queen Anne's reign, when it came through the lay-Reformers, the moral teachers Defoe, Steele, and Addison, in their penny folio half sheets, the *Review*, the *Tatler*, the *Spectator*, the *Guardian*," etc. . . . "In 1588 a small minority of the clergy, for the most part at work in towns, were intensely earnest, thoroughly pious, spiritually-minded men, but with a narrowness of view, and no great learning, and consequently with little general culture. At this time the bishops were thrusting hundreds of men into the ministry of the Church who were utterly unfit for their work."—Introduction to the *Epistle*, by E. Arber, p. viii.

II

THE MARTIN MARPRELATE CONTROVERSY, 1588—1590.

"I am called Martin Marprelat. There be many that greatly dislike of my doinges. I may haue my wants, I know. For I am a man. But my course I knowe to be ordinary and lawfull. I sawe the cause of Christs gouernment, and of the Bishops Antichristian dealing to be hidden. The most part of men could not be gotten to read any thing, written in the defence of the on[e] and against the other. I bethought mee therefore, of a way whereby men might be drawne to do both, perceiuing the humors of men in these times (especialy of those that are in any place) to be giuen to mirth. I tooke that course. I might lawfully do it. I [aye] for iesting is lawful by circumstances, euen in the greatest matters. The circumstances of time, place and persons vrged me thereunto. I neuer profaned the word in any iest. Other mirth I used as a couert, wherein I would bring the truth into light. The Lord being the authour both of mirth and grauitie, is it not lawfull in it selfe, for the trueth to vse eyther of these wayes, when the circumstances do make it lawful?

"My purpose was and is to do good. I know I haue don no harme, howsoeuer som may iudg Martin to mar al. They are very weake on[e]s that so think. In that which I have written I know vndoubtedly, that I haue done the Lord and the state of this kingdom great seruice. Because I haue in som sort discouered the greatest enemies thereof. And by so much the most pestilent enemies, because they wound Gods relligion, and corrupt the state with Atheism and loosnes, and so cal for Gods vengance vppon vs all, euen vnder the coulor of relligion. I affirm them to be the greatest enemies that now our state hath, for if it were not for them, the trueth should haue more free passage herein, then now it hath. All [e]states thereby would be amended: and so we should not be subject vnto Gods displeasure, as now we are by reason of them."—*Hay any Worke*, etc.

No account of English Puritanism and the desperate endeavour of the dominant hierarchy to strangle it in its cradle, would be at all complete if it contained no allusion to the famous Martin Marprelate Controversy,[1] "the Controversy," as Mr. Maskell calls it, "of the Elizabethan age." This controversy has a double interest, an interest to the student of English literature, as being the first successful, if not actually the earliest attempt to employ satire in ecclesiastical polemics, and also a very special interest to those who sympathise with the struggle for freedom of faith and conscience. These pungent tracts or pasquinades began to appear in 1588, the year of the Armada, and were issued under the *nom de plume* of Martin Marprelate. The proximate cause or

[1] We need scarcely say that for what appears under this head we are greatly indebted to the valuable reprints in *The English Scholar's Library of Old and Modern Works*, edited by Edward Arber, F.S.A., Lecturer in English Literature, etc., University College, London, *An Introductory Sketch to the Martin Marprelate Controversy*, and *The Epistle* [1588]; also to the well-informed, careful, and elaborate lecture on *The Martin Marprelate Controversy*, by the Rev. H. M. Dexter, D.D., of New Bedford, Massachusetts, in his work on *The Congregationalism of the last three hundred years, as seen in its Literature*; also on the principle—*Audi alteram partem*—to a *History of the Martin Marprelate Controversy*, by the Rev. William Maskell, M.A., a reprint, with considerable additions of an article, "Martin Marprelate," in the *Christian Remembrancer* of 1845. These three works form a complete thesaurus of information regarding this famous controversy. Chap. ii. and Appendix, in Hunt's *Religious Thought in England*, may also be consulted with advantage.

provocation of the Martinist pasquinades was the publication of a ponderous book by Dr. John Bridges, dean of Sarum, entitled, *Defence of the Government Established in the Church of England for Ecclesiastical Matters*, a reply to Travers' book on the *Discipline*, and an attempt to undermine the Puritan position generally.

The Epistle.—The rejoinder appeared in the shape of a quarto tract, which bore the descriptive title, *Oh read ouer D. John Bridges, for it is a worthy worke: Or an Epitome of the fyrste Booke of that right worshipfull volume, written against the Puritanes, in the defence of the noble cleargie, by as worshipfull a prieste, Iohn Bridges, Presbyter, Priest, or elder, doctor of Diuillitie, and Deane of Sarum. Wherein the arguments of the puritans are wisely prevented, that when they come to answere M. Doctor, they must needes say something that hath bene spoken. Compiled for the behoofe and overthrow of the Parsons, Fyckers, and Currats, that have lernt their Catechismes, and are past grace: By the reverend and worthie Martin Marprelate, gentleman, and dedicated to the Confocationhouse. The Epitome is not yet published, but it shall be when the Bishops are at conuenient leysure to view the same. In the meane time, let them be content with this learned Epistle. Printed oversea, in Europe, within two furlongs of a Bounsing Priest, at the cost and charges of M. Marprelate, gentleman.*

Without any preliminary skirmishing this broadside is at once discharged straight into the ranks of the bishops. "Right poysond, [puissant], persecuting, and terrible priests, the theame of mine Epistle vnto your venerable masterdomes, is of two parts (and the Epitome of our brother Bridges his booke, shall come out speedily). First, most pitifully complayning, Martin Marprelate, &c. Secondly, may it please your good worships, &c. Most pitifully complayning, therefore, you are to vnderstand, that D. Bridges hath written in your defence, a most senceles book, and I cannot very often at one breath come to a full point, when I read the same.

"Againe, may it please you to giue me leaue to play the Duns for the nonce as well as he, otherwise dealing with master doctors booke, I canot keepe *decorum personæ*. And may it please you, if I be too absurd in any place (either in this Epistle, or that Epitome), to ride to Sarum, and thanke his Deanship for it. Because I could not deal with his booke commendablie according to order, vnles I should be sometimes tediously dunsticall and absurd. For I haue heard som cleargie men say that M. Bridges was a verie patch [fool] and a duns, when he was in Cambridg. And some say, sauing your reuerence that are Bb. that he is as very a knaue, and enemy vnto the sinceritie of religion, as any popish prelate in Rome. But the patch can doe the cause of sinceritie no hurt. Naye, he hath in this booke wonderfully graced the same by writing against it. For I haue heard some say, that whosoeuer will read his booke, shall as euidently see the goodnes of the cause of reformation and the poore, poore nakednes of your gouernment, as almost in reading all Master Cartwrights workes. This was a very great ouer-sight in his grace of Cant. to suffer such a booke to come out. For besides that an Archb. is very weakely defended by masse Deane, he hath also by this meanes prouoked many to write against his gracious fatherhood, who perhaps neuer meant to take pen in hand."

There is no mincing of words. The *Epistle* abounds with unpruned and telling invective, what would be deemed in these days coarse vituperation. The bishops are "cogging and cosening knaues," "proud, popish, presumptuous, profane, paltry, pestilent, and pernicious prelates." They "lye like dogs"; as for "any maners," they might have been "brought up in Bridewell"; as for the Dean of Sarum, he deserves "a cawdell of Hempseed and a playster of neckweed, as weel as some of your brethren the papists."

This style was, of course, admirably fitted to catch the ear of the public. No plan, no methodised arrangement of their views, was striven after by these Puritan Free Lances who were fighting behind the shield of Martin Marprelate. They were anxious to avoid everything that was concatenated and formal. An elaborate and learned treatise, had it been within their power, and had the difficulty in getting it printed been less formidable than it was, would have defeated the object they had in view, which was to strike and to arrest attention, to make every point burn and scintillate, so that there should be no getting away from it, and no putting of the pamphlet down till it had been read (probably in most cases at one sitting) from beginning to end.

Not the least irritating feature of the *Epistle* must have been to the attacked prelates the assumption of perfect equality on the part of the writer. He poses as "The Rev. and worthy Martin Marprelate, gentleman," and addresses the bishops as "my learned brethren."

"Take head, brethren, of your rev. and learned brother, Martin Marprelate. But you see my worshipfull priestes of this crue to whom I write, what a perilous fellow M. Marprelate is: he vnderstands of all your knauerie, and it may be he keepes a register of them: vnlesse you amend, they shall al come into the light one day. And you brethren bishops, take this warning from me. If you doe not leaue your persecuting of godly christians and good subiects, that seeke to liue vprightly in the feare of God, and the obedience of her Maiestie, all your dealing shal be made knowen vnto the world."

Interpolated in the last part of the *Epistle* are "Conditions of Peace to be inuiolablie kept for euer betweene the reuerend and worthy master Martin Marprelate gentleman on the one partie, and the reuerend fathers his brethren, the Lord bishops of this lande." The bishops must promise—(1) to labour to promote the preaching of the word in every part of this land; (2) to admit to the ministry none but those who are known for their godliness and learning; (3) to suspend or silence none but those who show themselves unworthy to be ministers, though they refuse to wear the popish garments, and omit the corruptions of the Book of Common Prayer; (4) not to molest any for not kneeling at the communion, or for resorting on the Sabbath whither they would to hear the word preached; (5) to leave off private excommunication, and not to forbid public fasts, and never to slander the cause of reformation or the furtherance thereof, in terming the cause by the name of Anabaptisterie, schisme, etc., and the men puritans, and enemies to the state.

"These be the conditions, which you brethren bishops, shal be bound to keepe inuiolably on your behalfe. And I your brother Martin, on the other side, do faithfully promise vpon the performaunce of the premisses by you, neuer to make any more of your knauery knowne vnto the worlde."

Effect of the Epistle.—It is easy to imagine the flutter and excitement and consternation produced by this free-handed attack upon privilege and mitred tyranny. Such dare-devil impiety had never been heard of before. Not less to the people at large than to the pillars of Church and State, it appeared the very height of daring, a laying of sacrilegious hands upon the Lord's anointed. Its popularity, if that is to be measured by the number who read the pamphlet, was phenomenal. The Earl of Essex took a copy out of his bosom and handed it to the Queen. The students of Oxford and Cambridge hid them in the folds of their gowns.

Restrictions upon printing. — Officers and scouts were despatched in every direction to see if they could learn anything of the author, or those concerned in the origination of the libel, but they were one and all baffled in their efforts. The Primate and the Bishop of London had the entire control and censorship of the press, with the exception of two presses, one allocated to the University of Oxford and the other to that of Cambridge, both under clerical and equally vigilant supervision. There were in 1583, five years before the appearance of the Martin Marprelate tracts, only twenty-three printers in London, and the number of hand-printing presses in their possession was fifty-three. It was impossible for any anonymous pamphleteer to secure the aid of any of these. It would have been a capital offence for any printer to lend his press for any such purpose, and however carefully he might seek to conceal the secret, he could scarcely hope to elude detection and conviction. It was the duty of the Stationers' Company to make weekly search into all the printing houses in London, and report any suspicious circumstance or irregularity that might occur. "What with the daily observation of his own workmen and apprentices, the keen weekly search of his competitors in business, the censorship of the episcopal chaplains, etc., a printer and all his doings were perfectly well known; even to the kinds of type he used, the numbers he printed to an impression, and so forth, secret printing was, to one not in the trade, beset with innumerable difficulties. A recognised printer might keep secret presses in cellars, etc., despite the weekly searches, but it was forbidden to a private individual to acquire a press or type at all. There was always the further difficulty of finding the compositor who should be so hardy as to exercise his craft in antiepiscopal productions."[1]

The Epitome.—While the incensed bishops, fortified by the authority of the Queen, were putting into opera-

[1] See Arber's *Introductory Sketch*, p. 74.
The stringent measures that were adopted to prevent secret and unauthorised printing are well shown in the Star Chamber Ordinances of 1566 and 1586, as exhibited by Prof. Prothero in his *Select Statutes and Documents*, pp. 168–172.

tion all the machinery at their command in order to apprehend or discover the whereabouts of the miscreant or miscreants who had exploded the alarming shell, another explosion took place. This was the appearance of the *Epitome* which had been promised in the *Epistle*.

Martin, chuckling, as it were, in his hiding-place, begins by bantering the bishops: " Why my cleargie masters, is it euen so with your terriblenes ? May not a pore gentleman signifie his good will vnto you by a Letter, but presently you must put your selues to the paines and charges of calling foure Bishops together, Iohn Canterburie, Iohn London, Thomas Winchester, William of Lincolne, and posting ouer citie and countrie for poore Martin ? Why, his meaning in writing vnto you was not that you should take the paines to seeke for him. Did you thinke that he did not know where he was himselfe ? Or did you thinke him to haue bene cleane lost, that you sought so diligently for him ? I thanke you, brethren, I can be well though you do not send to knowe how I do. My mind towards you, you shal from time to time vnderstand by my pistles. I haue been entertayned at the Court. Euerye man talks of my worship. Many would gladly receiue my books if they could tell where to find them."

The four bishops were John Whitgift, John Aylmer, Thomas Cooper, and William Wickham, and for none of them has Martin a good word to spare. The first two were specially obnoxious. " Of all the bishops that ever were in that place, I meane in the see of Canterbury, none did neuer so much hurt vnto the Church of God as he hath done since his coming."

The Bishops on their defence.—The answer of the bishops to the *Epistle*—not to the *Epitome*, for beyond a mere general reference there was no answer to that—was issued in a quarto book of 252 pages, with the title, *An Admonition to the People of England: wherein are ansvered, not onely the slaunderous vntruthes, reprochfully vttered by Martin the Libeller, but also many other Crimes by some of his broode, obiected generally against all Bishops, and the chiefe of the Cleargie, purposely to deface and discredite the present state of the Church*, etc.

The preface was signed by " T. C.," bishop of Winchester. If the bishops had been anxious to do all in their power to write up Martin Marprelate, and confer notoriety on his tracts, they could not have had recourse to tactics more admirably adapted for this purpose. Where one bought and read " the solemn and apologetic *Admonition*," scores eagerly purchased the *Epistle* and *Epitome*, and gave willing credence to what they contained.

The fourth of these rattling pasquinades (we pass over the third) was a reply to the Admonition of Bishop Cooper. It opened with a lively appropriation of words used as one of the street cries of London—

Hay any worke for Cooper: or a briefe Pistle, etc. . . , wherein worthy Martin quits himselfe like a man, I warrant you, in the modest defence of his selfe and his learned Pistles, and makes the Coopers hoopes to flye off, and the Bishops' Tubs to leake out of all crye [out of all estimation, *i.e.*

excessively]. *Penned and Compiled by Martin the Metropolitane. Printed in Europe, not farre from some of the Bounsing Priestes.*

It was while printing this tract that the printing press of Martin Marprelate was seized at Manchester. But the effect in the way of arresting his surprising activity was only momentary. The dragon-teeth had been sown, and there sprang from them an unfailing progeny. Within a fortnight's time another press was at work, and another tract appeared, entitled, *The Protestatyon of Martin Marprelat, wherein notwithstanding the surprizing of the printer, he maketh it known vnto the world that he feareth neither proud priest, Antichristian pope, tiranous prellate, nor godlesse catercap* [four-cornered cap, hence, university student], etc.

By this time, however, others besides the bishops had taken up the cudgels, not so much, however, on their behalf as with the intention of retaliating upon Martin, and giving him as good as he gave. The ridicule of the stage was called into requisition, and pamphlets as scurrilous, if not quite as clever, as Martin's began to appear upon the other side. These were *Pappe with an Hatchet*[1] and *An Almond for a Parrot*, a rhyming tract of seven pages, entitled, *A Whip for an Ape*, etc. They were supposed to have been written by Thomas Nash, John Lyly, etc.

The Puritans renounce Martin and his works.—

---

[1] *Pappe with an Hatchet* is as characteristic as any, and may be read in *Elizabethan and Jacobean Pamphlets*, edited by George Saintsbury, London (Percival & Co.), where it is attributed to John Lyly.

It must not be supposed for a moment that in this series of pamphlets Martin was the acknowledged spokesman of the Puritans. The "sturdy Puritans, who were supposed to fight behind the shield of this visored knight," were, on the contrary, displeased with this rattling and abusive attack upon the authorities of Church and State.[1]

"The Puritans are angrie with me, I mean the puritane preachers. And why? Because I am to[o] open Because I iest. I did thinke that Martin shoulde not haue beene blamed of the puritans for telling the trueth openly."—*Epitome.*

It is not to be wondered at that Cartwright and many like-minded Puritans disapproved of the Martinist publications as a "kind of disorderly doings," and were at pains to disown all sympathy with them. They naturally wished that Presbyterianism should be seen in its sober-suited apparel; the motley garb of Martin Marprelate did not at all accord with their sense of the fitness of things, and, besides this, it tended to prejudice the discipline (so they thought) in the eyes of the people of England.

[1] Another proof of Mr. Maskell's temper as a controversialist is furnished by his affecting to doubt that they were disapproved *at the time* by the Puritan leaders. "It is not enough that they should disclaim him [Martin] *after*, before the council-board, with the terrors in the distance of the Tower and the rack, or before the Court of High Commission; it is not enough that Neal, their professed historian in after years, and their apologist, should speak of Martin in terms of reprobation, and (which proves either his utter ignorance or wilful lying) class him and his opponents in the same style as equally obnoxious to the members of the Government."—Maskell's *Martin Marprelate,* p. 102. See Mr. Hunt's comment on this, *History of Religious Thought,* vol. i. p. 105.

Martin Marprelate defended.—He who would play the rôle of apologist for the Martinist tracts would seem to need an unusual measure of courage, not to say effrontery, in view of the strictures and objurgations that have been cast upon them, not only by Anglican but by Puritan writers, and also by writers whose judgment runs no risk, apparently, of being deflected by ecclesiastical sympathies. They are "coarse, scurrilous, and indecent pasquinades," never surpassed in scurrility and malignity. "It is impossible," says Canon Curteis, "to give any extracts from these abominable and filthy lampoons." Had the Rev. Canon done what he says is impossible, this swearing at large might have been curbed, and his readers might have been left to judge for themselves (supposing the extracts had been at all copious and representative) how far they answer to the description he gives of them.

Well may Dr. Dexter say that English literature perhaps contains no clearer illustration than is furnished by this controversy of the tendency to speak strongly on scant or insufficient knowledge. Let us hear Mr. Arber, who, in the interest of historic truth, and with no bias other than the desire to unfold the real meaning of it, has made an independent and special study of this controversy. "Hitherto," he says, "the Martinists have been largely vilified, their works considered blasphemous, and their purposes treasonable. There is neither blasphemy nor treason to be found in their writings. Their authors, confessedly men of irreproachable moral character, merely adopted the 'extemporising' style of Richard Tarleton, the actor, to ridicule and affront a proud hierarchy endowed with large legal means of doing mischief, and not wanting in will to exercise those powers to the full." "They were the attempt of wit," says Mr. Arber, " to fight (though at desperate odds) against cruelty for permission to worship God according to the dictates of conscience. The Martinist attack was the New School of young Radicals attacking the Old School of aged Conservatives. And this partly explains why there was no compromise sought out by the bishops. They were too old to change, so they stood stiffly to their legal rights, and contemned anything like public opinion."

How the Martinist books could ever be called "blasphemous" passes all comprehension. Let those who have formed an unfavourable opinion in regard to them read the noble exhortation at the end of the *Epistle*.

Conclusion of the Epistle.—Now M. Prelates I will giue you some more counsell, follow it. Repent cleargie men, and especially bishopps, preach fayth Bb. and sweare no more by it, giue ouer your Lordly callings: reform your families and your children: They are the patterne of loosenesse, withstand not the knowen trueth no longer: you haue seduced her Maiestie and hir people. Praye her Maiestie to forgiue you, and the Lord first to put away your sinnes. Your gouernment is Antichristian, deceiue the Lord no longer thereby: You will grow from euil to worse vnlesse betimes you return. You are now worse than you were 29. yeeres ago: write no more against the cause of reformation: Your vngodlinesse is made more manifest by your writings: And because you cannot answer what hath bene written against you, yeeld vnto the trueth. If you should write, deale syllogistically: For you shame your selues, when you vse any continued speach, because your stile is so rude and barbarous. Raile no more in the pulpitt against good men, you do more hurt to your selues, and your owne desperat cause, in one of your rayling sermons, then you could in speaking for reformation. For euerie man that hath any light of religion in him will examine your groundes, which being found ridiculous (as they are) will be decided, and your cause made odious. Abuse not the high commission as you do, against the best subiects. The commission it selfe was ordained for very good purposes, but it is most horriblie abused by you, and turned cleane contrarie to the ende wherefore it was ordayned. Helpe the poore people to the meanes of their saluation, that perish in their ignorance : make restitution vnto your tenants, and such as from whome you haue wrongfully extorted anything : Vsurpe no longer, the authoritie of making of ministers and excommunication : Let poore men be no more molested in your vngodly courts : Studie more than you doe, and preache oftener : Fauor nonresidents and papists no longer : labor to clense ye ministery of the swarms of ignorant guides, wherewith it hath bin defiled : Make conscience of breaking the Sabboth, by bowling and tabling : Be ringleaders of prophanenes no longer vnto the people : Take no more bribes : Leaue your Symonie : Fauor learning more than you doe, and especially godly learning : Stretch your credit if you haue any, to the furtherance of the gospell : You haue ioyned the prophanation of the magistracie to the corruption of the ministerie : Leaue this sinne. All in a word, become good Christians, and so you shall become good subiects, and leaue your tyrannie. And I would aduise you, let me here no more of your euill dealing.

Giuen at my Castle between two wales, neither foure dayes from penilesse benche, nor yet at the West ende of Shrofftide : but the fourteenth yeare at the least of the age of Charing crosse, within a yeare of Midsommer, betwene twelue and twelue of the clocke.

Anno pontificatus vestri Quinto, and I hope *vltimo* of all Englishe Popes.—By your learned and worthie brother,

MARTIN MARPRELATE.

NOTES

WHO WAS MARTIN MARPRELATE?

The authorship of the Martin Marprelate tracts is enveloped in almost as much obscurity as that of the celebrated letters of Junius. It is a mystery how they ever got into print, a mystery still greater how Martin fought, and continued to fight, as he did, behind his closed visor, defeating the rage of the bishops and the vigilance of their scouts, while the secret of his identity was never rifled from him. Suspicion fell upon John Penry and John Udal. Strype says Penry "was reckoned the chief publisher, if not author, of those scandalous libels under the name of Martin Marprelate." Penry was imprisoned on the charge of being the author of *Hay any Worke for Cooper?* but, in the absence of evidence sufficient to convict him, he was released after a month's confinement.

By painstaking collation of evidence, and by a "process of exhaustion," Mr. Arber has arrived at the conclusion that John Penry and Job Throckmorton were the joint authors of the *Epistle* and other Martinist tracts. "Penry has long been known in our literary history. Henceforth Throckmorton must be placed by his side. The two together are the most eminent prose satirists of the Elizabethan age." "It is indubitable that John Penry was the managing director, the 'soul,' of this [Martinist] attack." It is right to say that Mr. Arber holds a very singular position in attributing to Penry the authorship of those tracts. The majority of those who have written upon this period, whether their sympathies are Anglican or Puritan, concur in admitting that Penry was not Martin Marprelate. "There is nothing in Penry's character or his writings that gives any countenance to the conjecture that he was Martin Marprelate." "The persistency with which the Marprelate tracts have been ascribed to Penry is a notable instance of the recklessness with which men write history when they have a purpose to serve."—Hunt's *Religious Thought*, vol. i. p. 83. Even Mr. Maskell, who never scruples to use his opportunity when he can fasten a damning charge upon "a Brownist, and most bitter enemy to the Church of England," says: "We must not overlook this, that no evidence was found, and also that Penry himself at the time (which I cannot give much weight to) and always after, even when about to die (when one is rather inclined to believe that he would speak the truth), denied that he had been concerned in the writing of those tracts."—Maskell's *Marprelate*, pp. 107, 108.

We think Dr. Dexter shows very strong and conclusive reasons for dissenting from Mr. Arber's opinion that Penry was the real author of the Martinist tracts.

He bases his dissent upon these four grounds—

1st. There is nothing in the affidavits bearing upon the case which implies that Penry was the author.

2nd. There is nothing in the style and manner of Penry's acknowledged works that makes it probable.

3rd. It is difficult to see how Penry could have found time with all the work he had to do in writing other books.

4th. The prelates did not dare to put him on trial as the author of the Martinist tracts.

5th. Contemporary opinions acquit Penry of their authorship.

6th. Penry solemnly denied that he was the author of these tracts.[1]

But though not the author of Martin Marprelate's pasquinades, Dr. Dexter thinks that Penry was the publisher. He it was that owned the press and the type that were used in their production, gave out the copy to the various workmen, corrected the proofs, used to pay the printers, and "appeared to be a principall dealer in all the action everywhere."

Who, then, was the author? Dr. Dexter has adventured the theory that the author was no other than Henry Barrowe, prisoner in the Fleet since 1586.

We shall have occasion to advert shortly at greater length to both Penry and Barrowe, and need only say here that Dr. Dexter has succeeded in constructing an ingenious if not convincing argument in support of his contention. See Dexter's *Congregationalism as seen in its Literature*, pp. 196-201, and Arber's *Introductory Sketch*, pp. 185-196.

Some impression of the effect produced in high quarters by the Martinist publications may be formed by reading section iv. of Mr. Arber's *Introductory Sketch to the Martin Marprelate Controversy*, containing State documents, etc.:—

1588.

Lord Burghley's autographic minutes of a letter to Archbishop Whitgift on the first appearance of the *Epistle*. Pp. 107, 108.

1589.

The Queen's proclamation against certain seditious and schismatical books and libels, etc., in which the *Epistle* and *Epitome* are undoubtedly aimed at. Pp. 109-111.

Archbishop Whitgift's report to Lord Burghley of the seizure of the Martinist press near Manchester. Pp. 112, 113.

Summary of the information in the hands of the Queen's Government at this date. Pp. 114-117.

---

[1] "Argument by the Rev. H. M. Dexter, D.D., of New Bedford, Massachusetts, U.S." Printed by Mr. Arber in *Introductory Sketch to the Martin Marprelate Controversy*, pp. 187-189.

The Puritan Martyrs

Contents of Chapter IX

Bishops incensed—John Udall—His crime, trial, declaration, and death—Martyrs for Independency—Roger Rippon—The Anabaptists—Six Separatists put to death—Henry Barrowe—His examination—Barrowe and Greenwood in prison—Reprieved—Executed—Barrowism—Barrowists and Brownists—John Penry—Cited before High Commission—His private papers seized—His protestation—Executed—Puritan martyrs, for what suffered—Religious toleration—Anglican animus towards Puritans — Puritans not seditious — Brownist petition.

CHAPTER IX

THE PURITAN MARTYRS

THE spirit of mutiny against the bishops, of which the Martin Marprelate tracts afford such audacious and indisputable proof, roused them to a state of frenzy, and they determined to leave nothing undone in order to bring home to all convicted or suspected persons the enormity of their crime.

John Udall.—Foremost among the early victims of episcopal tyranny was John Udall, a graduate of Cambridge and preacher at Kingston-upon-Thames, renowned not more for his Puritan leanings than for his learning and scholarship.[1] He was cited to appear before the High Commission at Lambeth; and for no other reason than that his opinions were obnoxious to the ecclesiastical authorities, he was forbidden to continue to preach. He was restored to his ministry through the intervention and influence of the Countess of Warwick and Sir Drue Drury; but in 1588 he was again suspended, and deprived of his living. He had in the meantime added to

---

[1] It is said that the first person James I. inquired after when he came to England was Master Udall. On hearing of his death he exclaimed, "By my sal, then, the greatest scholar in Europe's dedd."

his other offences by subscribing the *Book of Discipline*. He was the author of two remarkable tractates, known as *Diotrephes* and *A Demonstration of Discipline*, which have been printed by Mr. Arber in "The English Scholars' Library." The mere writing of such works was treason and rebellion against the bishops, and for quelling such mutiny they had endless resources at their command. They were at once the creators, judges, and administrators of the law, with an army of rapacious officials at their back, ever ready to do their bidding, and utterly unscrupulous as to the means employed. That feature upon which Lord Bacon, in his *Advertisement*, so strongly animadverts, "the solid obduracy of the bishops, their utter unwillingness to make the least concession, and so to satisfy moderate men"; this is strongly brought out in Udall's *Diotrephes*,[1] which, as the earliest of the anti-episcopal tracts, may, in relation to its Martinist successors, be regarded as the pilot-balloon sent up to see which way the wind was blowing.

Udall was charged with being concerned in the Mar-

[1] See Mr. Arber's Introduction to *Diotrephes—The State of the Church of England laid open in a Conference between Diotrephes a Bishop, Tertullus a Papist, Demetrius a Usurer, Pandochus an Innkeeper, and Paul a Preacher of the Word of God* [April, 1588]. This *Conference* is as vigorous a bit of Puritanism as anything that has come down to us from that age. Udall's other work is entitled, *A Demonstration of Discipline*, or *A Demonstration of the Truth of the Discipline which Christ hath prescribed in His Word for the Government of His Church in all times and places until the end of the World*. As has been pointed out already (p. 79), this proud claim was soon disposed of by the irony of events. In less than two generations, in England, at least, the Holy Discipline was discredited and rejected, though it revenged itself for this treatment by its retreat to, and its entrenchment in, the northern part of the kingdom.

tinist productions, and condemned to death on a charge
of libelling the bishops. "His trial," says Hallam, "disgraces the name of English justice. It consisted mainly
in a pitiful attempt by the Court to entrap him into a
confession that the imputed libel was of his writing, as
to which their proof was deficient. Though he avoided
this snare, the jury did not fail to obey the directions
they received to convict him. So far from being concerned in Martin's writings, Udall professed his disapproval
of them, and his ignorance of the author." His friends
made strenuous efforts in order to induce him to recant
his opinions, and sign a formal submission. Dean Nowell,
James VI. of Scotland, and Sir Walter Raleigh interested
themselves on his behalf, but unsuccessfully. Raleigh,
however, succeeded in drawing from him the following
declaration of his position, which was submitted to the
Queen: "I believe, and have often preached, that the
Church of England is a part of the true visible Church,
for which reason (1) I do still desire to be a preacher in
the same; I utterly renounce the schism and separation
of the Brownists. (2) I do allow the Articles of Religion,
as far as they concern the doctrine of faith and sacraments according to law. (3) I believe the Queen's
Majesty hath and ought to have supreme authority over
all persons, in all causes, ecclesiastical and civil. (4) I
believe the Church, rightly reformed, ought to be governed
as in the foreign Reformed Churches. (5) I believe the
censures of the Church ought merely to concern the soul,
and may not impeach any subject, much less any prince,
in liberty of body, goods, dominion, or any earthly
privilege." This declaration did indeed suffice for the

revocation of the death sentence, which appeared (even in the eyes of Whitgift) too iniquitous to be executed; but before his liberation could be effected, Udall died heart-broken in the Marshalsea Prison at the close of 1592, a true martyr to the cause of religious and constitutional liberty. "Solely for *Diotrephes* and the *Demonstration*, John Udall, an absolutely upright and pure-minded man, was cut off in the prime of life, a victim to the secular power and political influence of Queen Elizabeth's bishops."[1]

Martyrs for Independency.—Udall, as we have seen, disclaimed all participation in "the schism and separation of the Brownists." A Presbyterian and follower of Cartwright, he shared also Cartwright's disinclination to leave the Church of England. Those, however, who afterwards succeeded to the crown of martyrdom were men firmly convinced that the Established Church was no Church for them; that with a Church framed upon such lines, and opening its doors to all and sundry, whether moral or immoral, religious or irreligious, they could have no communion. Browne's doctrine of "a gathered Church" had been acting like leaven upon the minds of many who had no thought of ascribing to him its parentage. Fuller's pious and doubtless heartfelt wish in regard to Browne, "That his bad opinions had been interred with him," was not destined to be fulfilled. If the evil that men do lives after them,—and certainly this has been exemplified in the case of Browne,—the good, so far from being interred

[1] Arber's Introduction to *A Demonstration of Discipline,* p. vii.

with their bones, often has a resurrected vitality. The Brownists, as they were now called, continued to increase; and as they increased, persecution grew more bitter and relentless. Archbishop Whitgift had his officers and spies stationed wherever there was any likelihood of a meeting being held, and all surprised in the act of meeting for any kind of religious service were hailed off to prison. Separatism was construed into treason against the Queen, for it impugned her supremacy as head or governor of the Church, and was thus made synonymous with sedition and rebellion. How many were incarcerated and done to death in the foul, fetid, fever-reeking dungeons, we have no precise means of knowing, for their wretchedness and sufferings, endured silently and to the bitter end, have found no chronicler.

A brief account of one of these sufferers has come down to us. **Roger Rippon** died in prison, and his friends, moved with pity and indignation, carried, with great parade, before the house of Judge Young, who had passed the iniquitous sentence upon him, his coffin, bearing the inscription: "This is the corpse of Roger Rippon, a servant of Christ, and her Majesty's faithful subject, who is the last of sixteen or seventeen which that great enemy of God, the Archbishop of Canterbury, with his High Commissioners, have murdered in Newgate within these four years, manifestly for the testimony of Jesus Christ. His soul is now with the Lord, and his blood crieth for speedy vengeance against that great enemy of the saints, and against Mr. Richard Young, who in this and many the like points hath abused his power for the upholding of the Romish Antichrist, prelacy, and priesthood."

The Anabaptists.—It should be here stated that the first martyrs for religious liberty during the reign of Elizabeth are found, not among the Brownists, but among the hated, maligned, and much-suffering Anabaptists. The history of that remarkable sect has yet to be written, and when justice has been done to them a memorable and heroic chapter will have been added to the history of the world. The Anabaptists were Puritans before Puritanism had sprung into recognized existence, and held substantially all that the Puritans afterwards contended for. We have already seen how Foxe, the martyrologist, petitioned the Queen, unsuccessfully, for the lives of two members of this despised sect.[1] These were Dutch Baptists, John Wiel Macker and Heindrich Terwoort, who were burnt at Smithfield in 1575 for denying the function of the civil magistrate in matters of religion, and advocating the doctrine of separation of Church and State, and liberty of conscience. The bitter prejudice which these poor Anabaptists had to encounter may be gathered from the truculent tone adopted by Fuller when, speaking of the Queen's resistance to the plea urged in their behalf by Foxe, he says: "Indeed, damnable were their impieties, and she necessitated to this severity, who having formerly punished some traitors, if now sparing these blasphemers, the world would condemn her as being more earnest in asserting her own safety than God's honour. Hereupon the writ *de hæretico*

[1] P. 19.

comburendo (which for seventeen years had hung only up *in terrorem*) was now taken down and put in execution, and the two anabaptists burned in Smithfield *died in great horror, with crying and roaring.*"[1]

Six Separatist leaders suffered death upon the scaffold. One of them was **William Dennis**, concerning whom we have the voucher of Governor Bradford: "For Mr. Dennis, he was a godly man, and faithful in his place." Two other sufferers were **John Copping** and **Elias Thacker**, both of whom were hanged at Bury St. Edmunds in 1583, for "dispersinge of Browne's bookes." God gave them courage to bear it, says Bradford. This was their answer to the judge who sentenced them: "My Lord, your face we fear not; and for your threats, we care not; and to come to your read service, we dare not."

Henry Barrowe.—The three most notable of those who suffered and died for their attachment to the principles of Independency were Henry Barrowe, John Greenwood, and John Penry. The first and last of these names call for somewhat extended notice. Barrowe was "a gentleman of a good house," according to the testimony of Lord Bacon, who in his youth led a wild and dissipated life. He was educated at Cambridge, and took his degree of B.A. in 1569 to 1570. He became a member of Gray's Inn in 1576, and frequented her Majesty's Court. He dated his conversion to a sermon which he heard preached in a church into which he had casually strolled along with a boon companion, and, in the language of Bacon, "he made a leap from a vain and

[1] Fuller's *Church History*, vol. iv. p. 390.

libertine youth to a preciseness in the highest degree, the strangeness of which alteration made him very much spoken of." He became an ardent Puritan, and probably through the influence of Browne a convinced believer in those principles which the latter did so much to propagate.[1]

After Browne, Barrowe was the most remarkable of the early Independents, and he succeeded in communicating to an ever increasing number of his followers the impress of his strong character and vivid personality. His companion in tribulation was **John Greenwood**, who had been a clergyman of the Established Church, but had embraced Separatist principles, and was imprisoned for taking part in a conventicle meeting. It was while paying a visit to his friend in the Clink Prison that Barrowe was himself arrested and conveyed to Lambeth Palace, and there, after subjecting him to a brief interrogation, the archbishop committed him to prison. The charges brought against him may be best gathered from the examination he underwent before Whitgift, the Bishop of London, the Lord Treasurer, the Lord Chancellor, Lord Buckhurst, Justice Young, and others. This examination, the account of which we owe to his graphic pen, has become truly historic.

Examination of Barrowe.—We give just one or two extracts [2]—

[1] Bacon calls them (the Brownists) "a third kind of gospellers," and speaks of them as being directed by the great fervour of the unholy Ghost.—Bacon's *Works*, vol. i. p. 383.

[2] The whole of this examination is printed in Mr. Arber's *Introductory Sketch to the Martin Marprelate Controversy*, pp. 41-48.

"I being kneeled downe at the end of the table, the Lord Tresorer (Burghley) began and asked me my name; which when I had told him, he asked me if I had not ben sometymes of the Courte. I answered that I had sometymes frequented the Courte. He sayd he remembered me not.

"*The Lord Treasurer*—Why are you in pryson?

"*Barrowe*—I am now in pryson, my Lord, vppon the statute made for Recusantes.

"*Lord Treasurer*—Why will you not come to the Churche?

"*Barrowe*—My whole desyer is to come to the Churche of God.

"*Lord Treasurer*—Thou arte a fantasticall fellowe, I perceive, but why not to our churches?

"*Barrowe*—The causes are manye and great my Lord: and it were too longe to show them in particular, but breyflye, my Lord: I cannot come to your churches because all the wicked and prophane of the land are receyued in to the bodye of your churches; agayne you haue a false and Antichristian mynisterye set ouer your churches, neither worship you God aright, but after an Idolatrous and superstitious manner, and your Church is not gouerned by the worde of God, but by the Romish Courtes.

"*Lord Treasurer*—The Lord Tresorer . . . demanded of me whether I hold tithes lawfull.

"*Barrowe*—My Lord, they are abrogate and vnlawfull.

"*Lord Treasurer*—Why, thou wouldest haue the mynisters to liue by somewhat: whereof should they liue?

"*Barrowe—Ex pura elemosina*, of Cleane almesdeedes, as Christ and His Apostles did and in His Testament ordayned.

"*Lord Treasurer*—But how if the people will not give?

"*Barrowe*—Suche people are not the people of God.

"Then I beseeched the Lordes to graunt a publique conference, that it might appeare to all men what we holde and wherein we erred.

"*Archbishop of Canterbury*—The archbishop sayd, in great choller, we should haue no publicke conference: we had published inoughe alreadye, and therefore I commit you close prysoner.

"*Barrowe*—But contrary to Lawe.

"*Lord Treasurer*—The Lord Tresurour sayd that it be vppon such occasions done by lawe, and asked whether I had any learning or no.

"*Bishops*—Canterbury and London, with one consent, sayd I had no learninge.

"*Barrowe*—The Lord knoweth I am ignorant, I haue no lerning to boast of, but this I know, that you are voyd of all true learninge and good lives.

"As we were thus reasoning, the Lord Chauncellor asked me if I knew not these. 2. men, poynting to Canterbury and London.

"*Barrowe*—Yes (my Lord), I haue cause to knowe them.

"*Lord Chancellor*—But what? Is not thys the Bishop of London?

"*Barrowe*—I know him for no Bishop, my Lord.

"*Lord Chancellor*—What is he then?

"*Barrowe*—His name is Elmar [or Aylmer], my Lord.

"The Lorde pardon my fault that I layd him not open for a wolf, a bloudy persecuter, and an *Apostata*, but by that tyme the wardens man was plucking me vp.

"*Lord Chancellor*—And what is this man? (pointing to Canterbury).

"*Barrowe*—The Lord gaue me the spiryte of boldnes, so that I sayd, He is a Monster, a miserable Compounde; I know not what to call him, he is neither ecclesiasticall nor Cyvell, euen the second beast that is spoken of the Revelacion.

"*Lord Treasurer*—Where is that place? Shew it.

"*Barrowe*—So I turned to the place, 13 *cap.*, and read the verse 11, then I turned to 2 *Thessal.* 2; but the beast arose for anger and gnashed his teethe, and sayd, will ye suffer him, my Lord? So I was plucked vp from my knees by the wardens man, and carryed awaye."

One cannot but be struck by the unflinching and spirited way in which Barrowe bore himself during this prolonged examination. There plays, too, over the whole scene, flash upon flash of unconscious humour. Note, says Mr. Arber, Lord Burghley's keenness of mind. "Himself during his whole life a Puritan, he makes these innovators give chapter and verse for every statement they hazard. He must have chuckled when he asked Barrowe to prove out of Scripture that Whitgift was 'the man of sin,' 'the son of perdition.' Doubtless that story must have gone the round of the Court at the time. "If such an examination seems unseasonable at a time when Spain was preparing the Armada for England, which, if successful, would have swept

Prelate and Puritan away together, the unseasonableness is chargeable to Whitgift, who had kept Barrowe in prison since November 1586." Though in prison, Barrowe and Greenwood were not idle. It is a mystery that remains unsolved how they managed to secure the secrecy necessary to write so much as they did. Barrowe wrote no less than four or five volumes, one of which was a dense quarto of more than two hundred and fifty pages, entitled, *A Brief Discoverie of the False Church*, etc. These are admittedly from the pen of Barrowe; and, as we have already seen, Dr. Dexter argues (though with doubtful success) that his was the hand that penned the Martin Marprelate tracts, the 'copy' of which surreptitiously, and in some deftly concealed way, found its way into the hands of John Penry, to be by him, as the principal directing agent, printed and published, and scattered broadcast over the whole country.

Execution of Greenwood and Barrowe.—Greenwood and Barrowe were tried at the Old Bailey, March 23rd, 1592–1593, on a charge of writing and publishing sundry seditious books and pamphlets tending to the defamation of the Queen's Majesty. In the *Apology or Defence of such True Christians as are commonly (but unjustly) called Brownists*, written a day or two before his death, we have a description of what followed from Barrowe's own pen: "Upon the 24th, early in the morning, was preparation made for our execution: we brought out of the Limbo, our Irons smitten off, and we ready to be bound to the cart; when her Maiestie's most gracious pardon came for our reprieve." Certain "doctors and deans" being sent to "exhort and confer" with them, they expressed their willingness to debate the points at issue between them. But this was not what the authorities of the Church wanted. They wanted their retractation and submission, and to nothing that savoured of discussion and compromise would they be induced to listen. "Vpon the last day of the third month," says Barrowe, "my brother Greenwood and I were very early and secretly conveyed to the place of execution, where, being tied by the necks to the tree, we were permitted to speak a few words." After protesting their innocency of the charges preferred against them, just as they were offering up prayer for the Queen, the second sentence of reprieve arrived. This was the result of an appeal to the Lord Treasurer, urging that, "in a land where no Papist was put to death for religion, theirs should not be the first blood shed who concurred about faith with what was professed in the country, and desired conference to be convinced of their errors."

The ecclesiastical authorities, impatient of delay, took the law into their own hands, and on April 6th, 1593, contrived to have them secretly hanged. It is said, though there is not much proof for the story, that the Queen was displeased with the hurried and clandestine way in which the death sentence had been carried out. A letter in the State Paper Office, from one Thomas Philippes to William Herrell, reveals the fact that it was the fear of the Lower House of Parliament maiming a Bill against the Barrowists and Brownists, which had passed the Upper House, that made Whitgift and the bishops hasten the execution in the way they did. As the letter says: "The executions proceeded through malice of the bishops to the Lower House, which makes them much hated by the people affected that way."

Barrowism.—Barrowe is so commanding a figure in the annals of Puritan Separatism or early Independency, that some mention should be here made of the following he obtained, and of the Church system—afterwards set up more especially in the States of New England—to the shaping of which his influence so materially contributed. Barrowism, as it came to be called, was a system standing midway between Brownism and the system of Cartwright and Travers. It was an attempt to graft the Presbyterian eldership upon the simple Congregational idea of the Church; that eldership for which Udall, in his *Demonstration of Discipline*, claims the authority of Christ in His word, "in all times and places until the end of the world." The main difference of Barrowe's system of Church government and that of Browne is that, while the latter regards the authority of the Church as vested in the people themselves, Barrowe favours the idea of an *imperium in imperio* by the position he assigns to the elders of the Church, and by the power he would intrust to them. That he was in no danger of going over to the side of Cartwright is made clear by the way in which he speaks of Cartwright and his followers. "These Reformists, howsoever for fashion sake they give the people a little liberty to sweeten their mouths and make them believe that they should choose their own ministers, yet even in this pretended choice do they cozen and beguile them also, leaving them nothing but the smoky, windy title of election only, enjoining them to choose some university clerk,—one of those college-birds of their own brood,—or else comes a synod in the neck of them, and annihilates the election whatsoever it be."[1]

There is no marked difference that we have been able to discover, save in this matter of the eldership, between the principles held by the Barrowists and Brownists; yet there appears to have been as little *rapprochement* between them as between the ancient Jews and Samaritans. Greenwood had been charged by Giffard with being a Brownist, or sharing the opinions of the Brownists regarding the Church of England, and this is the answer he makes: "What opinion the Brownists hold of the Church of England, their worship, people, ministry, government, we neither know nor regard; neither is there any cause why we should be charged or condemned for their errors and faults for which themselves and this Church of England that receiveth and nourisheth all sectaries, heretics, wicked and abominable persons whatsoever shall account."[2] Greenwood goes back upon the subject and says: "You breathe out your accustomed lies, slanders, and railings. First you term us 'Brownists' and 'Donatists,' whereas *I never conversed with the men or their writings!* I detest Donatus' heresies. And if they had been instruments to teach us any truth, we are not therefore to be named with their names; we were baptized into Christ's. Browne is a member of *your* Church, *your* brother, and all Brownists do frequent *your* assemblies."[3]

It should be mentioned here that Browne, notwithstand-

---

[1] Dexter's *Congregationalism*, p. 239.
[2] Hanbury's *Historical Memorials*, vol. i. p. 66. [3] *Ibid.* p. 69.

ing his defence of Separatism, never enjoined upon his followers the duty of refusing to attend the services of the Established Church. This is what a Puritan opponent said of him: "Sometimes he would go to hear sermons, but that he accounted no active communion, and declared to his friends that he thought it not unlawful to hear our sermons, and therefore persuaded his followers in London so to do."

John Penry.—Few nobler spirits have been numbered among the noble army of martyrs than John Penry, the apostle of wild Wales, and its first missionary. He was born in Brecknorshire about the beginning of Elizabeth's reign. He was bred a Roman Catholic, "as arrant a Papist as ever came out of Wales," but contact with the influence of the Reformation seems soon to have wrought in him a great change. He matriculated at Cambridge, where he made acquaintance with Puritanism, and soon became a convinced and ardent disciple. Afterwards he removed to Oxford, influenced probably by the more positive Puritan spirit which there reigned, and took his degree of A.M. in 1586. The historian of Oxford, Anthony Wood, in his *Athenæ Oxonienses*, says: "He took holy orders, did preach in Oxon. and afterwards in Cambridge, and was esteemed by many a tolerable scholar and edifying preacher, and a good man." His heart was stirred within him on account of his countrymen, his kinsmen according to the flesh. In the *Protestation*, written before his death, and addressed to Lord Burghley, he says: "I am a poore young man, borne and bredd in the mountaynes of Wales. I am the first, since the last springing vpp of the gospell in this latter age, that publickly laboured to have the blessed seed thereof sowen in those barruyne mountaines."

For his zeal in preaching, and advocating by means of the press the preaching of the gospel,—ostensibly for his denunciation of "dumb or unpreaching ministers," who were scandalously ignorant and inefficient, contenting themselves with the lazy reading of a printed homily when they ought to be feeding the hungry sheep that looked up and were not fed,—he was cited before the High Commission, and sharply rebuked for the broaching of such heresy. Diligent study of the New Testament, and association with the Puritans and Separatist leaders, Barrowe and Greenwood, made him a strong believer in the principles they had espoused, and he became active in their advocacy by voice and by pen. In 1590, Penry was again cited before the High Commission, this time to answer for the part he had taken in the Martin Marprelate books or pasquinades. He was charged with being accessory to the writings of these tracts, and with having written some of them with his own hand. The latter charge is one that has never been substantiated. The evidence to the contrary is conclusive, and is admitted as being such by all versed in the history of this controversy.[1] But if not the

[1] Even by Mr. Maskell (p. 107), who loses no opportunity of pillorying a Puritan; even he is constrained to say: "We must not overlook this, that no evidence was found, and also that Penry himself at the time (which I cannot give much weight to), and always after, even when about to die (when one is rather inclined to believe that he would speak the truth), denied that he had been concerned in the writing of those tracts."

author of these famous tracts, clearly Penry was implicated in their production. "There can be no reasonable doubt," says Dr. Dexter, "that he was the publisher of them." He thinks that Barrowe and Penry were jointly responsible for them, the former as author, the latter as publisher. Suspicion fell upon Penry, and a warrant was issued for his apprehension; but he fled into Scotland, where he remained for three years, and continued to employ his pen in the advocacy of his opinions. On his return to England he was arrested and committed to prison. His private papers were seized, and among them was found a rough embryo sketch of a petition to the Queen, in which, using very plain words, he tells Her Majesty that "the Gospel was little beholden to her for anything," and that she suffered it "to reach no farther than the end of her sceptre."

This, be it remembered, was the rough first-hand impression of a petition which was intended to be addressed to the Queen, but was really drawn from his private diary. The extracts from this rough unfinished sketch form the basis of the charge that was brought against Penry. He was tried and found guilty, and sentenced to be hanged. The next day Penry wrote his *Protestation* to Lord Treasurer Burghley, written, as Hallam says, "in a style of the most affecting and simple eloquence," in which he protests that he had done nothing worthy of death, and that of sedition or disloyalty he was guiltless both in act and intention. "It was never known before this time," says Neal, "that a minister and scholar was condemned to death for private papers found in his study, nor do I remember more than one since that time, in whose case it was given for law *scribere est agere*, that to write has been construed an overt act; but Penry must die, right or wrong."

The first name on the warrant for his execution was Archbishop Whitgift, and, whilst Penry was at dinner, officers were despatched to bid him make ready, for he must die that afternoon. The sentence was carried out that same afternoon, May 29th, 1593, and thus died this young and intrepid martyr, an example of as unconquerable fidelity to the cause of truth and liberty as any of those emblazoned upon the martyr roll of fame.

This was his confession, written just before his death: "If I might live upon this earth the days of Methuselah twice told, and that in no less comfort than Peter, James, and John were in the Mount, and after this life might be sure of the kingdom of heaven, yet to gain all this I durst not go from the former testimony to the truth of Jesus Christ."

For what, then, did these Puritan martyrs suffer and die?—Was it for a particular form of Church government, to get Calvinism or Independency enthroned in the place of Episcopacy, or to have it established concurrently with Episcopacy? They were anxious, no doubt, that Independency should be a *religio licita*: but it was no mere polity they were contending for; it was the spiritual conception which lay at the root of Independency that they were supremely anxious to have recognised, not merely by one Church, but by all Churches; and that if there was to be one Church, that it should stand, not upon priestly rites, formalism, and magic, but upon the universal priesthood of all who worshipped God in the spirit and had no confidence in the flesh. Like the Free Churchmen of later times, they were battling for "the Crown rights of the Redeemer."

To say that Barrowe and Greenwood and Penry laid down their lives for their attachment to the principles of Independency, is to seem to expose them to the charge of perversity—it might seem of narrow-minded bigotry—at best, "the dissidence of dissent and the Protestantism of the Protestant religion." But really their attachment to Independency meant nothing more and nothing less than insistence on a Church in which Christ should be supreme Ruler and King, and in which all under-rulers should be in willing subjection unto Him. It was the vision of a purified Church, of the kingdom of heaven upon earth, in which there should be no unrighteousness, and in which, at least in their ideal aim, men should be holy and without blemish; it was this which stirred the moral passion that made them the Reformers, made them the Independents, made them the martyrs they were.

Like Browne before him, Barrowe assailed the principle of multitudinism in the existing Church of England, a Church in which there was no attempt "to discern between the righteous and the wicked, between him that serveth God and him that serveth Him not." Instead of the temple of the Church being composed of living stones, "they be rather of the refuse, common pebble chalk stones which cannot be used to any sound and sure building, even all the profane and wicked of the land, Atheists, Papists, Anabaptists, and heretics of all sorts, gluttons, rioters, blasphemers, purgerers, covetous extortioners, thieves, whores, witches, connivers, etc., and who not, that dwelleth within this land, or is within the Queen's dominions."[1]

Penry is not less clear in his perception and pronouncement: "We are to walk by the line of the word, and not after the judgments of men. Her Majesty's authority I acknowledge, but it doth no whit infringe her royal power and authority to deny that she hath any warrant, any power, any sword granted her of God, to establish either false religion, false and antichristian ordinances, or yet any other unwarrantable or unjust constitution. If Her Majesty and this High Court require of us that we resort unto the public assemblies of the land, and so to enter into the antichristian band, and continue therein, I answer again that it is against the written word of God, and therefore that Her Majesty hath no power, no authority from the Lord, to require this at our hand."

Religious Toleration.—It is not claimed for these Puritan Separatists that they were the apostles of religious toleration. Their attitude to this question we hope to consider more fully in a subsequent part of this work. Here a few words must suffice. The sun of toleration, "with healing in his wings," had not yet risen upon the world; or, rather, it had risen when Christianity was first planted, then it had become eclipsed in the deepening

[1] *A Brief Discovery of the False Church*, vi. 9.

shadows of the centuries that succeeded, until, in the darkness of the Middle Ages, it had become, we might say, quite extinguished. Between this period and the close of the sixteenth century, with the exception of the Mennonites or Anabaptists, who began to appear in Holland about 1522, it was not even professed by any body of people. Southey's assertion, however, that "No Church, no sect, no individual even, had yet professed the principle of toleration," [1] is not true. Not to speak of the Dutch Baptists, and William of Orange, who threw his shield over this persecuted sect, Robert Browne may fairly claim to have expiscated a doctrine of liberty of conscience, which, if heard of before in England, had been heard of only as a speculative conception. Dr. Dexter holds that "Robert Browne is entitled to the proud preeminence of having been the first writer claiming to state and defend in the English tongue the true and now accepted doctrine of the relation of the magistrate to the Church."

There is no doubt that succeeding Separatists fell behind Browne in the way in which they grasped, or rather failed to grasp, this doctrine. In the preface to a volume issued by Barrowe and Greenwood, they say: "We acknowledge that the princes ought to compel all their subjects to the hearing of God's word in the public exercises of the Church,"—a sentiment which seems strangely at variance with that which immediately follows: "Yet cannot the prince compel any to be a member of the Church, to receive any without assurance by public profession of their own faith, or to retain any longer than

[1] *Book of the Church*, vol. ii. p. 285.

they continue and walk orderly in the faith." To compel men to the hearing of God's word is not quite consistent with liberty of conscience. The time had not come for either Puritans or Prelatists to hoist that flag, and to march under it as the soldiers of a free spiritual commonwealth. The Separatists—perhaps unconsciously even to themselves—had their foot already upon the threshold of that new era.

Animus of Anglican writers in regard to the Separatists.—The vehemence with which the claims of these Puritan martyrs to the honour of martyrdom have been assailed by certain Anglican writers, is evidently the measure of their apprehension and alarm lest these claims should prove to be well founded. "They were not martyrs at all; they were condemned to death for defamation of the Queen, and for inciting to rebellion." "Penry was found guilty of a political crime by a British jury." Canon Curteis, in the Bampton Lecture for 1871, on *Dissent in its Relation to the Church of England*, surpasses himself in the endeavour to show that these men died for nothing more than a mere crotchet. "These" (Barrowe, Greenwood, and Penry) "all fell victims, not to the archbishop's anger, but to the indignation of the Queen and the whole country at the appearance of the scurrilous and blasphemous Marprelate tracts in 1588." What is to be thought of the accuracy of a writer that can so twist and misrepresent the plainest evidence? "For what was it," he goes on to ask, "in the name of common sense, that these men contested and suffered? It was not (as we have seen) for the great principles of

Independency as expounded by modern writers. It was for nothing in the world but for the mere 'crotchet' that the State was bound at the sword's point to establish Calvin's *divine* Church system (drawn from Eph. iv. 11) on the ruins of the existing *human* one. It was for the 'fixed idea' that the Queen and the Government, in resisting this interpretation of the infallible word of God, were resisting the Holy Spirit Himself, and going to perdition. It was for the insane fanaticism which led them to urge the overthrow of the ecclesiastical constitution of their country in language so violent and inflammatory that no court of justice, in such dangerous times as those were, could possibly forbear to put the Act of Parliament into execution." [1]

Such reckless statements as these, not one of which can be substantiated, serve only to reveal the *animus* by which a certain class of Anglican writers are moved when they essay to speak about Puritanism and the Church. Even granting that Barrowe, Greenwood, and Penry did hold such opinions as those attributed to them by Canon Curteis,[2] still they were only opinions; and why men should *be hanged for holding* them is a question on which he does not venture to enlighten us, though he evidently believes that hanging was no more than they deserved.

---

[1] Curteis' *Bampton Lectures*, p. 78.

In 1893 the Independents or Congregationalists of England celebrated the tercentenary of the martyrdom of Greenwood, Barrowe, and Penry, and this stirred—as was perhaps natural—the wrath of the *Church Quarterly*, the *Church Times*, and other organs of Anglican opinion, which did their best to discredit the celebration and pour contempt upon it.

[2] See Curteis' *Bampton Lectures*, note, p. 78.

The Puritan martyrs not guilty of sedition or any political offence.—As for saying that the offence of which these men were guilty was not ecclesiastical, not the holding of certain opinions in matters pertaining to Church and State, but was sedition and rebellion against the Queen, this is a fallacy too glaring and transparent to impose upon any but the credulous and those anxious to believe it. Speaking of the execution of Thacker and Copping, who were hanged for denying the Queen's ecclesiastical supremacy, " the proof of which was their dispersion of Browne's tracts, wherein that was only owned in civil cases," Hallam goes on to say : " This was according to the invariable practice of Tudor times. An oppressive and sanguinary statute was first made, and next, as occasion might serve, a construction was put upon it contrary to all common sense, in order to take away men's lives." Clearly, if the printing and circulating of obnoxious opinions is to be construed into an act of treason or disloyalty to the Crown, no reformation in Church or in State could ever have been carried through, and no hope of reprieve could ever have been indulged by those who set their hands to it. Under such a system as this, " justification by faith " becomes a treasonable doctrine, and Duke George of Saxony should not only have forbidden the circulation of his writings, but have brought Luther to the block.

It is a relief to turn from the prejudiced judgment of Canon Curteis to the judgment of another Churchman, who, though differing from Barrowe and Penry, and the contention of the Puritans in general, as decidedly as Canon Curteis, yet can do them the justice to say :

"Underneath the disputes about ceremonial and about Church discipline, underlying the accusations so freely cast against the Clergy that they were dumb dogs, an unpreaching ministry, against the bishops that they were lordly prelates and greedy wolves, beneath even the scurrility of the Martin Marprelate tracts, can be traced a true religious principle. The yearning after a more direct communion between God and the soul than was offered by a Church which had for the time deposed the sacraments from their place in the Christian system, was trying to find expression in a sense of personal election and individual mission."[1]

Meanwhile bonds and imprisonment and the prospect of lingering death did not stop the growth of Separatism. In the foul malarious atmosphere of Newgate, the Fleet, Bridewell, the Clink, and other prisons, sufferers for conscience' sake were dragging out a terrible existence.

The following,[2] from a petition by a number of Brownists, presented to Lord Burghley in 1592, gives some idea of the sufferings and misery these "poor Christians," as they styled themselves, were called upon to endure:—

"Pleaseth it then your Lordship to understand that we, Her Majesty's loyal, dutiful, and true-hearted subjects, to the number of threescore persons and upwards, have, contrary to all law and equity, been imprisoned, separated

---

[1] *The Church and the Puritans*, by Henry Offley Wakeman, M.A., Fellow of All Souls College, Tutor of Keble College, Oxford, pp. 42, 43.

[2] Strype's *Annals*, iv. 90; Neal, vol. i. p. 367.

from our trades, wives, children, and families, yea, shut up close prisoners from all comfort, many of us to the space of two years and a half, upon the bishops' sole commandment, in great penury and noisomeness of the prisons, many ending their lives, never called to trial: some haled forth to the sessions, some cast in irons and dungeons, some in hunger and famine; all of us debarred from any lawful audience before our honourable governors and magistrates, and from all benefit and help of the laws; daily defamed and falsely accused by published pamphlets, by private suggestions, often preaching, slanders and accusations of heresy, sedition and schism, and what not. . . . And seeing that for our conscience only we are deprived of all comfort, we most humbly beseech your good Lordship that some free and Christian conference, publicly or privately before your honour or before whom it would please you, where our adversaries may not be our judges (might be had), that our case, with the reason and proof on both sides, might be recorded by different notaries and faithful witnesses; and if anything be found in us worthy of death or bonds, let us be made an example to all posterity; if not, we entreat for some compassion to be shown in equity, according to law, for our relief: that in the meantime we may be bailed to do Her Majesty service, walk in our callings, to provide things needful for ourselves, our poor wives, disconsolate children, and families lying upon us, or else that we might be prisoners together in Bridewell, or any other convenient place at your honour's appointment, where we might provide such relief by our diligence and labours as might preserve life to the comfort both of our souls and bodies."

This petition was signed by fifty-nine persons immured in different prisons. Needless to say, it was rejected by the bishops and Privy Council. The reasons given are thoroughly characteristic, and the drift of them may be easily surmised.

Holland and the Exiled Independents

MEMORABLE EVENTS AND DATES

First Church of General Baptists in England . . 1611
First permanent Independent Church in England . 1616
John Robinson . . . . born 1575, died 1625

CONTENTS OF CHAPTER X

Number of Separatists—Causes—Indebtedness to Holland—Refugees in England—Influence of Holland on England—Holland birthplace of Puritanism—Bacon's opinion of the Separatists—Popular resentment at treatment of them—Act of Parliament to suppress Separatism—Exiles in Holland poor, but under strong and scholarly leaders—Francis Johnson—John Smyth—Church at Scrooby—John Robinson—Emigrates to Holland—Leyden—Robinson's attitude to the English Church—His farewell address to Pilgrims—Memorial tablet—Historic Independency—Helwys and first English Church of Baptists—First Independent Church in England—Henry Jacob—Robinson and Jacob semi-Separatists—Independents pioneers of liberty—Note on Robinson's farewell address.

CHAPTER X

HOLLAND AND THE EXILED INDEPENDENTS

WE have already adverted to the statement made by Sir Walter Raleigh in Parliament in 1580, that he was afraid that there were over twenty thousand Brownists in England. Considering that the entire population of England did not at that time exceed three millions of people, that is (according to Motley), about equal to the population of the Netherlands, this is a very considerable proportion, and it is little wonder that the statement has been generally supposed to be exaggerated. It is certainly grossly exaggerated if the statement is to be taken literally, for at the time it was made Browne was but beginning to be a conspicuous figure in public estimation, and could not have attracted to himself a very numerous following. Probably, however, Sir Walter used the word "Brownists" as descriptive of the Puritan Separatists generally, those who in substance had adopted the views of Browne, and were disaffected towards the Church and the existing ecclesiastical hierarchy. Taken in this extended sense, there seems no reason to suspect the truth of the statement.

But how had the Separatists grown to the number of twenty thousand? It would be a real, and, in our judgment, an insuperable difficulty to account for their rapid increase in so short a space of time, if we had no alternative but to attribute it to ordinary causes, say to the influence of the Marian exiles, who had returned home at the accession of Elizabeth imbued with the theology of Geneva and with the spirit of freedom which that theology generated wherever it was received. The leaven of their teaching and influence could not have been so great and so widely diffused as to spread the principles of Separatism among so numerous a section of the nation. It must have been circumscribed by the paucity of their numbers; and when in course of time these passed away, there were but few to take their place and carry on their work. But even if their successors had been equally numerous, equally zealous, their efforts to commend the doctrine of religious liberty to the great mass of the people would have been defeated by the inertness, ignorance, and brutality in which they were sunk. Very few of the latter could read, and it was believed by the ruling powers that the best way to make them contented was to keep them ignorant. In truth, when we consider the general condition of the people, the wonder is that Puritanism was not entirely crushed out while Elizabeth was on the throne. How, then, is the rapid growth of Puritanism to be explained? To answer this question we must mentally transport ourselves across the North Sea to the kingdom of the Netherlands or Holland.[1]

[1] In the middle of the seventeenth century, according to Motley, the population of Holland was as large as that of England, and much more wealthy. — *United Netherlands*, vol. iv. p. 557.

Puritanism in Holland.—The influence which this little kingdom, less than half the size of Scotland, and not one-fourth that of England, has exerted upon the historical development of Europe, and especially of our own country, in the matter of civil and religious liberty, has seldom, if recognised, been appraised at its true value.

In the brief notes which Professor Skeat has introduced at the commencement of his *Etymological Dictionary*, he takes credit for having been the first to point out with sufficient distinctness how great has been the indebtedness of England to Holland. " I am convinced that the influence of Dutch upon English has been much underrated, and a closer attention to this question might throw some light even upon English history. History tells us that our relations with the Netherlands have often been rather close. We read of Flemish mercenary soldiers being employed by the Normans, and of Flemish settlements in Wales, ' where ' (says old Fabyan, I know not with what truth) ' they remayned a long whyle, but after, they sprad all Englande ouer.' We may recall the alliance between Edward III. and the free towns of Flanders; and the importation by Edward of Flemish weavers." After Antwerp had been captured by the Duke of Parma, a third of the merchants and manufacturers of the ruined city are said to have found refuge on the banks of the Thames. A final stoppage of the trade with Flanders would have broken half the merchants in London.[1] Flemish weavers had come over with the Conqueror, then settled down in Norfolk, and suc-

[1] Green's *Short History*, p. 381.

ceeded to so great an extent in developing the industry at which they wrought, that Norwich became the second city in the kingdom. These Dutch refugees came to this country, not only for purposes of trade, but because they were driven out of their own country by stress of religious persecution. During the period the Netherlands were overrun and laid waste by the butcheries of Alva, it is computed that between fifty and one hundred thousand refugees found an asylum in England. In 1560 there were ten thousand, and in 1562 the number had reached thirty thousand.[1]

It was among the Flemish weavers that the preaching and doctrines of Wyclif caught hold and spread most rapidly, and during the persecution of the Lollards it is said more persons suffered death at the stake in Norfolk than in all the other counties of England put together.[2] The martyrs who suffered under Mary were most numerous in those counties where Lollardism exerted its greatest influence, and in those counties it was

[1] Green puts the number of refugees from the Netherlands at over 50,000. In the early part of the seventeenth century the population of London was not more than 130,000, and of these 10,000, were foreigners, mostly Walloons. In Norwich alone, as early as 1571, there were 3925 Dutch and Walloons, and in 1587 this number had risen to 4679, making a majority of the population.

[2] Professor Thorold Rogers' *Story of Holland*, p. 51 ; *The English Reformation of the Sixteenth Century*, by W. H. Beckett. Religious Tract Society. See the two maps. It is idle, in the face of such facts, to say, as Mr. Froude does, that the Lollard movement was an untimely birth, and that it completely died out. This much is certain, that it spread at first among the Walloon settlers ; and precisely in those parts—Norfolk and Suffolk and London—where these settlers were most numerous, there the Protestant reforming Puritan spirit was most active and vigorous.

that Puritanism flourished, and Separatism afterwards sprang up.

The influence of Holland upon England.—These refugees from the Netherlands brought with them the arts and sciences for which their country had already become famous, and they taught them to a people entirely ignorant of them; for it must be admitted, says Mr. Thorold Rogers, that for a long time in the industrial history of modern civilisation the English were "the stupidest and most backward nation in Europe." Holland, on the other hand, was the instructor of Europe in the most advanced kind of agriculture, the most enterprising commerce. It was the pioneer in navigation and in discovery, in physical research, in medical knowledge and skill, and produced the greatest jurists and the most learned scholars of the seventeenth century. It was a centre of varied literary activity when England lay enveloped in the gross darkness of ignorance, and more books teemed from its presses than from all other parts of the Continent.

But the greatest service which Holland rendered to our own country in the sixteenth century was the dissemination of Protestant convictions and sentiments—the right of private judgment, the duty of toleration, and liberty of conscience. The Netherlanders became missionaries to the people wherever they settled down, instructing them in the truths of the Bible, quickening at once their intelligence and aspirations, and leading them into the love and practice of virtue, which seemed indeed lofty and austere when compared with the morals of our own countrymen. The chief strongholds of English Puritanism were London and Norwich, and these were just the two cities where the Dutch community and influence were the most widely represented. It was in Norwich, as we have seen, that Robert Browne gathered the first Separatist or Independent Church, a church mainly composed of people from the Netherlands, who at that time formed the majority of the population of the city.

Holland the birthplace of Puritanism.—It seems clear, then, from what has been thus said, that the origin of Puritanism, strictly speaking, is to be sought, not in England, but Holland. It was in Holland that it first made its appearance, and when it began to appear in England at first it found a prepared soil, both among the Walloon settlers and among the people who came under the leaven of their influence. There can be no question that this powerfully contributed to its rapid growth, and to its indefinite expansion.

The debt of England to the Netherlands has been elaborately shown and emphasised in a work [1] to which reference has been already made, and the gist of which,

[1] *The Puritan in Holland, England, and America*; an Introduction to American History, by Douglas Campbell, A.M., LL.B., Member of the American Historical Association. The praise which Mr. Gladstone bestowed upon this work, it may be remembered, drew an indignant letter from Mr. Goldwin Smith, in which he characterised it as a laborious and prolix disparagement of one of the most glorious periods of English history. The contrast is certainly drawn between Holland and England in a way which is decidedly unflattering to the latter; but the body of facts which Mr.

so far as this part of the subject is concerned, is contained in the following words: "When the Reformation came in, in which North-Western Europe was new-born, it was the Netherlands which led the van, and for eighty years waged the war which disenthralled the souls of men. Out of that conflict, shared by thousands of heroic Englishmen, but in which England, as a nation, hardly had a place, Puritanism was evolved,—the Puritanism which gave the triumph to the Netherland Republic, and has shaped the character of the English-speaking race."

Continued oppression of the Puritan Separatists. —In the year 1592, that is, about ten years after Robert Browne began to disseminate his opinions, Lord Bacon wrote these words: "As for those which are called Brownists, being when they were at the most a very small number of very silly and base people here and there in corners dispersed, they are now (thanks be to God!), by the good remedies that have been used, suppressed and worn out, so that there is scarce any news of them."[1] This is, no doubt, excellent testimony

Douglas Campbell brings forward, and the evidence drawn from manifold sources, by which he sustains his conclusions, can hardly fail to carry conviction to every candid and unprejudiced mind, that he has made out a strong case in support of his contention, however humbling it may be to our insular pride to acknowledge it.

[1] "Bacon doubtless here expressed the feeling of all that were respectable in England's society," says Professor Masson, *Life of Milton*, vol. ii. p. 538. Doubtless he did; but considering how often the feeling of all that is respectable in England's society has gone against justice and principle, Bacon's opinion did not derive any added weight from this circumstance.

to the good and strong remedies which had been used against them; not equally good testimony, however, to their success, as appears from what follows.

Barrowe and Greenwood and Penry were the last who suffered death for their Separatist convictions. Their execution raised such a feeling of resentment against the bishops, both in the House of Commons and among the mass of the people, that the prelates took alarm; they saw clearly that the policy of murdering innocent men must be desisted from, or it would recoil with fatal effect upon themselves. Some other mode of quelling the spirit of dissent—the growth of Separatism—must be devised. Accordingly, about the very time that these martyrs for Independency were sent to their graves, an Act of Parliament was passed, making it penal for any person " to abstain from coming to church to hear divine service, or to receive the communion according to Her Majesty's laws and statutes aforesaid, or to be present at any unlawful assemblies, conventicles, or meetings under pretence of any exercise of religion contrary to Her Majesty's said laws and statutes." All persons convicted of such an offence were " to be committed to prison, there to remain without bail or mainprize, until they shall conform and yield themselves," etc. All persons refusing to make submission within three months were to be required to " abjure this realm of England and all other the Queen's Majesty's dominions for ever, unless Her Majesty shall license the party to return." The convicted person was required to make his submission in the following terms: " I, A. B., do humbly confess and acknowledge that I have grievously offended God in contemning Her Majesty's godly and lawful government and authority by absenting myself from church and from hearing divine service, contrary to the godly laws and statutes of this realm, and in using and frequenting disordered and unlawful conventicles and assemblies, under pretence and colour of exercise of religion; and I am heartily sorry for the same, and do acknowledge and testify in my conscience that no other person hath or ought to have any power or authority over Her Majesty," etc. In the last place, the Act provides " that every person that shall abjure by force of this Act, or refuse to abjure being thereunto required as aforesaid, shall forfeit to her Majesty all His goods and chattels for ever," etc.

This Act surely supplies a very striking comment upon Bacon's gratulatory deliverance. If these silly and base people, the Brownists, were, by the good remedies that had been used, suppressed and worn out, what need was there to pass an Act so drastic and designedly so woven as to enmesh and convict all persons guilty of the sin of Separatism? Drastic remedies usually imply the existence of desperate diseases.

The penalty which the Act visited upon those who refused to conform to its requirements left the Puritan Separatists no choice but to banish themselves as speedily as possible, and seek in some new land a freer air, a more hospitable asylum.

The Separatists or Independents in Holland.

—We propose now to accompany to Holland these expatriated Separatists, and note very briefly their fortunes and vicissitudes in that country till the great act of emigration to the far West was resolved upon, and at last became an accomplished fact. We propose to follow them further in their painful and adventurous quest, to trace the successive steps by which a small and feeble band of men and women became the heralds of a new faith, the pioneers of liberty, and the founders of a new world. This method of dealing with the subject of "Puritanism in the Old World and in the New" involves some little deviation from the chronological order of events, for it obliges us to pass over the development of Puritanism in England during the opening years of the reign of James I.; but more than what it loses in historic continuity, it is, we think, likely to gain in securing unity of impression, since it enables us to bring into effective juxtaposition the two continents and the two great fields on which Puritanism waged its struggles and won its distinctive triumph.

The limits within which the history we are relating must necessarily be compressed render it impossible to follow at any great length the fortunes of the exiles, or to do more than exhibit in barest outline the Church system which they endeavoured to construct. We can attempt little more than an enumeration of the leaders under whose direction they began and carried out the experiment.

"Not many wise, not many noble." The first emigrants belonged, almost without exception, to the humbler class of the people. They were miserably poor, so needy, indeed, that when they first landed in Holland the magistrates of the town in which they settled felt constrained to distribute among them a small sum of money for the relief of their necessities. They were glad to get any employment, and to accept such wages as were offered them, for " they were almost consumed with deep poverty, loaded with reproaches, despised and afflicted by all." We can form some idea of the difficulties which the exiles experienced in obtaining the means of subsistence from the statement of George Johnson (Francis Johnson's brother), that some who " had been students were content to card, spin, or to learn trades whereby to maintain themselves"; while of himself he tells that he had not above sixpence, sevenpence, or eightpence the week to live upon. Roger Williams said of Ainsworth, that " though a worthy instrument of God's praise, he lived upon ninepence in the week with roots boiled."

Those who figure as leaders of the small band of exiled Independents were indeed remarkable men, men of strong faith and vigorous personality, and they left their impress deeply graven upon the minds of the young struggling community. Francis Johnson, Henry Ainsworth, Henry Jacob, John Smyth, William Brewster, and especially John Robinson, were men who in any sphere of life would have made their mark, and have risen to a position of influence and ascendency over others. Like Browne and Barrowe, and Greenwood and Penry, they were nearly all university bred, all of them men of fair scholarly attainments, some of them pre-eminently so. Francis Johnson was a Fellow of Christ's College, Cambridge, as was also Henry Jacob and John Robinson. Ainsworth was a proficient Hebraist, and was spoken of as " the great rabbi of this age." " A very learned man he was; we have heard some, eminent in the knowledge of the tongues of the University of Leyden, say that they thought he had not his better for the Hebrew tongue in the university, nor scarce in Europe." Indeed, it is remarkable, considering the difficulties of their position, that nearly all the leading Puritans and Independents were not only men of parts, but men of real and solid learning. They carried this tradition and attachment with them, as we shall see afterwards, into the New World, and their descendants were ever distinguished for their " dread of an illiterate ministry."

Francis Johnson had at first leanings towards the Presbyterian system of Travers and Cartwright, but afterwards he embraced the principles of Independency, and connected himself with a little company of Separatists in London, described (but wrongly, as we have seen) as forming the first Independent or Congregational Church. Driven into exile, he settled at Amsterdam, and became pastor of a little flock, many of whom had been associated with him in England, and had accompanied him to Holland. The little Church settled at Amsterdam, having Francis Johnson for its pastor, and Henry Ainsworth for its teacher, was not long without embroilments and troubles. These were due, not merely to the circumstance in which the exiles were placed, though these were hard and untoward enough, but to the irruption of those human infirmities which in a free democratic society play a not inconsiderable part, and often, to a perilous degree, strain the loyalty of the professed and real friends of freedom. The mild scandals of that period have been sufficiently related elsewhere,[1] and need not further detain us.

Prominent among other causes of disturbance in the Church at Amsterdam was one whose name has been already mentioned, **John Smyth**, to whose influence and teaching the General Baptists trace their origin. He was a Fellow of Cambridge, became lecturer at London, and afterwards vicar of Gainsborough, in Lincolnshire. Here he embraced Separatist principles, and took steps to gather an Independent Church. This became the parent of the Church at Scrooby, which was founded in 1606, and removed to Leyden in 1609, and afterwards, in 1620, formed the company that sailed in the *Mayflower* to the shores of the New World.[2] After ministering for a short time to the Church at Gainsborough, Smyth transplanted himself and his little company to Amsterdam, and there they united with the Church of Francis Johnson. Meanwhile, however, Smyth had become a Baptist, being baptized, as some allege, by one John Morton, or, as others allege, having baptized himself. His views speedily became a source of trouble to the Church at Amsterdam, and it is not surprising to find that he had hardly connected himself with it than he seceded from it, carrying with him his little company.

John Robinson. — If Robert Browne was the

---

[1] See Dr. Dexter's *Congregationalism of the last Three Hundred Years*, "Fortunes and Misfortunes in Amsterdam."

[2] To that little Church in Scrooby belongs, therefore, the distinguished honour of being the mother Church of New England.

founder of Independency, in the sense that he was the first to grasp and give effect to its fundamental contention and principle, John Robinson was the father to whose fostering care and organising genius Congregational Independents are wont, by common consent, to ascribe their distinctive polity and faith. In him they recognise a leader of whom they have no reason to be ashamed, but have justly reason to be proud.

The obscurity that hangs over the history of many of the early Separatists is signally illustrated in the case of one who was in one sense the most distinguished of them all. Of the early life of Robinson [1] very little is known, not even his birthplace has been definitely ascertained, though it was probably in the neighbourhood of Scrooby, in Nottinghamshire. He was born in 1575 or 1576. He graduated at Corpus Christi College, Cambridge, in 1592, and became a Fellow probably in 1599. The year after, he removed to Norwich, where, according to Ainsworth, " the cure and charge of . . . sowles was committed to him." His Puritan leanings caused him to be suspended by the bishop of the diocese, and in 1604 he left Norwich, resolved to seek outside the Church the liberty which was denied him within its pale. There is evidence in the book which he afterwards published, entitled, *A Justification of Separation from the Church of England* that he did not take the step of severing himself from the Church in which he had been born and baptized

---

[1] The most complete account of Robinson and his opinions is that given by Dr. Dexter in his *Congregationalism of the last Three Hundred Years*. His life and works were published in three volumes by the Rev. R. Ashton, London, 1851.

without a keen pang of regret. He says: "Had not the truth been in my heart as a burning fire shut up in my bones, I had never broken those bonds of flesh and blood wherein I was so straitly tied, but had suffered the light of God to have been put out in mine own unthankful heart by other men's darkness." He resigned his fellowship, and repaired to Gainsborough, in Lincolnshire, where he joined a band of Christian men and women who had bound themselves by covenant with God "to walk in all His ways made known or to be made known unto them, according to their best endeavours, whatever it should cost them." This little company of Separatists numbered among them such men as John Smyth, Richard Clifton, William Brewster, William Bradford, Francis Jessop, and George Morton, all of them men shaped in no common mould, and some of them destined to leave upon a new world the impress of their strong character and personality. It was soon found convenient to repair to the old manor-house at Scrooby, occupied by William Brewster, a kind of factor to the Archbishop of York, where he had under his charge the mails of the Government, and kept a relay of post horses. The chapel attached to the manor-house formed a most suitable meeting-place, and Dr. Dexter thinks it probable that here the little company of those who afterwards formed the Mayflower Church were in the habit of worshipping. We have it on the testimony of Bradford, "they ordinarily met at his (Brewster's) house on the Lord's day, . . . and with great love he entertained them when they came, making provision for them to his great charge," and "continued to do so while they could stay in England." Robinson was associated with Clifton in the pastorship of the Church.

We may be sure that the meeting at Scrooby would not long escape the vigilance of the ecclesiastical authorities. "Some were taken and clapt up in prison, others had their houses beset and watched night and day, and hardly escaped their hands"; and the most were fain to fly and leave their houses and habitations, and the means of their livelihood. Seeing themselves thus molested, and that there was no hope of their continuance there, by a joint consent they resolved to go into the Low Countries, where, they heard, was freedom of religion for all men, as also how sundry from London and other parts of the land that had been exiled and persecuted for the same cause, were gone thither, and lived at Amsterdam and other places of the land. . . . To go into a country they knew not but by hearsay, where they must learn a new language, and get their livings they knew not how,— it being a dear place, and subject to the miseries of war, —it was by many thought an adventure almost desperate, a case intolerable, and a misery worse than death, especially seeing they were not acquainted with trades nor traffic (by which the country doth subsist), but had only been used to a plain country life, and the innocent trade of husbandry. But these things did not dismay them, although they did sometimes trouble them, for their desires were set on the ways of God, and to enjoy His ordinances. But they rested on His providence, and knew whom they had believed."

Robinson and his friends succeeded at last in evading the vigilance of the authorities, who put every hindrance they could in the way of their emigration, and managed to escape to Amsterdam. Their stay here, however, was only of short duration. It soon became evident to Robinson and the little band of Separatists he had brought with him from Scrooby, that the Church of Johnson afforded them no basis on which they could continue to associate and work together in peace and harmony. They resolved, therefore, to remove to Leyden, some miles distant, and there, in that "fair and beautiful city, and of a sweet situation, but made more famous by the university whither it is adorned," they took up their abode in 1609, and there for eleven years they continued to reside.

The members of the little Church worked at "such trades and employment as they best could," and by dint of honest industry "they came to raise a comfortable and competent living, but with hard and continual labour." In Leyden the able, prudent, and broad-minded Robinson found a congenial home and sphere of work where his gifts and powers could be fitly exercised. He became a distinguished member of the university, and in connection with it added greatly to his influence and fame by a public disputation he engaged in with Episcopius, in which he championed the tenets of Calvin against the Arminianism which was then coming into vogue. The Church under Robinson and Brewster continued to grow in numbers and strength. It may be justly regarded as the first Independent Church in which the principles of Independency found a congenial soil, and where they had free, fruitful, unhindered development. Robinson's definition of a Church is specially noteworthy; he defines it as "A company consisting though but of two or three separated from the world, whether unchristian or antichristian, and gathered into the name of Christ by a covenant made to walk in all the ways of God known unto them, is a Church, and so hath the whole power of Christ."

At first an ardent Separatist, and carrying his Separatist principles to the length of eschewing all communion with the Church of England, his opinion in regard to the latter gradually toned down, till at last he saw no wrong, but acknowledged that much benefit might be derived from "hearing the godly ministers preach and pray in the public assemblies" of the Church of England. His ultimate position in this matter is explicitly defined: "As to the lawfulness of communion with the Church of England," he says, "the error laid to our charge is our holding that every one of their assemblies are false churches. We profess we put a great difference between pure and impure among you, and do not doubt (God forbid we should!) but there are hundreds and thousands amongst you having assurance of saving grace, and being partakers of the life of God in respect of your persons; but considering you in your Church communion and ordinances, we cannot so difference you, but must truly testify against your apostasy as we do."

Robinson's farewell address to the Pilgrim Fathers. —In Robinson, both in his character and writings, was represented the breadth and catholicity of Independency in its best form, and with good reason he has been described, even by a bitter-minded opponent, as "the most learned, polished, and modest spirit that ever that sect enjoyed." His noble farewell words to the

Pilgrim Fathers, delivered on the eve of their departure from Holland to essay the perils of an unknown and new world, have become classical, and have done more perhaps to immortalise his name than all his other acts and writings together.[1] "We are now ere long to part asunder, and the Lord knoweth whether even he should live to see our faces again. But whether the Lord had appointed it or not, he charged us before God and His blessed angels to follow him no farther than he followed Christ; and if God should reveal anything to us by any other instrument of His, to be as ready to receive it as ever we were to receive any truth by his ministry; for he was very confident the Lord had more truth and light yet to break forth out of His Holy Word." Of this farewell address Mr. Motley says that "for loftiness of spirit and breadth of vision, it has hardly a parallel in that age of intolerance."

The fear which Robinson expressed, whether he should live to see again the faces of the friends from whom he was taking leave, was realised. He died in Leyden, and was buried in St. Peter's Church on March 4, 1625, nearly five years after the *Mayflower*, carrying with it the destinies of a great nation, set sail to the shores of the New World. Yet, like another Moses, he gained from

[1] The whole address, or that part of it which the writer has preserved, for he does not claim to reproduce all that Robinson uttered on this occasion, was written down, probably from memory, twenty-five years after, by Edward Winslow, one of the Fathers of New Plymouth, and published by him in a communication addressed to the Earl of Warwick and the Commissioners of the Plantations. This was printed in 1646 under the title, *Hypocrisie Unmasked*, a defence of the New England Colonies from the aspersions which had been cast upon them.

his Pisgah vantage ground some vision, dim it may be, but still real, of the glory that was to follow. It is his title to lasting fame that he incited, promoted, counselled, and directed, from its inception to its execution, the movement that was to be fraught with such signal consequences to the Church and to the kingdom of God and to the commonwealth of nations.[1]

Historic Independency.—We have now arrived at the point in the history of the Puritan Separatists when the name Separatist disappears, and is replaced by

[1] On July 24, 1891, a number of American and English Congregationalists, the lineal descendants (in faith and spirit at least, if not in fact) of the Pilgrim Fathers, and the representatives of the Mayflower Church, assembled at Leyden to witness the unveiling of a bronze tablet on the outside of St. Peter's Church, and directly opposite the house where John Robinson lived, taught, and died. The inscription on the tablet is as follows :—

THE MAYFLOWER, 1620

IN MEMORY OF

REV. JOHN ROBINSON, M.A.

PASTOR OF THE ENGLISH CHURCH WORSHIPPING OVER AGAINST
THIS SPOT, A.D. 1609–1625, WHENCE, AT HIS PROMPTING

WENT FORTH

𝕿𝖍𝖊 𝕻𝖎𝖑𝖌𝖗𝖎𝖒 𝕱𝖆𝖙𝖍𝖊𝖗𝖘

TO SETTLE IN NEW ENGLAND IN 1620

BURIED UNDER THIS HOUSE OF WORSHIP, 4TH MARCH 1625,
ÆT. XLIX. YEARS

IN MEMORIA ÆTERNA ERIT JUSTUS

ERECTED BY THE NATIONAL COUNCIL OF THE CONGREGATIONAL
CHURCHES OF THE UNITED STATES OF AMERICA, A.D. 1891

the historic title Independents. In Holland historic Independency began, and from that time its record is continuous and unbroken. In 1611 a number of "Brownists," who had been driven from the kingdom, returned, and founded in London the **first English Church of General Baptists**. Their leader was Thomas Helwys, who was associated with John Smyth in the oversight of the Church which seceded from the Church of Francis Johnson, thus forming the second congregation of Separatists or Independents in Amsterdam. In 1616, five years afterwards, a number of other exiles returned, and founded, also in London, the **first permanent Independent or Congregational Church**, under the ministry of Henry Jacob.

Henry Jacob was one of the most remarkable of the early Independents, and both in style and manner resembled the modern Independent perhaps more closely than any of his contemporaries. He was originally a clergyman in the county of Kent, and showed his zeal as a Churchman by writing a work, entitled, *A Defence of the Churches and Ministry of England*, written in two treatises, against the reasons and objections of Mr. Francis Johnson and others of the separation commonly called Brownists. This drew forth an answer from Johnson in a series of propositions which are still worthy of being read as a specimen of clear and admirable reasoning. It is said that Jacob himself was so impressed by Johnson's reply, that soon after he renounced his position as a clergyman, and espoused the cause of the Separatists. Whether due to this cause or not, it is certain that Jacob became a convinced and sturdy Independent. "He was a person," says Anthony Wood, "most excellently well read in theological authors, but withal a most zealous Puritan, or, as his son Henry used to say, 'the first Independent in England.' Jacob defines a true Church to be a number of faithful people formed by their willing covenant in a spiritual outward society or body politic, ordinarily coming together in one place;[1] instituted by Christ in His New Testament, and having power to exercise ecclesiastical government, and all God's other spiritual ordinances—the means of salvation —in and for itself immediately from Jesus Christ." "When each ordinary congregation giveth their free consent in their own government, then certainly each congregation is an entire and *independent* body politic, and indued with power immediately under and from Christ, as every proper Church is and ought to be." This appears to be the first use of the name "Independent"; but no importance, we think, is to be attached to it in this respect, as Jacob evidently uses it more as a description than as an appellation.

John Robinson and Henry Jacob were called semi-Separatists, because they did not share the aversion or reluctance of many of the Separatists to worshipping in the parish churches, maintaining that in them there were true Christians, "tender and gracious souls," to whom

[1] Not, however, "ordinarily coming together in one place," as did the Separatists during the reign of Elizabeth, and even that of her sister Mary; for from the way in which he expands the definition, it is clear that Jacob contemplates a less fluid, casual, and altogether more permanent system of Church order and discipline.

Christ's presence was revealed, though their assemblies were not constituted according to Christ and the model and authority of the New Testament.

In both Robinson and Jacob is seen in a very eminent degree the irenical temper and the constructive instinct of the wise, broad-minded Christian statesman. It is probable that the influence of Holland did much to cultivate in them and the Separatists generally much of this instinct and temper. They were out of the reach of persecution, and away from all the baleful influences which goad and irritate and rankle in the breasts of those who suffer wrongfully the ills and miseries of oppression. Naturally the points of antagonism between them and the dominant hierarchy and Church would become less sharpened and less acutely felt, and as naturally, not the negative, but the positive side of their faith, and of those Church principles which they had come to look upon as the pure deposit of a far-back apostolic age, would begin more and more to strengthen its hold upon them. They had, as it were, leisure from themselves, leisure from strife and contending, and under the more genial conditions in which they now found themselves placed, their minds gradually expanded and ripened; they became enamoured of a new fruitful ideal of strength and beauty, and this ideal they sought patiently and not without success to translate into the life and polity of the Church and Independency of the future.

The Independents the pioneers of religious liberty. —We do not claim for these early Independents that they succeeded in mastering the lesson of religious toleration.

That came later, but the advances they made towards it entitle them to be regarded as the first pioneers, in England at least, of toleration and religious liberty. In 1609, Henry Jacob published his famous tract, entitled, *An Humble Supplication for Toleration and Liberty to enjoy and observe the Ordinances of Jesus Christ.*

This Dr. Fairbairn speaks of as the *earliest plea* for toleration in the English language; but while technically this may be allowed, it is due to that much-maligned and "poor shattered renegade," Robert Browne, to say that this is scarcely to do justice to the position he took up a whole generation before Henry Jacob or Leonard Busher ever penned a line in defence of toleration. The consideration of this question we must, however, relegate to a later period, and to a subsequent portion of the history with which we propose to deal.

NOTE ON ROBINSON'S FAREWELL WORDS TO THE PILGRIM FATHERS

It is not to be denied that there is a certain class of thinkers who are more than others enamoured, we might say violently enamoured, of these words. They have been adopted as the special motto of those who claim to be *par excellence* "liberal theologians." It would seem as if the fair, broad-minded historian of *Congregationalism as seen in its Literature* had been tried, not to say irritated, by the pretensions of this school, for he enters into an elaborate attempt to prove that in the matter of theological latitude Robinson was guiltless of the "liberalism" which is imputed to him. A careful examination of Dr. Dexter's argument has left upon our mind the impression of his overproving, *i.e.* of not proving, his case.

We think he proves to the hilt that the primary reference of these remarkable words of Robinson is not to dogma but to polity, or, to use Dr. Dexter's words, that "polity, and not dogma," is the keynote of this noble farewell. "More light on those questions of bishops, elders, and synods and presbyters must be expected to break forth, as guided by providence and experience, humble piety shall further interpret the word." This undoubtedly is the primary reference of the words, but we submit that they do not on this account exclude the natural and logically implied conclusion which "the self-styled advanced thinkers of the day" have drawn from them.

Robinson must have been aware, in his own consciousness at least, that the words which he uttered were susceptible of the utmost width and scope: and improbable as it may be that he anticipated the construction which has since been put upon them, certainly the words, looked at by themselves, lead one to think that if this construction had been present to his mind, he would still have been unflinching in their expression. And probably, if someone had pointed out to him the peril of sending out with his imprimatur so free and bold a deliverance, he would have replied that he was responsible for the deliverance itself, and not for conclusions which others might draw from it. Whatever use may have been made of these words, whatever extreme opinions they have been employed to buttress up, the words themselves are noble words, and in every way worthy of the enlightened and broad-minded father of Independency.

PART II

PURITANISM IN THE NEW WORLD

Founding of New Plymouth

Memorable Events and Dates

James I. reigned	1603-1625
Richard Bancroft, Archbishop of Canterbury	1605-1610
George Abbot, do. do.	1611-1633
America discovered by Columbus	1492
Virginia successfully colonised; first permanent English settlement in America	1607

Mayflower set sail, September 6, 1620; arrived at Plymouth Bay, December 21, 1620.

Contents of Chapter 1

The Pilgrim Fathers—Founders of a New World—Residence in Holland—Negotiations concluded and leave-taking—The *Speedwell* and the *Mayflower*—The *Mayflower* alone—Compact signed—Cape Cod—Plymouth Rock—Cold of winter—Indians—Mortality among settlers — Honour that belongs to the Fathers — Independency — Growing prosperity.

Leaders in Colony

William Brewster, John Carver, William Bradford, Miles Standish, Edward Winslow.

CHAPTER I

FOUNDING OF NEW PLYMOUTH

The Pilgrim Fathers.—There are dates and epochs in the history of our sea-girt isle which will never fade from the memory of men: the Norman Conquest in 1066; the signing of Magna Charta in 1215; the defeat of the Spanish Armada in 1588; the Revolution of 1688. But one tolerably familiar with the great landmarks of history would probably be puzzled to remember what there was specially remarkable about the year 1620. Yet that year was signalised by a movement which, whether we consider its beginning, or the far-reaching and fruitful issues that sprang from it, is absolutely without parallel in the history of the world. It was the year the *Mayflower* cast anchor in Plymouth Bay. Its crew all told did not number more than one hundred and two, and of these twenty-eight were women.

"Giants in heart they were, who believed in God and the Bible."

They had crossed the then comparatively untraversed path of the Atlantic for love of God, and in search of liberty of conscience.

They were the founders of a New World.—The rock on which they set foot—Plymouth Rock—may be described as the corner-stone of that mighty Republic which now covers a territory of 3,557,000 square miles, and extends from the Atlantic on one side to the Pacific on the other, and comprises a population of nearly seventy millions of people. " Behold how great a matter a little fire kindleth." It is safe to say that never in their most visionary mood did it enter into the mind of these exiles for liberty of conscience to imagine that out of their sowing would spring the mighty harvest which is being reaped to-day.[1] They had no other motive in leaving their native land than that of the hunted partridge which flies to the mountains. They simply wanted an asylum, where, free from all molestation and disability on account of their faith, they could worship the Great Being to whom they owned no doubtful or wavering allegiance.* They were, as Milton says, " faithful and freeborn Englishmen, good Christians, . . . constrained to forsake their dearest home, their friends and kindred, whom nothing but the wide ocean and the savage deserts of America could hide and shelter from the fury of the bishops."

It was no new idea struck out of their minds by the force of relentless persecution that made the expatriated Puritans turn to the Far West, in the belief that there was to be found a land that would afford them a safe

[1] " They little thought how pure a light
With years should gather round that day;
How love should keep their memories bright,
How wide a realm their sons should sway."

asylum, and where they might breathe the pure air of liberty. Their enemies must be credited with the justice (such as it was) of keeping them well informed in regard to that. "Why do you not take yourselves off to Virginia?" was the taunting question which had been again and again repeated in their hearing—indeed, ever since Raleigh had added that not inconsiderable strip of territory to the English Crown. It was the iron entering deeper and deeper into their soul which gave to the idea substance and shape. It was partially arrested by their sojourn in Holland, where they enjoyed full civil and religious liberty; but even there it could not be uprooted. Holland was no home to them. They could not forget that they were in a foreign country, where the language and customs and habits of the people served only to accentuate the feeling of estrangement. The "hardness" of the country, and the difficulty of obtaining the means of subsistence, not to speak of comfort, made it repugnant to their children and to intending settlers from their native land. But most of all, their religious scruples and convictions were offended by the easy-going laxity of the Dutch. The latter had no respect for the Sabbath, and many other observances which their Puritan neighbours prized and held in reverent and jealous regard, they treated with indifference. Their standard of morals was correspondingly low, and the exiles feared, not without reason, that by association with them the fibre of their children's principles would become flaccid. Moreover, they had constantly present to their mind the dread that their posterity "would in a few generations become

Dutch, and would lose their language and their name of English," and so, " if God would be pleased to discover some place unto them, though in America," they might " more glorify God, do more good to their country, better provide for their posterity, and live to be more refreshed by their labours than ever they could do in Holland, where they were"; or in this way they cherished " a great hope and inward zeal of laying some good foundation for the propagation and advancement of the gospel in those remote parts of the world; yea, though they should be but stepping-stones unto others for the performance of so great a work."

It is not needful to enter into minute details in regard to the negotiations which had to be conducted, and the difficulties which had to be overcome, before the purpose which the exiles had conceived could be carried out. As may be readily imagined, a step like this was not resolved upon without much and anxious deliberation. Fears and lions were in the way, and there were not wanting those, even among their own number, who prophesied failure and disaster. Objections were heaped up even to the danger arising from change of air and food; and the drinking of water instead of beer would, it was averred, infect their bodies with sore sickness. Bolder and more daring counsels, however, in the long-run prevailed, and apparently with one heart and mind the exiles set themselves to the achievement of their great task. But so many were the obstacles and mountains that had to be laid low, that nearly three years elapsed before they found themselves on board the vessel which was to carry them and their families to the New World. It was in

June 1620 that the step which actually committed the pilgrims to their new venture was definitely taken. This was the securing of the ship—the *Mayflower*—which was to transport them across the sea. In addition to this, the *Speedwell*, a vessel of sixty tons, was purchased in Holland; she was to convey the Leyden contingent to Southampton, whence both vessels were to commence their distant and adventurous voyage.

There are few scenes that figure in the pages of history more impressive and solemn than that leave-taking between the emigrants and their friends in Leyden—solemn as the farewell of death itself, for it could not but be present in the minds of both that they were looking into each other's faces for the last time. Who that heard it ever forgot the text from which the beloved Pastor Robinson—himself restrained from being of the number of the emigrants—preached to them: "And there at the river by Ahava I proclaimed a fast, that we might humble ourselves before our God, and seek of Him a right way for us and for our children, and for all our substance." The fast was succeeded by a frugal feast, and in the words of a participator and actor in the scene: "They that stayed at Leyden feasted us that were to go at our pastor's house (being large), where we refreshed ourselves with our tears and singing of psalms, making joyful melody in our hearts as well as with the voice (there being many of the congregation very expert in music); and, indeed, it was the sweetest melody that ever mine ears heard." The *Speedwell* was anchored at Delfthaven, some fourteen miles distant, and hither many of their brethren accompanied the exiles. So "they left the goodly and pleasant city which had been their resting-place near twelve years." We can imagine the feelings of the pilgrims as they came within sight of their native land, and realised that only for a too brief season could they look upon the old familiar places and green fields of England. For they loved England passionately, notwithstanding it had been to them a cruel stepmother: loved it "as a Roman loved the city of the seven hills, as an Athenian loved the city of the violet crown." It was in connection with this leave-taking, though the time at which they were spoken is not precisely known, that Robinson uttered those memorable words, which have probably done more to immortalise his name than all his other writings and acts together.

The Mayflower.—It was on the 5th August 1620 that the *Mayflower*, a vessel of about one hundred and eighty tons, and the *Speedwell* set sail from Southampton. No sooner were they fairly embarked than the *Speedwell* was found to be so leaky that it was unsafe for her to proceed farther, and both vessels put back to the port of Dartmouth. Eight days were spent in making the necessary repairs, and once more the two vessels were unfurling their canvas to the winds. They had not got out of sight of Land's End when the captain of the misnamed *Speedwell* (intimidated, there is little doubt, by the prospect, not only of the voyage over the Atlantic, but of what awaited them on the other side) declared that he must return or sink. The ship, he said, was not strong enough to undertake such a voyage. There was no other course open than for both vessels to return again, and this they did, this time to Plymouth. Here the *Speedwell* was discharged, and it was agreed that those of the emigrants who were least fitted "to bear the brunt of this hard adventure" should be left behind, while the *Mayflower* should proceed with the rest of the company. After the loss of much valuable time, the *Mayflower*, with her crew of one hundred and two passengers, set sail from Plymouth to the great Western World, September 6th, 1620.

It is not too much to say that in a very real and profound sense the *Mayflower* carried with her the moral destinies of the world. Her crew were not only the pioneers of civil and religious liberty, they were the heralds of a faith which, tested by the heroic men it has formed, and the heroic actions it has produced, may indeed challenge comparison with any faith by which men have been moulded and inspired. The struggle they were called upon to wage was a struggle for liberty, not only in the New World, but in the Old; and but for the planting of Puritanism in New England, the victory of Puritanism in the mother country would have been shortlived, and shorn of its most characteristic features and products. These expatriated exiles—self-expatriated by conscience and by principles which were dearer to them than life itself—indulged in no vain and Utopian hopes as to that which awaited them on the other side of the Atlantic. They saw, in the first place, that in the absence of any existing form of government whose protection they might invoke, it would be necessary to set up a government of their own; and seeing that there were those among their own number "not well affected to unity and concord," before they came within sight of land they set to work, like the sagacious and practical men they were, to formulate a code of their own.

Compact on board the Mayflower.—A compact—a solemn league and covenant it might well be called—was drawn up and signed in the cabin of the *Mayflower*: "In the name of God, amen. We whose names are underwritten, the loyal subjects of our dread sovereign King James,[1] having undertaken, for the glory of God and advancement of the Christian faith, and honour of our king and country, a voyage to plant the first colony in the northern parts of Virginia, do by these presents, solemnly and mutually, in the presence of God and one of another, covenant and combine ourselves together into a civil body politic for our better ordering and preservation, and furtherance of the ends aforesaid; and by virtue hereof to enact, constitute, and frame such just and equal laws, ordinances, acts, constitutions, and offices from time to time as shall be thought most convenient for the general good of the colony. Unto which we promise all due submission and obedience."

This instrument was signed by the entire body of men who were on board the *Mayflower*, forty-one in number. It has been truly said: "This was the birth of popular constitutional liberty. The Middle Age had been familiar

---

[1] It would have been well for them if they had professed no such allegiance. In this unwitting acknowledgment they were heaping up trouble for themselves and their descendants (see p. 302).

with charters and constitutions, but they had been merely compacts for immunities, partial enfranchisements, patents of nobility, concessions of municipal privileges, or limitations of the sovereign power in favour of feudal institutions. In the cabin of the *Mayflower* humanity recovered its rights, and instituted government on the basis of 'equal laws' for 'the general good.'"[1] Mr. John Carver, who had acted as governor during the voyage, was confirmed in this office for the first year.

It was on the 21st November 1620 that the pilgrims set foot for the first time on the soil of the New World. Their purpose was to find a place farther south than that at which they landed; but, finding themselves among dangerous shoals, and encountering adverse winds, they were glad to find refuge in the harbour of Cape Cod. Just before the *Mayflower* dropped anchor, "they fell upon their knees and blessed the God of heaven who had brought them over the vast and furious ocean, and delivered them from all the perils and miseries thereof, again to set their feet on the firm and stable earth, their proper element." The hearts of the emigrants must have, indeed, sunk within them as they surveyed the bleak, barren, inhospitable coast on which

[1] Bancroft's *History of the United States*, vol. i. p. 234, revised edition, p. 244, Macmillan & Co. 1876. Critics have pointed to this statement of the historian of the United States as an instance of his enthusiasm running away with him. Dr. Borgeaud, while allowing that perhaps some objection may be made to it on the score of exaggeration, adds: "It is not the less true that, in spite of all that has been said to lessen its importance, the agreement of the *Mayflower* remains one of the most remarkable documents of modern history."— *The Rise of Modern Democracy in Old and New England*, p. 110.

they found themselves landed. With a lively prescience of coming evil our Lord said to His disciples: " Pray that your flight be not in the winter." So cold was the season, that it is told of the first party of explorers that the spray of the sea froze as it fell on them, and made their clothes like coats of iron. Their strength was greatly reduced by the hardships which they had undergone during their rough and inclement voyage, especially with the scanty supply of food.

"Short allowance of victual and plenty of nothing but gospel;"

and now with their retreat cut off by the ocean on one side, and their progress by the wilderness on the other,—especially such a waste howling wilderness as it must then have seemed,—their condition was as hopeless and desperate as could well be imagined. " Because there were no graves in Egypt, hast thou taken us away to die in the wilderness? would to God we had died by the hand of the Lord in the land of Egypt, when we sat by the flesh-pots, and when we did eat bread to the full "— might have been the language of the angry remonstrants had there been some Moses to whom they could affix the responsibility of their position; but this was not the temper of the gallant, intrepid, God-fearing band of men and women who came out, like Abraham of old, not knowing whither they were going, except that they were going at the bidding of Abraham's God. The next day was the Sabbath, and according to their invariable custom they rested, and observed it as a day of worship. Monday had no sooner dawned than the women were astir, improving the opportunity with housewifely zeal. "Joyful was that washing day,—odours of pine and sassafras in the air, and 'coals of juniper' under their kettles,—not less joyful than toilsome, for their feet were at last on the soil of New England." Two explorations into the adjacent country—one by land and the other by sea— were conducted without leading to any satisfactory result. They resolved to make one more attempt to find a suitable harbour, and, after braving hardships and dangers which made them well-nigh give up in despair, they ran their boat aground in Plymouth Bay. The *Mayflower* "furled her tattered sails" in Plymouth Bay just five weeks after she had anchored in Cape Cod. The name Plymouth had been given to the bay six years before by an earlier explorer, Captain John Smith, and seeing that they had set sail from Plymouth, the pilgrims concurred in the retention of the name.

It was on the 21st of December 1620 that the pilgrims disembarked in Plymouth Bay. There is probably no more sacred spot in the world than **Plymouth Rock,** which commemorates the landing of the Pilgrim Fathers on the wild New England shore.

". . . Plymouth Rock, that had been to their feet as a doorstep
    Into a wild unknown, the corner-stone of a nation."

"Setting rhetorical exaggeration aside, we need not doubt that in watching that sad yet hopeful procession of men, women, and children, we are witnessing one of the great events and one of the heroic scenes of history."[1] "The consequences of that day," says the historian of the United States, "are constantly unfolding themselves as

[1] *The United States: An Outline of Political History*, 1492–1871, by Goldwin Smith, D.C.L., p. 4.

time advances. It was the origin of New England; it was the planting of New England institutions as the pilgrims landed. Their institutions were already perfected. Democratic liberty and independent Christian worship at once existed in America." Plymouth Rock, famous throughout the world as the stepping-stone upon which the pilgrims landed, still occupies the same position as when the pilgrims' shallop first grazed its side. The only alteration is that it has been raised somewhat, and is now covered by an architectural canopy of granite. De Tocqueville says: "This rock has become an object of veneration in the United States. I have seen bits of it preserved in several towns of the Union. Does not this sufficiently show that all human power and greatness is in the soul of man? Here is a stone which the feet of outcasts pressed for an instant; and this stone has become famous; it is treasured by a great nation; its very dust is shared as a relic. And what has become of the gateways of a thousand palaces? Who cares for them?"[1]

The numbers of the little company had been greatly reduced by disease and death, and those who were spared, unprovided with anything but the barest necessaries of life, were ill-fitted to encounter the cold and rigour of the New England winter. So rapid was the mortality, that, when spring returned, and "the birds sang in the woods most pleasantly," scarce fifty of the original hundred remained. "In those hard and difficult beginnings there were discontents and murmurings among some, and mutinous speeches and carriage in others; but

[1] De Tocqueville, *Democracy in America*, vol. i. p. 29.

they were soon quelled and overcome by the wisdom, patience, and just and equal carriage of things by the governor and better part." So passed the sorrowful first winter in Plymouth, but the spirit of the little company was unbroken. In April the *Mayflower* was despatched home to England, yet, notwithstanding the losses they had sustained, and the hardships and privations they were still enduring, not one of the brave company signified their willingness to return.

"Oh, strong hearts and true! not one went back in the *Mayflower*. No! not one looked back who had set his hand to that ploughing."

Governor Carver was among those who had succumbed to the fatal cold and hardships, and **William Bradford**, who had been a member of the little Church in Scrooby, was chosen to fill his place. He was governor of Plymouth for nearly thirty years, and to his graphic and picturesque chronicle we are indebted chiefly for what we know of the migration from Scrooby, the transplanting of the Church to Holland, and the settlement of the Fathers in New Plymouth. The other notable leaders in the colony were—**William Brewster**, the hospitable provider of the first place of meeting in Scrooby, and the stout Puritan soldier, **Miles Standish**, whose courtship is so quaintly related by Longfellow.

The Pilgrims entered into friendly relations with the various tribes of Indians round about them. One tribe alone refused their overtures, and showed their hostile intentions by sending a bundle of new arrows tied up in a rattlesnake's skin. The said skin was stuffed by Miles Standish full of powder and shot, and sent back as the response and challenge of the young colony, and this the messenger was directed to carry back to the Indian sachem. Yet it would appear that at one time the colonists were only saved from extermination by an epidemic of sickness which broke out among the Indians; but for this they had all probably been tomahawked to death. Their number increased very slowly, as compared with what might have been expected. At the end of ten years the colony contained no more than three hundred souls. It was all the settlers could do to wring from the infertile soil the means of subsistence. Inured to hardship and privation by their sojourn in Holland, as well as by their previous manner of life, they were well-fitted—better fitted probably than any similar number of men that could have been selected from the population of England—to encounter the rigour of the climate, and to perform the hard task of colonisation. Such heartening as the friends they had left behind had it in their power to give, they received from time to time. "Let it not be grievous to you that you have been instrumental to break the ice for others. The honour shall be yours to the world's end."[1] "Out of small beginnings," said Bradford, "great things have been produced; and as one small candle may light a thousand, so the light here kindled hath shone to many; yea, in some sort, to our whole nation."

The Pilgrim Fathers the founders of a new empire.
—The attempt has sometimes been made to belittle the

[1] "To the world's end the honour is theirs. If Columbus discovered the New Continent, they discovered the New World."—*The United States: An Outline of Political History*, by Goldwin Smith, p. 5.

importance of New Plymouth, and the position of the Fathers in relation to the future of America. Mr. Doyle[1] says "that if the Plymouth settlement had never been made, the political life of New England would in all probability have taken the same form, and run the same course as it did." This is like saying that if Columbus had not discovered America, it would very probably have been discovered. But how does Mr. Doyle know that the political life of New England would have run the same course without the Fathers as it did run? He will say perhaps that the character of the men who afterwards colonised Massachusetts lends support to his conjecture; but suppose these had not been the Puritans they were, suppose the first settlers had been Royalists, as was the case in Virginia, is it likely that democracy would have taken root as it did, or that free institutions would have spread over America as they have done to-day? In making the assertion he does, Mr. Doyle most seriously underestimates the influence of New Plymouth upon the settlers in Massachusetts. He forgets that Independency became the religion of the latter, and that, though in time the colony of New Plymouth became incorporated with Massachusetts, it parted with its autonomy, as Greece parted with her independence by inoculating her conquerors with her own ideas, manners, and character. There can be no doubt that the Pilgrims were historically, and in the most real and unimpeachable sense, the founders of the American Republic. "In pursuit of religious freedom, they estab-

[1] *The English in America: The Puritan Colonies*, by J. A. Doyle, vol. i. p. 61.

lished civil liberty, and meaning only to found a Church, gave birth to a nation, and in settling a town, commenced an empire."

Congregationalism or Independency was in New Plymouth the prevailing form of Church government, and the special character it assumed was that which had been impressed upon it by the revered and trusted Robinson. William Brewster was the ruling elder of the Church, and there being as yet no ordained minister among the little band of emigrants, he performed all the duties of this office, except the administration of the sacraments. It cannot be said, however, that in the young rising colony the principles of Separatism won their way and triumphed without a struggle. The devoted band of men and women who had joined themselves in Church covenant at Leyden, with John Robinson as their pastor, did not constitute the whole company that had come over in the *Mayflower*. In England they had been joined by others; others again came over afterwards to New England, some of them not of the most reputable sort, and made common cause with the colonists of New Plymouth. Among these were a number of Conforming Puritans, and these, instigated by their friends and sympathisers in England, sought to subvert the constitution of the Church at Plymouth, and "capture" it in the interest of their own anti-Separatist principles. In this, however, they were signally defeated, and at the end of ten years, after fortune and prosperity had begun to smile upon their labours, and the Fathers had succeeded in quelling all opposition, and living down all serious prejudice, it fell out that the little handful of men and women gathered into the Church at Scrooby, and there cradled, and afterwards nurtured into strength at Leyden, became the nucleus of **the first Free Church of America**, the founders of a new free commonwealth of Churches, destined to sow over a vast continent the seed of religious faith and religious liberty.

Growing prosperity of Plymouth.—In 1627 the partnership with the "Adventurers," or merchants in London who had advanced the money necessary to enable the Fathers to emigrate, came to an end. The whole of their stock and interest in the colony were made over to the settlers, and they were relieved of the burden of pecuniary obligation which for seven years had been weighing heavily upon them. The sun of prosperity had begun at last to shine upon them; the wilderness had become a fruitful field, and gave promise of yet further increase of growth and fruitfulness. There is no better or more pleasing picture of the condition and appearance of New Plymouth than that furnished by Isaac de Rasières, secretary of the Dutch colony at New Netherlands, who visited Plymouth in 1627. It stood on rising ground, separated from the sea by some twenty yards of sand. The buildings were laid out like a Roman city in miniature. Two streets crossing one another formed the town, and at their meeting stood the governor's house. Before it was an open space, guarded by four cannon, one to command each of the ways which there met. On an eminence behind the town, but within its precincts, stood the little meeting-house, which, besides serving the purpose of worship, was also a public storehouse, a powder magazine, and a fort all in one, protected with battlements and six cannon—a combination of law and gospel, which not only served the convenience, but was essential to the safety of the little community. Each house was a substantial log-hut, standing in its own enclosed patch of ground. Round the whole ran a palisade, the *tun*, which, as a distinguishing feature, so often gave its name to the Teutonic settlements. Of the four entrances three were guarded by gates, the fourth being sufficiently protected by the fort or by the sea. Along the stream to the south was the arable land divided into small patches of corn. Beyond lay the common pasture, consisting of meadow and wood and jungle. But it is not necessary to expand this description. Enough has been noted to indicate the thrift and growing resourcefulness of the young vigorous colony. New Plymouth is now fairly started on its epoch-making career.

The Founding of Massachusetts

MEMORABLE EVENTS AND DATES

Charles I. reigned 1625-1649
John Endicott arrived at Naumkeag (Salem) . 1628
Massachusetts colonised 1629

CONTENTS OF CHAPTER II

Massachusetts Bay Company—Non-Separatists—Endicott and his Company at Salem—Joined by Higginson and his Company—Second Independent Church—Voting by ballot—Bancroft on State and Church at Salem—Prelatists expelled—Pilgrim Fathers—Puritans and Separatists—Robinson's counsel and prediction—Antipathy to Separatism disappearing—Democracy—Church Membership a condition of franchise—Not so in New Plymouth—Increase of Massachusetts.

LEADERS IN COLONY

Francis Higginson, John Cotton, Thomas Hooker, John Winthrop, Thomas Dudley, Henry Vane, John Harvard, Hugh Peters.

CHAPTER II

THE FOUNDING OF MASSACHUSETTS

NINE years after the planting of New Plymouth, another band of exiles, unable to endure longer the yoke of an overbearing and prelatical Church, and enamoured with the prospect of enjoying liberty and purity of worship, set sail to the shores of New England, and formed themselves into a colony on Massachusetts Bay. They were fortunate enough to secure a charter from the King, empowering them to form themselves into a corporation, and assume the title, "The Governor and Company of the Massachusetts Bay in New England." The readiness with which the Royal charter was granted is doubtless explained by Charles' desire to rid himself of those who had become to him and his government a source of trouble and annoyance, though afterwards, like Pharaoh, he seems to have hardened his heart and repented for having let the people go. The number of new settlers was between three and four hundred; they were a mixed body of emigrants, consisting mainly of Puritans whose leanings were rather towards Presbyterianism than Independency, and did not favour the Separatist principles of the latter. "They esteemed it their honour to call the Church of England their dear mother, and could not part from their native country, where she specially resided, without much sadness of heart and many tears in their eyes; ever acknowledging that such hope and part as they had attained in the common salvation, they had received in her bosom and sucked from her breasts." Among them were probably some sincerely attached to episcopal order and worship. Driven out as they were from their native land by the high-handed tyranny of Laud, they remembered only as it faded out of their sight that it was the land of their birth and their fathers' sepulchres. "We will not say,"—such are the words ascribed to Higginson,—"as the Separatists were wont to say at their leaving of England, Farewell, Babylon! farewell, Rome! but we will say, Farewell, dear England! farewell the Church of God in England, and all the Christian friends there; we do not go to New England as Separatists from the Church of England, though we cannot but separate from the corruptions in it; but we go to practise the positive part of Church reformation, and propagate the gospel in America."

Prior to the arrival of this company a number of Puritans, including men of wealth and wide social influence, had obtained from the Council of New England a tract of land of considerable extent, from the Merrimack to the Charles River. This was made over to an association of six gentlemen, one of whom, John Endicott, a stern and resolute Puritan, was installed as governor over the new plantation. He was to be aided by "a plentiful provision of godly ministers," and enjoined to bear in mind—so ran the letter of instructions from the directors in London—that "the propagating of the gospel is the thing we do profess above all to be our aim in settling this plantation." Endicott and his following made their way to Naumkeag, and here they joined themselves to a number of others, and the name Naumkeag was changed to Salem, or "peace," in token of the amicable agreement which had been concluded with the earlier settlers. By the accession of the company led by Francis Higginson, **Salem** rose at once into strength and importance, and Endicott became governor of a colony that took the lead of all others, at once distancing New Plymouth, which had been in existence for nine years.

The second Independent or Congregational Church in America.—By this time Endicott's Puritan convictions had carried him to the extreme verge of Separatism, as is evidenced by a letter he wrote to Governor Bradford of Plymouth prior to the arrival of Higginson and his company: " Touching your judgment of the outward forms of God's worship, it is, as far as I can yet gather, no other than is warranted by the evidence of truth, and the same which I have professed and maintained ever since the Lord in mercy revealed Himself unto me." On the arrival and settlement of the new-comers the whole matter of the Church standing of the colony came up for consideration, and after a day spent in fasting and prayer, and after Higginson and Skelton had given a detailed statement of their views, a ballot was taken, "every fit member voting"; and Skelton was chosen pastor, and Higginson teacher. This is **the first recorded instance of voting by ballot in America.** They were solemnly inducted into their office, the Plymouth Church being invited to send delegates; and Bradford and others who were present with him gave to pastor and teacher the right hand of fellowship, "wishing all prosperity and a blessed success to such good beginnings."[1] A Confession of Faith and Covenant according to the Holy Scriptures, was drawn up by Higginson in the following terms—the same substantially, it will be observed, as that adopted by the little Church at Scrooby:—"We covenant with the Lord, and one with another, and do bind ourselves, in the presence of God, to walk together in all His ways, according as He is pleased to reveal Himself unto us in His blessed word of truth." Thus the Church of Skelton and Higginson was the second Independent or Congregational Church in America.

"To the great European world," says Mr. Bancroft, "the few tenants of the mud-hovels at Salem might appear too insignificant to merit notice; to themselves they were as the chosen emissaries of God. . . . The emigrants were not so much a body politic as a Church in the wilderness, with no benefactor round them but nature, no present sovereign but God. An entire separation was made between State and Church; religious worship was established on the basis of the independence of each separate religious community. The Church was self-constituted. It did not ask the assent of the King, or recognise him as its head; its officers were set apart and ordained among themselves; it used no liturgy; it rejected unnecessary ceremonies, and reduced the simplicity of Calvin to a still plainer standard. The motives

[1] Bradford's *History of Plymouth Plantation*, p. 265.

which controlled their decisions were so deeply seated in the character of their party, that the doctrine and discipline established at Salem remained the rule of Puritan New England."[1]

It was not to be expected, in so mixed a body of colonists, that this doctrine and discipline would secure perfect conformity. There were those who were favourers of Prelacy, and were sincerely attached to "the Common Prayer worship." These naturally took umbrage at what they regarded as an unwarrantable invasion of their liberty. "You are Separatists," they said to their fellow-colonists, "and you will shortly be Anabaptists." "We separate," was the answer, "not from the Church of England, but from its corruptions. We came away from the Common Prayer and ceremonies in our native land, where we suffered much for nonconformity; in this place of liberty we cannot, we will not use them. Their imposition would be a sinful violation of the worship of God." The stronger party proceeded by force to suppress the convictions of the weaker,—thus showing how, in their zeal for freedom, men may be recreant to the very genius of freedom,—and they seized upon the two leaders of the episcopal section, and at the instance of Endicott, who told them "that New England was no place for such as they," shipped them off to England by the first returning vessel. They were banished from Salem because they were Churchmen. For such summary retaliation no defence can be offered.[2] It was

[1] Bancroft's *History of the United States*, vol. i. p. 262; in revised edition, pp. 271-272, in which the phraseology is slightly altered.

[2] Yet Dr. Palfrey, in his *History of New England*, vol. i. pp. 299, 300, does essay to defend it. "The right of the Governor and Com-

the first upcropping of the persecuting spirit in New England.

The Fathers of New Plymouth Puritans and Separatists.—A very sharp line of distinction is sometimes drawn between the religious, or, speaking more strictly, the ecclesiastical position of the early colonists of Massachusetts and the Pilgrim Fathers of Plymouth. It is maintained that the inclusion among the former of Episcopalians and Presbyterians and Con-

pany of Massachusetts Bay to exclude at their pleasure dangerous or disagreeable persons from their domain they never regarded as questionable, any more than a householder doubts his right to determine who shall be the inmates of his home. No civilised man had a right to come or to be within their chartered limits except themselves and such others as they, in the exercise of an absolute discretion, saw fit to harbour. . . . Religious intolerance, like every other public restraint, is criminal wherever it is not needful for the public safety; it is simply self-defence whenever tolerance would be public ruin." True, but who will maintain that the safety of the colony was endangered by the presence of "one, two, or more surpliced priests conducting worship in accordance with the Book of Common Prayer"? It is probably quite true that behind the surpliced priest the colonists saw the intolerance of Laud and the despotism of the Court of High Commission; but seeing that the surpliced priest had no power to threaten them with either the one or the other, they might just as well have left him alone. It is not pretended that these men were guilty of insubordination or of not being "conformable to the government." Had that been any ground of accusation against them, they should have been dealt with, not as Churchmen, but as rebels. As Churchmen (Dr. Palfrey's specious pleading notwithstanding) justice and religious toleration required that they should be protected, and the rulers of the colony could well have afforded to extend toleration to them. "Master, we saw one casting out devils in Thy name, and we forbade him, because he followeth not with us." Will Dr. Palfrey say that this exorcist was a dangerous or disagreeable person, whom the disciples had a perfect right to "exclude," or interdict? The Master had a very different opinion.

formists parts them by a deep and wide gulf from the uncompromising Separatists who had come over in the *Mayflower*. The distinction certainly needs to be borne in mind, but in our judgment it is not of that vital importance which is sometimes claimed for it. It does not seem to us that much is gained by contending that the Pilgrim Fathers were not Puritans, but Separatists.[1] We know no valid or sufficient reason for refusing them their right of inheritance in the great name and traditions of Puritanism. They were both Puritans and Separatists. It were as unreasonable to deny their right to be called Protestants. The Separatists in the Puritan party were only extreme Puritans; they were the vanguard of the Puritan host, that is to say, they carried their zeal for reform and purity of doctrine and worship to its implied and, as they believed, necessary conse-

[1] See pamphlet entitled, *The Pilgrim Fathers neither Puritans nor Persecutors*. A Lecture delivered at the Friends' Institute, London, on the 18th January 1866. Reprinted in 1891, with Preface, by the late Benjamin Scott, Esq., F.R.A.S., Chamberlain of the City of London. Third edition. (Elliot Stock.) Mr. Scott makes much of the hostility existing between Puritan and Separatist—the fact that the former was sometimes more bitter against Separatism than against Prelacy or Popery—as an evidence of the marked and radical difference between them, but this by no means sustains his contention. It is unhappily only too common for those who are members of the same household of faith, whether in politics or in religion, to regard each other with inveterate dislike. The feeling which the Whig sometimes has for the Radical and the Radical for the Whig, the feeling which the general Baptist sometimes has for the strict Baptist, and the strict Baptist for the general, not to speak of numerous other instances, should have led him, we think, to suspect the conclusiveness of such evidence. The old classification of "moderate" Puritans and "rigid" Puritans (see Fletcher's *History of Independency*, vol. iii. p. 28), or Puritans and Puritan Separatists, seems on every ground to be preferred to that of Puritans *and* Separatists.

quence. To borrow a political illustration, the Whigs may be said to compose the right, and the Radicals the left wing of the Liberal party, but the right of both to be designated Liberals is allowed and recognised.[1] In the same way there is no reason to deviate from traditional usage in regarding those who were zealous for separation from the Church of England as members of the great Puritan party.

But there are other reasons why this distinction should not be pressed, and not the least influential is that derived from the character of New Plymouth Independency, as impressed upon it by Robinson. Quoting once more from the memorable address: "Another thing he commanded to us that we should use all means to avoid and shake off the name of Brownist, being a mere nickname and brand to make religion odious and the professors of it odious to the Christian world. For," said he, "there will be no difference between the unconformable ministers and you when they come to the practice of ordinances out of the kingdom." This prediction was literally fulfilled. Separatists and conforming Puritans, as they were called, found no difficulty in composing their differences on the free soil of New England. The fact

---

[1] "The English Reformation was brought about, as every other great change is brought about, by the co-operation of two classes of men, who are, on the whole, content with the principles by which they have hitherto guided their lives, though they think some changes ought to be made in matters of detail; and those who start upon an entirely new principle, and who strive to realise an ideal society which commends itself to their own minds. They answer, in short, to the Whigs and Radicals of modern political life, whilst the Conservatives are represented by a third class, averse to all change whatever."—Gardiner's *Puritan Revolution*, p. 1.

that there was no Church to dissent from was an effectual guarantee that this apple of discord would not be introduced among them. The seed of liberty soon found a congenial nidus in the prolific soil of New England. Its growth could not be checked. The Conformists soon found themselves making common cause with the Separatists; not only did scruples and differences begin to melt away, but they found themselves also, by a spontaneous and rapid process, assimilating the extreme principles of the latter.[1]

The Puritans in England were amazed as well as alarmed at the boldness of their brethren in Massachusetts, and the correspondence that passed between them—expostulation on the one side and self-defence on the other—is instructive and entertaining.[2] It shows that no sooner had Endicott and the Puritans who came with him begun to breathe the air of the free wilderness, than they began to lose the antipathy of their party against Separatism, and to see that the theory of the Pilgrims concerning "the outward form of God's worship" was "warranted by the evidence of truth." In the Utopia of New England there was no room for the

[1] The case with which rigid Puritanism drifted into Separatism in New England, is signally illustrated in the case of John Cotton, formerly rector of St. Botolph's Church in Boston, Lincolnshire. "As long as he abode in England, in all his opposition to the episcopal corruptions, went not beyond Cartwright and the Presbyterians. So soon as he did taste of the New English air he fell into so passionate an affection with the religion he found there, that, incontinent, he began to persuade it with a great deal more zeal and success than before he had opposed it."—Palfrey's *History of New England*, vol. ii. p. 84, note.

[2] See Hanbury's *Historical Memorials*, vol. ii. chap. xxxv., entitled, "Nine positions sent to New England—Answers—Reply."

propagation or assertion of erroneous opinions, even about "things indifferent."[1] It will thus be seen that the Church position taken up by the colonists at Salem was substantially the same as that which had been outlined by Robinson and adopted by the Fathers at Plymouth.

There is no preciser form of democracy extant than that which was established as the basis of the government of Massachusetts. Voting by ballot was introduced from the beginning, and "government of the people, for the people, by the people"—to use the memorable words of Abraham Lincoln—gave token that it was nevermore to "perish from the earth." The time was not yet ripe for universal suffrage, but, with this exception, representative democracy was as perfect in New England as it is in the America of to-day.

Church membership a condition of the franchise.—In their zeal for religion the colonists of Massachusetts went beyond the Fathers of New Plymouth, for "to the end the body of the commons may be preserved of honest and good men, it was ordered and agreed that for the time to come no man shall be admitted to the freedom of this body politic but such as are members of some of the Churches within the limits of the same." On this account the accusation of narrowness has been freely brought against the colonists of Massachusetts. But it does not appear that, in this instance, the accusation has any firm basis on which to rest. The condition imposed seemed to the members of

---

[1] *The Genesis of the New England Churches*, by Dr. Leonard Bacon, pp. 456, 462.

a theocracy such as Massachusetts aspired to be, the most suitable and the most natural thing possible under the circumstances. Unquestionably it would have been wiser if they had seen their way to the broad position taken up by Cromwell: "The State, in choosing men to serve it, takes no notice of their opinions. If they be willing faithfully to serve it, that satisfies." But in Massachusetts things were not ripe for such a principle of selection. Indeed, it is difficult to see how they could have acted upon any other principle than that which they did, though it was sure to be found unworkable as the colony grew stronger and more numerous. We may say, with Dr. Palfrey,[1] that the conception, if a delusive and impracticable, was a noble one. "Nothing better can be imagined for the welfare of a country than that it shall be ruled on Christian principles; in other words, that its rulers shall be Christian men—men of disinterestedness and integrity of the choicest quality that the world knows—men whose fear of God exalts them above every other fear, and whose controlling love of God and of man consecrates them to the most generous aims. The conclusive objection to the scheme is one which experience had not yet revealed, for the experiment was now made for the first time."

In New Plymouth church membership was not made a condition of the elective franchise. As we shall have occasion to show in what falls to be said upon this subject, the spirit of toleration was more prevalent among

[1] *History of New England*, vol. i. p. 345. See also, for defence of Massachusetts, Dr. Dexter's *Congregationalism as seen in its Literature*, p. 420.

the Fathers than among any of the early colonists. It is even said that Miles Standish, the stout-hearted soldier and leader at Plymouth, was a Roman Catholic, and considering the fiery hatred of Rome which, even more than their zeal for liberty, distinguished the early Puritans, this fact (if it were a fact) registers considerable width of view and catholicity. "Their residence in Holland had made them acquainted with various forms of Christianity; a wide experience had emancipated them from bigotry; and they were never betrayed into the excesses of religious persecution, though they sometimes permitted a disproportion between punishment and crime."

Leading men in Massachusetts.—The early history of Massachusetts is the history of a class of men as remarkable for gifts of statesmanship and organising power as for their moral and religious qualities. **Francis Higginson**, the leader of the first party of emigrants, had been rector of a church in Lincolnshire, and had been deprived of his living for nonconformity. **John Cotton**, a fellow of Emmanuel College, Cambridge, had been for more than twenty years rector of St. Botolph's, Boston, and, rather than continue in a position which had become intolerable to his conscience, chose to give up his living, and quit the most magnificent parish church in England to officiate in the rude meeting-house in Boston, Massachusetts. In the same ship came **Thomas Hooker**, also fellow of Emmanuel College, and afterwards known as "the light of the Western Churches." Other emigrants were **Hugh Peters**, afterwards the friend and chaplain of Cromwell, and who, for the part he took in connection with the execution of King Charles I., suffered death as a regicide; **John Harvard**, the founder of the celebrated university, which is now the glory of the literary republic; **Henry Vane**, the younger, "young in years, but not in sage counsel old," one of the greatest of Puritan statesmen, a prominent actor in the Cromwellian republic, and who preferred to die upon the scaffold rather than desert the "righteous cause" of liberty, or abate his testimony against kingly and tyrannical usurpation.

The accession, however, which bore most closely on the immediate interests of the colony was the arrival of John Winthrop and **Thomas Dudley**, men cast in very different moulds, but both destined to exercise great influence upon the young rising republic. Dudley, like Endicott, was a stern and unbending Puritan, but less liberal, a good hater, and hating nothing so much as tolerance of what he deemed laxity and error. A quatrain found among his papers after his death reveals not only a foible for making verses, but also the spirit of the man and of the age in which he played his part—

> "Let men of God in courts and churches watch
> O'er such as do a Toleration hatch,
> Lest that ill egg bring forth a cockatrice
> To poison all with heresy and vice."

John Winthrop was a gentleman of wealth and position who, at the age of forty-two, left his manor-house in Sussex to help in the planting of faith and freedom in New England. In Winthrop is seen the noblest type of Puritanism; the same mingling of firmness and charity, purity and grace, which is exhibited in the character of

Colonel Hutchinson, and imparts to it such singular charm and beauty. In the art of managing men, and in the power of winning confidence and commanding respect, he has been compared to Washington, and, indeed, in this and in other respects he bears no little resemblance to that most stainless of all patriots. The fortitude of his mind, and the disciplined patience and sweetness of his temper, enabled him to encounter and to endure what would have been insupportable to others, nor did all the hardships and untoward circumstances of New England lead him to cast one longing, lingering look behind at the treasures he had quitted in the Egypt of his native land. Writing to his wife, whom he had left behind in England, he says: "We here enjoy God and Jesus Christ, and is not this enough? I thank God I like so well to be here, as I do not repent my coming. I would not have altered my course though I had foreseen all the afflictions. I never had more content of mind."

Winthrop and Dudley were associated together, the one as governor, the other as deputy-governor, of the colony for many years, indeed, with one or two breaks, during the whole term of their natural life. The accession of such leaders to the colony of Massachusetts was the means of originating a tide of emigration, which, with more or less intermission, did not cease to flow till the rising of the English nation against Charles and Laud, and the success which attended it was the means of inducing a goodly number of the exiles to return to their native land. It was in 1630 that Winthrop and Dudley reached New England, and before the year had expired seventeen ships had come to New England, bringing not far from fifteen hundred passengers. The major part of these were Puritans,—eight hundred of them belonging to the Independent party,—and comprising not a few clergymen, scholars, and men of ample means and fortune. The depth of their emotion, and the pain which it cost them to wrench themselves away from their friends in England, are revealed in their parting words: " Our hearts shall be fountains of tears for your everlasting welfare when we shall be in our poor cottages in the wilderness." By the year 1634, Massachusetts had received an accession of nearly four thousand settlers, and about twenty villages or parishes, with an average population of two hundred each, had been founded.

"Thus was founded the theocratic commonwealth of Massachusetts, with none like it to be found in history, except the republic of Calvin; like it, brave, austere, but intolerant of inquiry, persecuting heresy without pity and without mercy."[1] We shall be able better, by and by, to form a correct estimate of the justness (or otherwise) of this description.

[1] Dr. Borgeaud's *Rise of Modern Democracy*, "Massachusetts," p. 149.

Roger Williams: the Beginnings of Religious Controversy in New England

MEMORABLE EVENTS AND DATES

William Laud, Archbishop of Canterbury . 1633-1645
Roger Williams founded first Baptist Church
   in America   . . .   1639

CONTENTS OF CHAPTER III

Liberty needing safeguarding—Roger Williams—His individualism and love of toleration—His personal character—Call to church at Salem—Banishment—Wanderings among Indians—Settles in Rhode Island and founds town of Providence—Becomes Baptist and founds Baptist Church—Deposed by Salem Church—Visit to England—"The Bloody Tenet of Persecution"—Father of Voluntaryism—His position stated, and exaggerations refuted—First to found a free Church in free State—Rhode Island Settlement—Anne Hutchinson and Antinomianism—Expelled from Massachusetts—Founding of Portsmouth and Newport.

CHAPTER III

ROGER WILLIAMS: THE BEGINNINGS OF RELIGIOUS
CONTROVERSY IN NEW ENGLAND

THE colonists of Massachusetts, like those of New Plymouth, had left their native land to enjoy a civil and religious freedom which was denied them by an oppressive and prelatical Church; yet when this object had been attained, and it became necessary to frame a Constitution of their own, they found it a task hard and formidable enough. Even liberty requires to be checked and safeguarded, or it becomes an insufferable tyranny. Apart from the character and stamp of men who gave in their adhesion to it, even Robinsonian Independency furnished no guarantee for the preservation of liberty and order. The very theory of Church Independency fosters, as Professor Masson says, the development of theological differences and their strenuous expression. The very freedom it encourages, the direct appeal it makes to the individual conscience, or, as it is now termed, the right of private judgment, seemed to these early colonists to call for some safeguarding provision, some outward regulative control. "The New England Church was a State Church [we should rather call it a Church State] after a fashion. The pious Puritans, who had expatriated themselves from cruel England, had no other idea than that of founding in the wilderness a commonwealth pervaded and regulated by the strictest legislation of the Bible, and every man, woman, and child in which should walk all their lives long in the ways of Puritan Christianity."[1] Troubles were in store for the rising colony,—troubles inseparable from the new order of things,—and these were precipitated by the action, the strident individualism it may be called, of one man, to whose character and doings we venture to devote a considerable, and what may even seem a disproportionate, space.

Roger Williams.—" In the year 1654 a certain windmill in the Low Countries, whirling around with extraordinary violence by reason of a violent storm then blowing, the stone at length, by its rapid motion, became so intensely hot as to fire the mill, from whence the flames, being dispersed by the high winds, did set a whole town on fire. But I can tell my reader," says this lively and graphic writer,[2] " that above twenty years before this there was a whole country in America like to be set on fire by the rapid motion of a windmill in the head of one particular man." This particular man was Roger Williams, and certainly no more picturesque figure, no more daring and untemporising, though erratic mind, ever impressed itself upon the early history of America. This remarkable man was a Welshman, born in Carmarthenshire about the year 1606, that is, fourteen years

[1] Masson's *Milton and his Time*, vol. ii. pp. 564, 571.
[2] Cotton Mather.

before the *Mayflower* set sail. He received his education at Charterhouse School, London, and afterwards at Pembroke College, Cambridge. If he ever contemplated entering the ministry of the Church, the way soon became barred through his Separatist leanings and subsequent Separatist convictions. He found an influential friend and patron in Sir Edward Coke. Writing afterwards to the daughter of that eminent lawyer, he says: "That man of honour and wisdom and piety, your dear father, was often pleased to call me his son; and truly it was as bitter as death to me when Bishop Laud pursued me out of the land, and my conscience was persuaded against the National Church, and ceremonies and bishops, beyond the conscience of your dear father,—I say it was as bitter as death to me when I rode Windsor-way to take ship at Bristowe, and saw Stoke House, where that blessed man was, and durst not acquaint him with my conscience and my flight." When he arrived at Nantasket in 1631, he was about twenty-five years of age, "a young minister, godly and zealous, and having precious gifts." He at once began to promulgate the great doctrine with which his name has become identified —the right and duty of every man to form his own opinions and act upon his religious convictions without restraint or interference of any kind whatever. The principle of authority never found a more strenuous assailant, the principle of toleration a more uncompromising advocate. He said: "The doctrine of persecution for cause of conscience is most evidently and lamentably contrary to the doctrine of Christ Jesus." The civil magistrate, he averred, had no right to compel attendance on public worship, no right to punish any breach of the fourth commandment, no right to impose fines or oaths, or to levy any tax whatever for the maintenance of religion. "The civil magistrate may not intermeddle even to stop a Church from apostasy and heresy; his power extends only to the bodies and goods and outward estate of men." He likens the commonwealth to a ship manned by a motley crew composed of men of various religious creeds. Each one is free to follow his own creed and worship God according to his own conscience. All this is perfectly compatible with the captain having sole charge of the ship and enforcing discipline among the crew. "No one shall be bound to worship, or maintain a worship, against his own consent." "What?" said his opponents. "Is not the labourer worthy of his hire?" "Yes," replied Williams, "for them that hire him." He retorted upon those who contended that only members of the Church should be magistrates, that it were as unreasonable to select a "doctor of physick or a pilot" according to his skill in theology and his standing in the Church. Every Church, Williams maintained, was absolutely independent of every other Church, and to this principle of Independency he saw nothing but danger, a perilous approximation to Presbyterian tyranny, in the so-called conferences between ministers and Churches. "He pushed Brownism to its logical conclusions — the complete separation of civil and religious matters, and absolute democracy."[1] Professor Masson speaks of him as "the arch-individualist, Roger Williams." No doubt many before Williams had reached the same conclusions; it is his

[1] Borgeaud's *Rise of Modern Democracy*, p. 156.

pre-eminent distinction that he did not hesitate to carry them out to their extreme logical and practical consequences, and that in the face of prejudice, obloquy, and persecution. Williams claimed not only the fullest toleration for his own opinions, however repugnant they might be to others; he claimed also a like toleration for the opinions of others, however repugnant they might be to himself. He would be no party to imposing any disability on Turk or Infidel, Mohammedan or Jew, Catholic or Protestant, Conformist or Separatist. He held that it was unlawful to take possession of lands without having purchased them from the Indians, the original occupiers. The King of England could not make a valid grant of lands which did not belong to him. To take them and make them over to the colonists was, in Roger Williams' eyes, nothing less than thievery. The consternation produced by the promulgation of such views, and put forward with extraordinary zeal and vehemence, can be easily imagined.

Let no one suppose, however, that extreme as his opinions were, extravagant as they seemed to the soberminded colonists, that Roger Williams was either fanatic or firebrand. His excesses were tempered by a rich glowing and affectionate nature, one of those natures, contact with which disarms prejudice and hostility. No one could succeed in hating him who came under the spell of his personal influence. Those who knew him best, said Cotton Mather, declared him, from "the whole course and tenor of his life and conduct, to have been one of the most disinterested men that ever lived, a most pious and heavenly-minded soul."

The people of Salem desired to have him as their teacher. This raised in headquarters such a storm of opposition that Williams found it prudent to withdraw from Salem, and accordingly betook himself to Plymouth, where he remained for two years in association with Brewster and the Fathers. But the people of Salem would not be baulked in their intention, and on the death of their pastor, Skelton, they elected Williams to fill his place. This was the occasion for a manifesto from Governor Haynes and the ruling magistrate. Summoned before the General Court, and in presence of his accusers, he "maintained the rocky strength of his grounds," and declared himself "ready to be bound and banished, and even to die in New England," rather than renounce his opinions. At a meeting of the Court in Boston the following edict was passed: "Whereas Mr. Roger Williams, one of the elders of the Church of Salem, hath broached and divulged divers new and dangerous opinions against the authority of magistrates, and also writ letters of defamation both of the magistrates and Churches here, and that before any conviction, and yet maintaineth the same without retractation, it is therefore ordered that the said Mr. Williams shall depart out of this jurisdiction within six weeks now next ensuing."[1]

The refractoriness of Williams gave the authorities considerable trouble. They tried to entrap him and his wife and child, and ship them off secretly to England, but Williams, getting wind of their design, fled to the woods, and took refuge with the Pokanokett Indians, in

[1] See p. 345 for brief discussion of the alleged injustice of the banishment of Roger Williams.

company with whom he wandered about for fourteen weeks in the depth of winter, "not knowing what bread or bed did mean." He wrote letters of admonition to all the Churches whereof any of the magistrates were members, inciting them to admonish the magistrates of their injustice. This was the breaking point of the strain between Williams and the Churches themselves; they could not justify his recusant and impenitent attitude. His own wife was constrained to set herself in opposition to him. Often in the stormy night he had neither fire nor food nor company; often he wandered without a guide, and had no house but a hollow tree; but his unconquerable spirit, winsomeness of disposition, power of inspiring others with affection and trust, stood him in good stead. He grappled to himself the hearts of the Indians as with hooks of steel. "God," he says, "was pleased to give me a painful, patient spirit to lodge with them in their filthy smoky holes (even while I lived at Plymouth and Salem), to gain their tongue." "The barbarous heart of Canonicus, the chief of the Narragansetts, loved him as his son to the last gasp." He said: "The ravens fed me in the wilderness." "That ever-honoured Governor Winthrop privately wrote to me to steer my course to the Narragansett Bay, encouraging me from the freeness of the place from English claims or patents. I took his prudent motion as a voice from God." To this bay Williams and his family, with five other companions, steered their course. They landed in Rhode Island in June 1636, and Williams named the spot at which they landed "Providence," for, he said, "I desired it might be a shelter for persons distressed for conscience." Such was the foundation of the town of **Providence,** such the beginning of the settlement of Rhode Island. With the utmost cordiality and goodwill the Narragansett Indians ceded to him the extensive territory in the midst of which he had made his home, and so confirmed him in possession of it that, as he says, he could claim the soil as "his own as truly as any man's coat upon his back." Here at once was to be tried the experiment of setting up a democracy of the most thoroughgoing type. Something like a community of goods was at once established. Williams reserved to himself not one foot of land, not one tittle of political power more than he granted to servants and strangers. "He gave away his lands and other estate to them that he thought were most in want, until he gave them away all." As Professor Masson observes, it was probably the most absolutely democratic community on the whole face of the earth. But if it was a democracy, it was also a theocracy, for it was laid down from the beginning that God was their King, the ruler of conscience to be implicitly obeyed, "only in civil things" were they free to frame their own laws and regulations.

Though Williams had stoutly protested against the injustice of his being banished from Massachusetts, though he had undergone untold hardships, and was still under the sentence of outlawry, not the least feeling of resentment or ill-will towards those who had been the means of inflicting this suffering upon him found place in his large and generous heart. "I did ever, from my soul, honour, love them, even when their judgment led them to afflict me." Many hearts in Massachusetts were stirred with relentings at the exhibition of such unruffled patience and sweetness. "That great and pious soul, Mr. Winslow, melted, and kindly visited me, and put a piece of gold into the hands of my wife for our supply."

Williams was at once the founder of the new settlement and its pastor and teacher. Surrounded by congenial associates, and strong in his own religious principles and rectitude of purpose, he set to work to complete the hard task he had taken in hand. It might have been supposed that the work of organising the small community, as well as of sowing broadcast the seed of the new faith in the new country, would have consumed all his energies; especially when to this was added the necessity of labouring for the maintenance of his family, for, as he says: "Time was spent day and night, at home and abroad, on land and water, at the hoe and at the oar, for bread." But there was another difficulty, not less formidable that it was of his own creating. Williams had a very clamant and pertinacious creditor to satisfy in the shape of his own conscience. It was all he could do to keep pace with its requirements. Three years after his settlement in Rhode Island we hear of his having embraced Baptist principles, and with a consistency from which he never shrank, he induced a poor man, who, like himself, had come all the way from Salem, to baptize him; then he baptized his baptizer, along with ten others, thus founding what was practically **the first Baptist Church in America.**

This was a great scandal to the Church at Salem, of which Williams and his wife were still nominally members, and at the instance of its new pastor, Hugh Peters, the Church solemnly deposed them, along with others, from its membership. Even then, Williams could not satisfy that uneasy and clamorous conscience of his, that he had a right to be baptized, and that even if he had, that the administration of baptism was valid, and in accordance with the will of God. This raised in Williams' mind the whole question of Church order and Church ordinances. Was there divine authority for any of them? Was not the God who spake to Abraham and Saul of Tarsus calling him to cut himself adrift from external forms, and cast himself upon the unmediated revelation and teaching of God Himself?[1] "Let the reader fancy him," says Professor Masson, "in 1640, a man of thirty-four, of bold and stout jaw, but with richest and softest eyes, gazing out upon Narragansett Bay, a spiritual Crusoe, the excommunicated even of Hugh Peters, and the most extreme and outcast soul in all America."[2]

It does not fall within the scope of our purpose to relate the history of Roger Williams. This has been abundantly done by others. All we are endeavouring to do is to indicate his position in the New England theocracy, and the religious and political developments to which his influence so powerfully contributed. We pass over his visit to England in 1643, when he made the acquaintance of Milton, and became intimate with the leading divines of the Westminster Assembly; simply noting how he threw himself with characteristic vehem-

[1] In his fiery and polemical tract, *George Fox digged out of his Burrowes*, written many years after, in 1676, he says: "I profess that if my soul could find rest in joining unto any of the Churches professing Christ Jesus now extant, I would readily and gladly do it, yea, unto themselves whom I now opposed."

[2] Masson's *Life of John Milton and History of his Time*, vol. ii. p. 563.

ence into the controversy which was then raging round the question of toleration, and wrote his famous tract, entitled, *The Bloody Tenet of Persecution for cause of Conscience discussed in a Conference between Truth and Peace.* The tract was a most forcible plea for unlimited toleration, a toleration which should embrace all sects and all opinions—Papists and Jews, Mohammedans, Pagans, and Infidels. Yet he was well aware of the hopelessness of his task, for he writes: " I confess I have little hope till these flames are over that this discourse against the doctrine of persecution for cause of conscience should pass current, I say not amongst the wolves and lions, but even among the sheep of Christ themselves. Yet *liberavi animam meam.* I have not hid within my breast my soul's belief."

Professor Masson designates Roger Williams as the father and apostle of what, since his time, has figured anywhere in Great Britain, or in the United States, or in the British Colonies, under the name of **Voluntaryism.** Says the eloquent historian of the United States, he was the first person in modern Christendom to assert in its plenitude the doctrine of the liberty of conscience, the equality of opinions before the law; and in its defence he was the harbinger of Milton, the precursor and the superior of Jeremy Taylor. For Taylor limited his toleration to a few Christian sects; the philanthropy of Williams compassed the earth.[1] Williams would permit persecution of no opinion, of no religion, leaving heresy unharmed by law and unprotected by the terrors of penal statutes. He believed in liberty and equality, as he believed in

[1] *History of the United States*, revised edition, vol. i. p. 298.

the gospel. "He had the robust faith—a faith without scruples and without reservations—of the men of old time."[1]

Exaggerated claims put forward on his behalf.— The error into which some of the panegyrists of Roger Williams have fallen, is that of placing him on too lofty a pedestal, and claiming for him too commanding a position among the pioneers of progress and the apostles of "soul-liberty." We certainly cannot follow Mr. Straus[2] in bracketing Williams with Luther and Cromwell as one of the three epoch-making men of modern history; nor can we subscribe to the eloquent eulogy of Mr. Bancroft, in which he says that he was "the first person in modern Christendom who asserted in its plenitude the doctrine of the liberty of conscience, the equality of opinions before the law." This honour belongs, more justly, to the despised Anabaptists and Mennonites of Holland, who, a hundred years before, suffered in the cause of "soul-liberty" the most rancorous persecution. William, Prince of Orange, himself threw his shield over them, and in commanding the magistrates of Middleburgh to desist from persecuting the Anabaptists, used these remarkable words—most remarkable when we consider the time when they were spoken: "We declare to you that you have no right to trouble yourselves with any man's conscience, so long as nothing is done to cause private harm or public scandal. We therefore expressly

---

[1] Dr. Borgeaud, *Rise of Modern Democracy*, p. 164.
[2] *Roger Williams, the Pioneer of Religious Liberty*, by Oscar S. Straus (1894).

ordain that you desist from molesting these Baptists," etc. This was in 1577. But there are other claimants, who must, in all fairness, be regarded as having priority over Roger Williams in asserting and advocating the doctrine of toleration and religious liberty; or: Robert Browne, for example, on behalf of whom it is claimed that he was the first writer clearly to state and defend in the English tongue the true and now accepted doctrine of the relation of the magistrate to the Church. It was in 1581 that Browne was inhibited from preaching his "seditious" doctrines in Norwich. A generation later, and a whole generation before Roger Williams, Leonard Busher wrote his *Religious Peace; or, A Plea for Liberty of Conscience*.[1] In 1611, in a Confession of Faith put forth by the English Baptists of Amsterdam, it is clearly stated that "the magistrate is not to meddle with religion or matters of conscience, nor compel men to this or that form of religion: because Christ is the King and Lawgiver of the Church and conscience."

Williams' title to honour and pre-eminence rests, not upon the ground that he was the *earliest* champion of soul-liberty, or that, as Mr. Bancroft says, he was the

[1] Leonard Busher, who was a member of the first English Church of General Baptists founded by Thomas Helwys (see *ante*, p. 221), published his tract in 1614, in which he says: "As kings and bishops cannot command the wind, so they cannot command faith; and as the wind bloweth where it listeth, so is every man that is born of the Spirit. You may force men to church against their consciences, but they will believe as they did before, when they came there." This was written thirty years before the *Bloody Tenet of Persecution*. A valuable catena of references to this subject will be found in a note on p. 414, vol. i. of Dr. Palfrey's *History of New England*. We propose to advert again to this subject, pp. 357-379.

first person in modern Christendom who asserted in its plenitude the doctrine of liberty of conscience, but that he planted the first civil government in which the principle of toleration and religious liberty was explicitly proclaimed and consistently upheld and maintained. His title to fame is, that he was the originator and founder of "a free Church in a free State."[1]

Rhode Island Settlement.—Slate Rock, to all lovers of freedom, ought to have an interest second only to Plymouth Rock. It was the spot where Williams and his four companions landed, and where, upon the neighbouring hillside, they commenced the first settlement of Rhode Island, to which, in recognition of "God's merciful providence to him in his distress," he gave the name "Providence."[2] In the course of time the first four or five settlers were joined by others, and to a nucleus of thirteen associates the lands granted by Canonicus and Miantonomoh, the Indian sachems, were made over for a sum of thirty pounds. These were formed into townships, the settlers stipulating for themselves and for those who should be afterwards admitted to the same, to render "an active or passive obedience to all such orders or agreements as shall be made for public good," but it was expressly added, "only in civil things."

[1] "The theories of freedom in Church and State, taught in the schools of philosophy in Europe, were here brought into practice in the government of a small community," etc.—Professor Gervinus in his *Introduction to the History of the Nineteenth Century*, p. 65.

[2] The town of Providence has since raised a statue to the memory of its founder. Roger Williams is represented in the attitude of addressing an assembly, and on the book which he holds may be read the inscription: "Soul-Liberty. 1636."

The name Providence was given, as we have seen, in token of its founder's desire that "it might be a shelter for persons distressed for conscience." The latitude of this invitation proved, as might naturally be supposed, dangerously wide. Those who chafed under the more stringent laws and regulations of Massachusetts and of other colonies, and those who for other reasons found them intolerable, had a city of refuge conveniently near at hand to which they could flee. Inevitably, Providence became "a harbourage for all sorts of consciences." Thither fled the disaffected, the turbulent, fanatics of all kinds and all shades of belief; every description of "cranky" persons, "some half-crazed with those teeming maggots of the brain which so breed in times of exasperating religious controversy; others possessed by harmless vagaries of illogical thought, which spring up in such seasons in some minds, and which, if they have a meaning to those who cherish them, are incomprehensible to everybody else."[1] Happily for the future of this settlement, arrest was at length laid upon the tendency to religious anarchy and political disorder, and out of this primal chaos order and restraint and progress gradually emerged.

Anne Hutchinson and the "Antinomian Dispersion."
—In the wake of the disturbance occasioned by Roger Williams, and by his expulsion from Massachusetts, there followed another controversy, bitterer by far than any that had yet broken out. This was theological, and raged round what was known as the doctrines of

[1] *A Popular History of the United States*, by Bryant and Gay, vol. ii. p. 40.

Antinomianism. The leader in this controversy was a woman of such " busy spirit, competent wit, and voluble tongue, yet profitable and sober carriage," that she soon drew companions and disciples round her, and extorted even from her enemies testimony to her masculine understanding and power of eloquent persuasiveness. Mrs. Anne Hutchinson, the harbinger of the " revolt of woman," as she has been termed, had followed her favourite minister, the Rev. John Cotton, from Lincolnshire to New England. She had brought over with her, says Winthrop, " two dangerous errors—first, that the person of the Holy Ghost dwells in a justified person ; second, that no sanctification can help to evidence to us our justification." In exposition of her views, she lectured in Boston twice a week, and large numbers of her own sex flocked to hear her, many forsaking their own ministers and proclaiming themselves her followers. " It began to be as common," says Winthrop, " to distinguish between men by being under a covenant of grace or a covenant of works as in other countries between Protestants and Papists." Mrs. Hutchinson found staunch supporters in her brother-in-law, the Rev. John Wheelwright, and Sir Henry Vane, at that time governor of the colony ; even the sober-minded and judicious Cotton declared in her favour ; and a considerable number of persons of influence in the colony adopted her views, and abetted her arraignment of ministers and priest-ridden magistrates living under a covenant of works. She claimed to possess, and to live and teach under, the influence of special divine inspiration, a claim which of all others the more sober-minded Puritans of that age were least able to tolerate. The contest grew hot and furious, and at length issued in what is known in the history of Massachusetts as the Antinomian Dispersion. Anne Hutchinson was brought to trial before the Court of Massachusetts. Sentence of expulsion was passed upon her, and she, accompanied by a goodly number of friends and sympathisers, made their way to Providence, where they were hospitably received by Roger Williams, and, at his advice, settled down in Rhode Island, and founded the two towns of **Portsmouth** and **Newport.**

Says Professor Masson: " These two, I should say,— this man in his prime from Carmarthenshire and this woman from Lincolnshire, now with wrinkles round her eloquent eyes,—were the two spirits in New England that had most of the incalculable in them, and had shot furthest ahead in the speculative gloom." [1]

[1] Masson's *Milton and his Time*, vol. ii. p. 577.

Growth and Development of New England

MEMORABLE EVENTS AND DATES

Long Parliament met	1640
Charles I. beheaded	. 1649
Four Colonies of New England united	. 1643
Commencement of Protestant missions	. 1646

CONTENTS OF CHAPTER IV

Connecticut colonised—Thomas Hooker, father of American democracy—Connecticut professes no allegiance to British Crown—New Hampshire—New Haven—The Pequot Indians—Roger Williams as peacemaker—Pequots implacable—Exterminated—Missionary labours—John Eliot, apostle to the Indians, translates Bible—First missionary corporation—United colonies—Rhode Island left out—Massachusetts predominant—Expansion of New England—Attitude of England—A Governor-General of Commission threatened—Resistance of colonists—False relation between colonies and mother country—Measures to prevent emigration, especially of clergymen—Eight ships arrested—Cromwell and Hampden not on board—Loss to mother country by New England—Long Parliament—Emigration stayed—Prosperity and longevity of colonists—Contrasted with Europe—Winthrop's fine description of liberty.

LEADERS

In Rhode Island .	. Roger Williams.
In Connecticut .	. Thomas Hooker.
In New Haven .	. John Davenport and Theophilus Eaton.

CHAPTER IV

Growth and Development of New England

It is quite beside the purpose of this work to give any detailed and connected history of the colonies of Connecticut, Rhode Island, New Hampshire, and the way in which they rose into political importance. Only as this bears upon the establishment of the Puritan theocracy in New England does it come within the scope of our present purpose.

Colonisation of Connecticut.—We do not propose, therefore, to give any extended description of the new communities that were formed, and the Puritan villages which rose in rapid succession upon " the delightful banks " of the Connecticut, nor of the rich harvest that sprang from the cultivation of these alluvial lands. Thomas Hooker, " the light of the Western Churches," was the chief pioneer in this movement. He was one of the most learned and eloquent of the Puritan leaders, and was specially distinguished for his broad and advanced views in regard to the self-governing power of the people. Winthrop and Cotton held such views to be both inexpedient and dangerous. Winthrop defended the restriction of the suffrage, on the ground that " the best part is always the least, and of that best part the wiser part is always the lesser." Hooker, on the other hand, held that "in matters which concern the common good, a general council, chosen by all, to transact businesses which concern all, I conceive most suitable to rule, and most safe for relief of the whole." To this position Hooker steadfastly adhered, and in the course of a sermon preached by him, after Connecticut had commenced its separate and independent existence, he maintained that "the foundation of authority is laid in the free consent of the people; that the choice of the public magistrates belongs to the people of God's own allowance; and that they who have the power to appoint officers and magistrates have the right also to set the bounds and limitation of the power and place unto which they call them." The government of Connecticut was settled on a purely democratic basis, and its Constitution was the "first written Constitution of modern democracy,"[1] and more, perhaps, than any other man, **Thomas Hooker deserves to be called the father of American democracy.** "Well knowing," its preamble recited, "where a people are gathered together the Word of God requires that to maintayne the peace and union of such a people there should be an orderly and decent government established according to God, to order and dispose of the affayres of the people at all seasons as occasion shall require; doe

---

[1] "We have passed from the world of unwritten to that of written Constitutions, from a world of government by usage, tradition, and chartered privileges, wrested from kings, to a world of government by public reason embodied in codes of political law."—*The United States, an Outline of Political History*, by Goldwin Smith, D.C.L., p. 20.

therefore associate and conjoyne ourselues to be as one Publicke State or Commonwealth, and doe, for ourselves and our successors, and such as shall be adjoyned to us hereafter, enter into Combination and Confederation together, to maintayne and preserve the liberty and purity of the Gospel of our Lord Jesus Christ which we now professe, as also the discipline of the Churches; which, according to the truth of the said Gospell, is now practised amongst us: as also in our civill affairs to be guided and governed according to such Lawes and Rules, Orders and Decrees as shall be made, ordered, and decreed, as followeth:"[1] ... What is omitted from the written Constitution is almost as significant as what it contains. Such expressions as those introduced into the compact drawn up in the cabin of the *Mayflower*, "dread sovereign," or "gracious King," are conspicuous by their absence. Connecticut recognised no allegiance to the British Crown, nor to any government outside its own bounds. It refused to make church membership a condition of exercising the franchise, and also church attendance compulsory, in this respect departing from the practice of Massachusetts, and conforming to the example of New Plymouth. "More than two centuries have elapsed; the world has been made wiser by the most varied experience; political institutions have become the theme on which the most powerful and cultivated minds have been employed, and so many constitutions have been framed or reformed, stifled or subverted, that memory may despair of a complete catalogue; but the people of Connecticut have found no reason to deviate essentially

---

[1] Dr. Borgeaud's *Rise of Modern Democracy*, p. 121.

from the frame of government established by their fathers."[1]

New Hampshire.—The settlement of New Hampshire in 1623 need not detain us further than to note that of its four towns, two were founded by Antinomians driven out from Boston. The other two were founded by Episcopalians, and were the first-fruits of the colonising efforts of Gorges and Mason. In 1641, at the request of a majority of the settlers, this colony was added to Massachusetts.

New Haven. — The colony of New Haven was founded in 1638 under the leadership of John Davenport, a clergyman, and Theophilus Eaton, a merchant, possessed of considerable substance. Davenport was very apprehensive lest his flock should be led away by the Antinomian heresy which had broken out in Massachusetts, and for this and other reasons connected with the insufficiency of Massachusetts as a place of trade, they wished to withdraw from its jurisdiction and set up an independent government of their own. Each of the towns was to be governed by seven ecclesiastical officers, known as "pillars of the Church." These seven were to gather round them others who were eligible for membership in the Church, and these were to be the nucleus of the new State. The Bible was their statute-book, and "the choice of magistrates, legislation, the rights of inheritance, and all matters of that kind were to be decided according to the rules of Holy Scripture."[2] They re-

[1] Bancroft's *History*, vol. i. p. 302, revised edition, p. 319.
[2] *Records of the Colony and Plantation of New Haven*, ed. Ch. J. Hoadley (Hartford, 1857), p. 12.

jected trial by jury, that being no part of the Mosaic law. Church membership was the condition of citizenship; he who was not fit for that was unfit for this, for the State must be "according to God." This law had the effect of disfranchising more than half the settlers in the town of New Haven, nearly half in Guildford, and less than one-fifth in Milford. "The first leaders of the colony of New Haven represent the clerical tendencies of Congregationalism."[1] Thus New Haven, even as to its basis of government, was the very opposite of Connecticut; it was less democratic even than Massachusetts: it was indeed an absolute theocracy, but founded upon the voluntary concurrence of the people themselves. It maintained its separate existence, however, for only about twenty-five years; at the end of that time it was annexed to Connecticut.

The Pequot Indians.—Immediately after the little federation of towns in Connecticut had been formed, and before they had taken the step of separating from Massachusetts, they found themselves threatened by a new and alarming peril. The various tribes of Indians inhabiting the regions in the midst of which the colonists had made their home, always regarded the latter as game to be hunted down, tomahawked, and, if possible, exterminated. Of these tribes the Iroquois and the Pequots were the most cruel, vindictive, and ruthless. The latter were living in close neighbourhood to the settlers in the Connecticut valley, and they had seven hundred warriors at their command. The Pequot Indians formed an alliance with their hereditary enemies, the

[1] Dr. Borgeaud's *Rise of Modern Democracy*, p. 135.

Narragansetts, and conceived the design of falling upon the colonists, who were less than two hundred in number. This conspiracy was frustrated by Roger Williams, who, with consummate skill and courage, succeeded in dissolving this ill-starred alliance. Writing many years afterwards, he says : " I had my share of service to the whole land in that Pequot business . . . the Lord helped me immediately to put my life into my hand, and scarce acquainting my wife, to ship myself all alone, in a poor canoe, and to cut through a stormy wind, with great seas, every minute in hazard of life, to the sachem's house. Three days and nights my business forced me to lodge and mix with the bloody Pequot ambassadors, whose hands and arms, methought, reeked with the blood of my countrymen massacred by them on Connecticut river, and from whom I could not but nightly look for their bloody knives at my own throat also."[1] Williams was so far successful that he was able to prevail upon the Narragansett chiefs to refrain from their design, and the result was, they made a treaty of alliance with the English. But the Pequots were implacable, and were not to be turned from their hostile purpose. Connecticut appealed to Massachusetts and Plymouth for aid, which was readily granted. A fierce battle ensued, one fought at desperate odds on the part of the colonists; but the savages could make no stand

[1] "Williams' opportunities of studying the Indian character were perhaps greater than those of any other man of his time. He was always an advocate for justice towards them. But he seems to have had no better opinion of them than Mr. Parkman (see his *Jesuits in North America*), calling them sharply and shortly wolves endowed with men's brains."—Lowell's *Among my Books, New England Two Centuries Ago*, p. 277.

against the disciplined forces of the white men, and the deadly precision of their arms. A terrible rain of English bullets, assisted by a still more terrible conflagration, did most effectually the work of extermination. It is computed that some six hundred Indians perished, while of the English only two were killed, and about twenty wounded. "Thus," exclaimed the exultant leader, "did the Lord judge among the heathen!" "There remained not a sannup or squaw, not a warrior nor child of the Pequot name." A nation had been wiped out of existence. It was a bloody but decisive arbitrament. It led to the establishment of a peace which lasted for forty years. No doubt, as Mr. Goldwin Smith observes, the Puritan had his cruel moods, and his notions about smiting the Canaanite in New England as well as in Ireland; but in this instance the fierceness of the founders of Connecticut was not without provocation and excuse. They were fighting not only in self-defence, but for their very lives, and for the very existence of their hearths and homes.

First Protestant missionary labours.—It is pleasant to turn from such scenes of carnage to scenes in which humanity and Christian philanthropy are seen at work, redressing the wrongs and ameliorating the sufferings which man's inhumanity to man has been the means of inflicting. The settlers did not deal with the Indians they dispossessed of the lands which had been their hunting grounds and those of their ancestors from time immemorial as men who had no right to justice and compensation. They paid for the lands they occupied, and for the seed-corn they used. But there were those among their own number who could not allow that justice and even-handed dealing exhausted their obligation to the tribes around them. It is interesting to remember that it was within the Puritan commonwealth that the first Protestant missionary movement originated. The Pilgrim Fathers were the first to move in this good work. One of their number was set apart " to promote the conversion of the Indians." In December 1621, Robert Cushman appealed to England on behalf of " these poor heathen," and in 1636 the colony legislated for the "preaching of the gospel among them." **John Eliot, the apostle to the Indians**, famous both as a linguist and preacher, moved with pity for a race so benighted, and living in such ignorance and misery, gave up his settled ministry at Rosebury, near Boston, and devoted himself for forty years to the conversion and civilising of the Indians in their forests and wigwams. He published an Indian grammar and a complete translation of the Bible in the Indian language. This was the first Bible printed in America, and remains to this day, though printed in a language which has become extinct, and which very few living scholars are able to read, a monument of his prodigious industry and patience and skill. Through the labours and influence of this devoted man and others like-minded, it is estimated that in 1674 there were no fewer than four thousand " praying Indians," as they were called. Schools were established, and many learned to read and write. The effect of these labours was to a large extent nullified by internecine strife among the various tribes, and by their gradual retreat and disappearance before the march of civilisation; but the spiritual harvest which sprang from the seed thus sown is beyond all human power to compute, and is bearing fruit even to the present day. It is interesting to note in this connection that the first Protestant Missionary Corporation was that called into existence by the Long Parliament, and was formed for the "Propagation of the Gospel in New England." To assist this object Oliver Cromwell, then Lord Protector of England, issued an order for a collection to be made in all the parishes of England and Wales.

The United Colonies of New England.—The time had now come when it was felt that the federal principle, which has since received such majestic embodiment in the Republic of the United States, might with great advantage be applied to four of the then existing colonies. Accordingly, in 1643, Massachusetts, New Plymouth, Connecticut, and New Haven entered into a confederation " to advance the kingdom of our Lord Jesus Christ, and to enjoy the liberties of the gospel in purity with peace." This was deemed necessary in view of their exposure to common dangers arising from the " people of several nations and strange languages" by whom they were surrounded, also because "the sad distractions of England" cut off from the mother country all hope of assistance. They entered, therefore, " into a firm and perpetual league of friendship and amity, for offence and defence and succour upon all just occasions, both for preserving and propagating the truth and liberties of the gospel, and for their own mutual safety and welfare." These four colonies were " made all as one," under the name, "The United Colonies of New England." Rhode Island was left out of this arrangement. The attitude of the people of that island had been so independent and defiant, that to them no terms of union could be proposed; they must be abandoned to their own perversity and condition of isolation. Rhode Island determined to get from the old country the protection she could not obtain in the new. With this object in view Roger Williams departed for England, and after making a brief acquaintance with its stormy politics, returned, bringing with him a charter, thanks to the good offices of Sir Henry Vane—"the sheet anchor of Rhode Island," confirming the new colony in the possession of the most absolute rights and privileges. For some time Rhode Island seemed to be drifting rapidly in the direction of anarchy, on account of its "headiness and tumults"; but the character of the men chosen to administer the government was happily the means of keeping the vessel right, and enabling it to steer at length a straight prosperous course, and "Rhode Island was not long in showing the world that civil society could subsist, and political order could be maintained, without imposing shackles on spiritual life."[1] This federated union did not work at first without considerable

---

[1] In his *Records of Rhode Island*, Lieutenant-Governor Arnold claims for his country the honour of having been the cradle of American democracy. But, as Dr. Borgeaud says, "the historians of the other States of New England assert their claims also to this honour, each for his own, with no less talent and no less convincing proofs." Those who cannot be suspected of bias either the one way or the other will probably concur in his judgment, that democracy is not the heritage of any one single State, but of all the States of New England, though it may be in differing proportions.

friction. The predominance of Massachusetts—a predominance naturally created by her superior size and strength, and exacerbated, there can be little doubt, by a domineering spirit—was resented by her weaker sisters, and instead of harmony there was jealousy and strife. But this was incident to the initial stage of the movement rather than to its subsequent development, and in spite of all drawbacks the Confederacy grew and flourished.

Expansion of New England.—A nation had now been planted, and had taken firm and fruitful roothold in the soil of New England. The population embraced by it had reached nearly 24,000, of which 15,000 may be assigned to Massachusetts, 3000 to New Plymouth, 3000 to Connecticut, and 2500 to New Haven. During the twenty-three years which had elapsed since the *Mayflower* had cast anchor in Cape Cod, fifty towns and villages had been planted, between thirty and forty churches had been erected, " and more ministers' houses, a castle, a college, prisons, forts, cartways, causeys many, and all these upon our own charges, no public hand reaching out any help, having comfortable houses, gardens, orchards, grounds fenced, corn fields," etc.[1]

Attempted interference on the part of the mother country.—Nations, like individuals, sometimes profit by the misfortunes of others. The civil war in England broke out in 1642, just about the time that the four colonies of Massachusetts, New Plymouth, Connecticut,

[1] *New England's First Fruits*, etc. (London, 1643); Palfrey's *History of New England*, vol. ii. p. 6.

and New Haven entered into federated union. But for this circumstance, the colonists of New England would probably have been involved in a most bitter and disastrous struggle for their rights and liberties. The English Church and hierarchy had from the first maintained towards them a hostile attitude. They looked upon them as escaped victims, as runaway slaves were afterwards regarded by the planters of Virginia; and the tidings which reached England from time to time of the freedom enjoyed by the settlers in the New World, and of their growing prosperity, did not make them feel any more favourably disposed towards them. The resentment of the Royalist and High Church party was fanned and intensified by malcontents and seditious persons, who, finding the rule and discipline of New England too oppressive, had returned to their native land, and now sought to revenge themselves upon the colonists by setting in circulation all manner of defamatory reports. They said that New England was torn with religious factions; that religious sanctions were disregarded; that marriage was no longer held to be a sacrament, but a contract celebrated by the civil magistrate; that the colonists held the Church of England in utter detestation; and that they were determined to owe no sort of subjection to the English Crown. This was to excite the deepest susceptibilities of the then rulers in Church and State.

The King was induced to sanction the appointment of a Governor-General of Commission, with full power to revise the laws of the colonies, and to introduce what form of government they judged necessary to bring it into subjection to the English Crown. At the head of this Commission was Laud, the Archbishop of Canterbury. It was proposed to send out a Governor-General, and to revoke every patent or charter which had been previously granted. This struck at the foundation, at the very life, of the rising commonwealth. There was a consultation of the Puritan leaders at Boston, and the resolution come to was: "If a Governor-General were sent we ought not to accept him, but defend our lawful possessions if we were able; otherwise to avoid or protract." The colonists met this threatened invasion of their liberties with earnest but dignified remonstrance. The letter addressed by Winthrop to the Commissioners concludes by saying: "If the patent be taken from us, the common people will conceive that His Majesty hath cast them off, and that hereby they are freed from their allegiance and subjection, and therefore will be ready to confederate themselves under a new government, for their necessary safety and subsistence, which will be of dangerous example unto other plantations, and perilous to ourselves of incurring His Majesty's displeasure." They asked nothing of His Majesty but the favour of neglect.

It will thus be seen that the colonists had no thought of disowning the authority of the British Crown, to which, rather than to Parliament, they held themselves bound. At the same time, they clung jealously to their own independence, claimed and exercised the right of framing their own laws, administering their own affairs, and entering into any compact or alliance they deemed necessary for their own safety or advantage, without waiting for any mandate or authorisation from the mother country. For, said Winthrop, "if we in America should forbear to unite for offence and defence against a common enemy till we have leave from England, our throats might be cut before the messenger could be half seas through." This relation of dependence upon the mother country was unhappily established from the very beginning. It was enshrined in the covenant signed in the cabin of the *Mayflower*: "We whose names are underwritten, the loyal subjects of our dread sovereign King James," etc. The colonists thus never suffered themselves to forget that they were liegemen of a sovereign on the other side of the Atlantic. "Herein lay the fatal seeds of misunderstanding—of encroachment on the side of the home Government, of revolt on that of the growing colony, and ultimately of revolution. This was the beginning of woes, the full measure of which came in 1765."[1]

The Government, represented by Strafford, Laud, and the ecclesiastical hierarchy, saw that, powerless as they were to check the rising liberties of the colonies, they could, at any rate, succeed in reducing the dimensions of the evil by staying the tide of emigration. None but the poorest, and socially the most uninfluential, were allowed to leave the country without a special permission, and these were required to take the oath of supremacy and allegiance to the King. On April 30, 1637, the following proclamation was issued: "The King being informed that great numbers of his subjects are yearly transported into New England with their families and whole estates, that they might be out of the reach of

[1] See Goldwin Smith's *United States*, pp. 6, 7.

ecclesiastical authority, His Majesty therefore commands that his officers of the several ports should suffer none to pass without licence from the Commissioners of the Plantations, and a testimonial from their minister of their conformity to the orders and discipline of the Church." To stop the flight of the ministers, the following Order of Council was published: "Whereas it is observed that such ministers as are unconformable to the discipline and ceremonies of the Church do frequently transport themselves to the plantations, where they take liberty to nourish their factions and sysmatical humours to the hindrance of the good, conformity, and unity of the Church, we therefore expressly command you, in His Majesty's name, to suffer no clergyman to transport himself without a testimonial from the Archbishop of Canterbury and Bishop of London." This edict did not produce any appreciable effect in restraining those who were bent on leaving the country. A squadron of eight ships in the Thames, preparing to set sail for the New World, was arrested by order of the Privy Council. It has been alleged that Hampden and Cromwell, with other illustrious patriots, were on board this fleet, intending to seek in the New World the rights and privileges which they had sought vainly in the Old; but this statement appears to rest upon no basis of fact, and on the face of it, it is a most improbable story; and yet, improbable as it is, it is avouched by Hallam,[1] Hume, and other historians.

---

[1] Hallam's *History*, vol. ii. p. 58: "Men of a higher rank than the first colonists, and now become hopeless alike of the civil and religious liberties of England; men of capacious and commanding

Loss to the mother country represented by New England.—Neal, the Puritan historian, basing his statements on Mather's *History of New England*, says that during twelve years of Laud's administration there went over the sea about four thousand planters, carrying with them materials, in money and cattle, etc., to the value of not less than one hundred and ninety-two thousand pounds. "Upon the whole, it has been computed that the four settlements of New England, viz. Plymouth, Massachusetts Bay, Connecticut, and New Haven, all which were accomplished before the civil wars, drained England of four or five hundred thousand pounds in money (a very great sum in those days); and if the persecution of the Puritans had continued twelve years longer, it is thought that a fourth part of the riches of the kingdom would have passed out of it through this channel." [1]

The Long Parliament met in 1640. This marked the turn of the tide for the Puritans both at home and abroad. It not only stayed the tide of emigration, but induced many to return to their native land. The population of New England, fed by the continuous stream of emigration

minds, formed to be the legislators and generals of an infant republic, —the wise and cautious Lord Say, the acknowledged chief of the Independent sect; the brave, open, and enthusiastic Lord Brooke; Sir Arthur Haselrig Hampden, ashamed of a country for whose rights he had fought alone; Cromwell, panting with energies that he could neither control nor explain, and whose unconquerable fire was still wrapt in smoke to every eye but that of his kinsman Hampden,—were preparing to embark for America, when Laud, for his own and his master's cause, procured an Order of Council to stop their departure."

[1] *Neal*, vol. i. p. 546; Palfrey's *History of New England*, vol. i. p. 584.

between the years 1620 and 1640, reached to between twenty-three and twenty-four thousand. But from 1640 there set in a return tide, which did not cease to flow for that same century and a quarter, so that, in that period, more persons passed from New England to the mother country than came out from the mother country to New England. It must not be supposed, however, on this account, that New England continued to be the sterile, inhospitable soil and clime that it was to the first settlers. Nowhere was man's power to subjugate by his indomitable will the forces of nature, and make them subservient to his happiness and prosperity, more singularly displayed. When the persecutions ceased in England there were dwelling in New England thousands who would not change their country for any other in the world. At one time Cromwell offered the colonists the rich and sunny land of Jamaica in exchange for their own. At another time he proposed to transplant them to Ireland; but, wisely for themselves and for the world, they preferred to remain where they were. "As Ireland will not brook venomous beasts, so will not that land vile livers." One might dwell there "from year to year, and not see a drunkard, or hear an oath, or meet a beggar." The consequence was a marked increase of health and longevity. The average duration of life in New England, as compared with Europe, was doubled; and the human race was so vigorous that of all who were born into the world, more than two in ten, full four in nineteen, attained the age of seventy. Of those who lived beyond ninety, the proportion, as compared with European tables of longevity, was still more remarkable. "I have dwelt the longer," continues Mr. Bancroft, " on the character of the early Puritans of New England, for they were the parents of one third the whole white population of the United States as it was in 1834.[1] Within the first fifteen years—and there was never afterwards any considerable increase from England—we have seen that there came over twenty-one thousand two hundred persons, or four thousand families. Their descendants were in 1834 not far from four millions.[2] Each family has multiplied on the average to one thousand souls. To New York and Ohio, where they then constituted half the population, they carried the Puritan system of free schools; and their example is spreading it through the civilised world."

The progress which had been made in New England in the planting of free institutions, and the measure in which civil and religious freedom was possessed and enjoyed, can be best appreciated, as De Tocqueville[3] has pointed out, by running our eye, even rapidly, over the then existing condition of Europe. In every portion of that continent absolutism still reigned. The aspirations of the people were stifled; they were systematically exploited in the

[1] "It would probably be coming somewhere near the truth to divide the present [this was written in 1858] white population of the United States into three equal parts—one part belonging to the New England stock, one the posterity of English who settled in the other Atlantic colonies, and another consisting of the aggregate of Irish, Scotch, French, Dutch, German, Swedish, Spanish, and other immigrants, and their descendants."—See Preface to Palfrey's *History of New England*, ix.

[2] Bancroft's *History of the United States*, revised edition, vol. i. p. 375. The population of the United States is now not far from seventy millions.

[3] De Tocqueville, *Democracy in America*, vol. i. 42, 43.

interest of a governing class; were left for the most part to sink further and further in ignorance and degradation and misery, and anything like independence or liberty was withheld from them. And yet, "at that very time, those principles, which were scorned or unknown by the nations of Europe, were proclaimed in the deserts of the New World, and were accepted as the free creed of a great people. . . . In the bosom of this obscure democracy, which had as yet brought forth neither generals nor philosophers nor authors, a man[1] might stand up in the face of a free people and pronounce the following fine definition of liberty: 'I observe a great mistake in this country. There is a twofold liberty—natural (I mean as our nature is now corrupt) and civil or federal. The first is common to man with beasts and other creatures. By this, man, as he stands in relation to man, simply hath liberty to do what he lists; it is a liberty to evil as well as to good. This liberty is incompatible and inconsistent with authority, and cannot endure the least restraint of the most just authority. The exercise and maintaining of this liberty makes men to grow more evil, and in time to be worse than brute beasts: *omnes sumus licentia deteriores*—we all become worse by licence. That is the great enemy of truth and peace, that wild beast which all the laws of God are bent against, to restrain and subdue it. The other kind of liberty I call civil or federal; it may also be called moral, in reference to the covenant between God and man in the moral law, and the political covenants and constitutions among men themselves. This liberty is the

[1] Governor Winthrop.

proper end and object of authority, and cannot subsist without it; and it is a liberty to that only which is just, good, and honest. This liberty you are to stand for at the hazard, not only of your goods, but of your lives, if need be. Whatsoever crosseth this is not authority, but a distemper thereof. This liberty is maintained and exercised in a way of subjection to authority; it is of the same kind of liberty wherewith Christ hath made us free.'"

Such was the Puritan ideal of a well-ordered and free commonwealth.

Religious and Social Aspects of New England

MEMORABLE EVENTS AND DATES

Harvard College founded	1636
First code of laws, "The Body of Liberties" adopted	1641
The Bay Psalm Book, the first book printed in America, printed in Cambridge, Massachusetts	1640
The "Cambridge Platform" adopted	1651

CONTENTS OF CHAPTER V

Congregational Independency, indigenous to new state of things—Led to democracy—The Cambridge Platform—Cotton on Independency—Platform adopted—New England Way—Barrowism—Growth of Independency—The Sabbath in New England—Passion for worship—First meeting-house—Saturday evening—Wintry meeting-houses—Miss Earle's description—Judge Sewall—Social Life in New England—Satires on Puritanism—Austereness of American Puritans—Amusements and luxuries proscribed—Temperance, not abstinence—Regulations as to dress, concession to "dignities"—Old Testament and Mosaism—Nathaniel Ward—The Body of Liberties—Ten capital offences—Church attendance—Penalty more stringent in Virginia—Laws more humane than those of England—Prevalence of vice—Measures for its suppression abortive through their severity—Education in New England—Dread of illiteracy—Common schools—Harvard College.

CHAPTER V

RELIGIOUS AND SOCIAL ASPECTS OF NEW ENGLAND

Congregational Independency.—We have seen how Congregationalism or Independency was the system of Church government which was carried over in the *Mayflower* to the shores of the New World. We have seen, too, how its principles gradually infiltrated into the minds of the main body of succeeding settlers, even of those who were at first hostile and disaffected, till at last it came to be seen that Congregational Independency was the only practicable polity, the only system suited to the necessities of the young rising Puritan Republic. The colonists of Massachusetts, who were at first the least friendly to this system, "yielded," as Dr. Borgeaud has it, "to the necessities of the case, and also, there is no doubt, to a sincere conviction, developed by example, that such an organisation was what was sanctioned by Holy Scripture." So it may be said that Independency rose to the ascendency which it gained through the operation of "the law of the survival of the fittest." It is not too much to say that it was the only mould into which the new molten metal could have been run, or, changing the figure, the only vessel capable of holding the new generous fermenting wine of faith and liberty. True, it might have been run into other vessels, but in that case it would not have been the same wine, its quality would have been altogether changed. This was what happened in Virginia; there it acquired a "tang" that was peculiarly its own, and bore witness to the more ancient, aristocratic vine from whose clusters it had been pressed. "Its principles" (those of the Confederation of the Colonies), says an unfriendly historian, "were altogether those of Independency, and it cannot easily be supported by any other."[1] "It may be said that as a general rule Congregationalism produced democracy wherever it was interpreted by laymen, or by pastors who had broken away completely and radically from the ideas of the Anglican clergy, and who followed out the logical consequences of the premises laid down."[2]

[1] Chalmers' *Annals*, p. 178, quoted by Dr. Palfrey, vol. i. p. 633.
[2] *Rise of Modern Democracy*, p. 119. In the panegyrists of this system Dr. Borgeaud detects a strain of irritating self-complacency, even while doing justice to their contention. "The share of influence which Congregationalism can claim in the formation of the national institutions of the United States has been insisted upon by its literary representatives. Their zeal, which was occasionally excessive, and not always free from the feeling, so provocative of criticism, which certain interpreters of Holy Scripture call *self-righteousness*, caused a reaction." So a new school has risen up, "in which may be counted some distinguished historians," which makes American democracy descend in a direct line from Teutonic institutions. But, as pointed out on pp. 22, 23, the credit of giving rise to democracy, both in the Old World and in the New (whatever that credit may be, and as shown conclusively by Dr. Borgeaud), certainly belongs to Puritanism and Independency. The Church covenants, on the basis of which free government and free institutions, in a word, democracy, were modelled, were "the essential cause of the Independent congregations."—*Rise of Modern Democracy*, pp. 137–140, also p. 32.

The Cambridge Platform.[1]—It will be well here to advert briefly to an event which took place in 1651, which, though occurring at a later period than this work professes to embrace, has a unique importance, "as completing the theocratic organisation of the Puritan commonwealth in Massachusetts." This was the adoption of the famous Cambridge Platform, which was agreed upon at a synod of Churches meeting in Cambridge in 1648. It contained some seventeen chapters, and its credal confession was substantially that of the Westminster Assembly of Divines. The time had come when, as Cotton Mather says, it was convenient that "the Churches of New England should have a system of their discipline, extracted from the word of God, and exhibited unto them with a more effectual acknowledged and established recommendation; and nothing but a council was proper to compose the system." This system was to embody the Congregational idea or conception of the Church in preference to that denoted by the name Independency. In his *Way of the Congregational Churches Cleared*, John Cotton, who did perhaps more than any other leader to make Independency a working system, objects to Independency as "a fit name of the way of our Churches," describing it as "too strait," "because we do profess dependence upon magistrates for civil government and protection; dependence upon Christ and His word for the sovereign government and rule of our administrations; dependence upon the counsel of other Churches and synods, when our own variance or ignorance may stand in need of such help from them." This

[1] See Dexter's *Congregationalism as seen in its Literature*, p. 439.

broader conception of the Church, and of the relation of one Church to another, was embodied in the Cambridge Platform. It is easy to see in this measure of retreat and recession from the hard and fast line of Independency the indirect influence of the spirit of Presbyterianism, which had been brought over from the mother country by a large body of the colonists. The number who resisted the assimilative process by which the majority of their brethren became Independents, and who still remained zealous for Presbyterianism, were ever on the alert to stir up agitation on its behalf, and the victory secured by the Presbyterians in England under the Long Parliament made them only the more restless and aggressive. Partly, therefore, to disarm their antagonism, but chiefly in order to consolidate and unify the Churches themselves, and lift them out of their unintegrated condition and position of isolation, a plan of government was adopted, entitled, " A Platform of Church Discipline, gathered out of the Word of God, and agreed upon by the Elders and Messengers of the Churches assembled in the Synod at Cambridge in New England, to be presented to the Churches and General Court for their consideration and acceptance in the Lord." This was presented accordingly, and after various changes and modifications—none, however, affectting the substance of the Platform—it was adopted in 1651.[1]

[1] "This Platform is the most important document produced by the Congregationalists of the seventeenth century, for it most clearly represents the belief of the Churches and their system of government for more than one hundred years. It was, indeed, the legally recognised standard till 1780."—*Congregationalists in America*, by Rev. Albert E. Dunning, D.D., p. 149.

The judgment of Dr. Dexter is, that the early Congregationalism of America was Barrowism, and not Brownism, a Congregationalised Presbyterianism, or a Presbyterianised Congregationalism, which had its roots in the one system, and its branches in the other; which was essentially Genevan within the local congregation, and essentially other outside of it. The forty or fifty churches which, "for the substance of it," adopted the Cambridge Platform, held this general system, indeed, with varying degrees of strictness, from the almost Presbyterianism of Hingham and Newbury to the large-minded and large-hearted Robinsonism of the mother *Mayflower* Church.[1] This system came to be designated and known as **The New England Way.**

Growth of Independency or Congregationalism in New England.—The following is a brief summary of the position of Independency in New England at the close of 1648, the year when "The Cambridge Platform" had been agreed upon as the common basis of Church government. These twenty-eight years since the landing of the Fathers in Plymouth may be regarded as the creative era of American Congregationalism. The Plymouth Church remained alone till 1629. In 1648 the number of churches in New England had grown to fifty-one. Thirty of this number were planted in Massachusetts, nine in New Plymouth, five in Connecticut, five in New Haven, two in New Hampshire. To this number must be added two or three on Long Island, and one in Virginia. The leading or

[1] *Congregationalism as seen in its Literature*, pp. 463, 464.

organising minds were Cotton, Hooker, Norton, Davenport, and the learned and credulous Cotton Mather. In less than fifty years after this, *i.e.* in 1696, there were, according to President Hills, one hundred thousand souls in New England, and one hundred and thirty Congregational churches.[1]

The Sabbath in New England.—It must never be forgotten that New England, to use the words of the excellent Francis Higginson, "was a plantation of religion, not a plantation of trade." "New England was the colony of conscience; if they make religion as twelve and the world as thirteen, such an one hath not the spirit of a true New England man." This religious character, impressed upon it in its nascent condition, it has never lost; it has permeated its whole history and character and institutions. "The principles of New England," says De Tocqueville, "spread at first to the neighbouring States; then they passed successively to the more distant ones; and at length they imbued the whole Confederation." The government of New England was as near an approach to a theocracy as the world has seen since that of the Jewish Church. As truly as to the Jews which came out of Egypt, it had been said by their sovereign ruler to these expatriated exiles: "Ye shall be unto me a kingdom of priests and a holy nation." To these early settlers in the West worship was a necessity and a passion. "It had been as unusual for a right New England man to live without an able ministry as for a

[1] Punchard's *History of Congregationalism in America*, vol. i. p. 627, note.

smith to work his iron without a fire." It was liberty to worship God according to their own conscience which had brought them over the sea, and now that this liberty was within their reach, they enjoyed it in no stinted measure. It was with keen and ardent joy

"They rolled the Psalm to wintry skies."

Their first meeting-house was a "timber fort," both strong and comely, with flat roof and battlements, and was erected on an eminence behind the town. It thus served a threefold purpose. It was an observatory from which they could observe the approach of scout and Indian marauder; it was also a powder-magazine, protected on all sides by a cannon-mounted rampart; and it was also a meeting-house for worship,—a combination of war and gospel, which was necessary both for their safety and comfort. This was the house of worship for twenty-eight years. The settlers were eager and glad to build their meeting-houses, for they looked upon them as the visible sign of the theocracy which the Most High had established in their midst, and of the covenant they had made with Him. But lest some future settlements should be slow or indifferent about doing their duty, it was enacted in 1675 that a meeting-house should be erected in every town in the colony; and if the people failed to do so at once, the magistrates were empowered to build it, and to charge the cost of its erection to the town.

In Massachusetts we find, among other rules and regulations framed by the Company for the colonists, that the inhabitants were to "surcease" their labour every Saturday throughout the year at three of the clock in the afternoon, and to spend the rest of that day in catechising and preparation for the Sabbath, as the ministers should direct. "From sunset on Saturday until Sunday night they would not shave, have rooms swept, nor beds made, have food prepared, nor cooking utensils and tableware washed." The ministers of New England laid great stress upon this prolonged preparation for the Sabbath. It was a prevalent belief among the early colonists that the practice of working on the eve of the Sabbath was one certain to call down the judgment of heaven upon them. One man who had worked an hour after sunset at the repairing of a mill-dam went home to find that his child had fallen into an uncovered well in the cellar of his house, and was drowned. This is related by Winthrop as an instance of divine retribution, and, adds the pious and good man, "the father freely, in the open congregation, did acknowledge it the righteous hand of God for his profaning His holy day." "Sweet to the pilgrims and to their descendants was the hush of their calm Saturday night and their still, tranquil Sabbath—sign and token to them, not only of the weekly rest ordained in the Creation, but of the eternal rest to come." The universal quiet and peace of the community showed the primitive instinct of a pure simple devotion, the sincere religion which knew no compromise in spiritual things, no half-way obedience to God's word, but rested absolutely on the Lord's Day, as was commanded. No work, no play, no idle strolling was known; no sign of "human life or motion was seen except the necessary care of the patient cattle and other dumb beasts, the orderly and quiet going to and from the meeting, and at the nooning, a visit to the churchyard to stand by the side of the silent dead. This absolute obedience to the letter as well as to the spirit of God's word was one of the most typical traits of the character of the Puritans, and appeared to them to be one of the most vital points of their religion."[1] In her charming book, *The Sabbath in Puritan New England*, Miss Earle gives a graphic and amusing description of the early meeting-houses, with their old-fashioned pews and their seats allocated with nice discrimination according to the position and character of their occupiers. The description given of the icy temperature of the meeting-house is enough to affect us with a fit of shivering, even as we read it at the fireside. "One can but wonder whether that fell scourge of New England, that hereditary curse, consumption, did not have its first germs evolved and nourished in our Puritan ancestors by the Spartan custom of sitting through the long winter services in the icy, deathlike meeting-houses." This is an entry from the diary of Judge Sewall: "The communion bread was frozen pretty hard, and rattled sadly into the plates. Extraordinary cold storm of wind and snow. Blows much more as coming home at noon, and so holds on. Bread was frozen at the Lord's table. Though 'twas so cold John Tuckerman was baptized. At six o'clock my ink freezes, so that I can hardly write by a good fire in my wife's chamber. Yet was very comfortable at meeting." In the bitter winter weather women carried to meeting little foot-stoves. This, however, was done furtively,

[1] *The Sabbath in Puritan New England*, by Alice Morse Earle.

as not quite comporting with New England ideas of enduring hardness. It is told of one worshipper that when it was proposed to introduce a stove into the wintry meeting-house, he withheld his subscription, on the ground that "good preaching kept him hot enough without stoves."

"Sadly down through the centuries is ringing in our ears the gloomy rattle of that frozen sacramental bread on the church plate, telling to us the solemn story of the austere, comfortless church life of our ancestors. Would that the sound could bring to our chilled hearts the same steadfast and pure Christian faith that made their gloomy, freezing services warm with God's loving presence! . . . Patient, frugal, God-fearing, and industrious,—cruel and intolerant sometimes, but never cowardly,—sternly obeying the word of God in the spirit and the letter, but erring sometimes in the interpretation thereof, surely they had no traits to shame us, to keep us from thrilling with pride at the drop of their blood which runs in our backsliding veins. Nothing can more plainly show their distinguishing characteristics, nothing is so fully typical of the motive, the spirit of their lives, as their reverent observance of the Lord's day."[1]

 **Social Life in New England.** — The austerity and gloom of Puritanism is a theme on which it does not require much ability to grow eloquent. It lends itself

---

[1] *The Sabbath in Puritan New England.* The book abounds with lively and attractive etchings, and there is an absence of the straining and exaggeration which so often occurs in books and essays professing to describe Puritan life and manners.

only too easily to satire and criticism, and much that is entertaining, if not quite true, has been written about it. In New England, as elsewhere, life was a stern, solemn, and colourless thing. How could it be otherwise with men trained in such a school as these settlers had been, inured from their very birth to toil, hardship, and privation, and with no leisure to cultivate the graces and amenities of human life. It would have been a miracle if the history of such a people had been other than "dry and unpicturesque." "There is no rustle of silks, no waving of plumes, no clink of golden spurs." Instead, we have the noise of axe and hammer and saw, an apotheosis of dogged work, work for mere subsistence, for the sheer necessaries of life,—work, the dignity of which Carlyle chants in his pæan, and in comparison with which all else is chaff and dust—"Extrinsically, prosaic; intrinsically, it is poetic and noble." "It has been the fashion lately," adds Mr. Lowell,[1] "with a few feeble-minded persons to undervalue the New England Puritans, as if they were nothing more than gloomy and narrow-minded fanatics." It is more than thirty years since these words were written, but the word "lately" may as well stand to-day; nor need the fashion be restricted to a few feeble-minded persons. The error has a wider and more reputable currency; but inveterate as it is, it has no support, save that which imagination or unreasoning prejudice is able to supply.

There can, of course, be no question as to the austereness of these American Puritans. They had crossd the sea, not only to get rid of a persecuting Church, but also to

[1] *Among my Books*, p. 232.

get out of the reach of profligacy, social corruption, and contagion. "Merry England," the England of the *Book of Sports*, of holiday saturnalias, with their drinking bouts and their bear-baitings and cock-fightings; this was the Babylon which had cast them forth, and every shred and trace of which they were determined to extrude from the land of their adoption. They set up, as they believed, in sheer self-protection, a system of wholesale proscription which was bound in the long-run to react injuriously upon them and their children. Everything that savoured of lightness, cheerfulness, and recreation was discouraged and frowned upon. There were to be no amusements save such as could be extracted from the social accessories of religion and worship. No persons might possess cards, or dice, or other means of gambling. Dancing was condemned as an encouragement to wantonness, or as inconsistent with a sober and grave carriage. The "worldly luxury of long hair" on the part of men was denounced as sinful, or, if not sinful, "uncomely and prejudicial to the common good." "The sale of everything was regulated by law, with such minuteness as to reach the cost of a meal at an inn, and even the price of a pot of beer between meals. The law fixed the price of all commodities, of all labor, and of all servants' wages. The use of tobacco was early forbidden in all public-houses and places; and though one might smoke it in his own house, it was unlawful to do so before strangers, or for one person to use it in company of another."[1] Puritan asceticism does not seem to have

---

[1] See chapter on "The Boston Puritans," in Bryant and Gay's *Popular History of the United States*, vol. ii. p. 62.

extended to matters of food and drink, and though frugality and temperance were the rule, what was thought of the attempt to make it a binding, self-denying ordinance may be gathered from an extract from a letter from Thomas Shephard, minister of Cambridge, to Governor Winthrop in 1639 : "This also I doe humbly entreat, that there may be no sin made of *drinking in any case one to another,* for I am confident that he that stands here will fall and be beat from his grounds by his own arguments; as also that the consequences will be very sad, and the thing provoking to God and man to make more sins than (as yet is seene) God Himself hath made."[1]

Extravagance, or any kind of insobriety in dress, was specially distasteful to the Puritans of New England. They felt moved to declare against " the ordinary wearing of silver, gold and silver laces," against " immoderate great sleeves," and " slashed apparel." The size of sleeve which women were allowed to wear in their dress was limited to the width of half an ell; and none were to be made " with short sleeves, whereby the nakedness of the arm may be discovered in the wearing thereof." The General Court (of Massachusetts), however, had at length to acknowledge the difficulty of enforcing such sumptuary laws, on account of " the blindness of men's minds, and the stubbournnes of theire wills," and they found it necessary to exempt from their operation persons of education and employment " above the ordinary degree." At the same time, the Court reaffirmed their " utter detestation and dislike that men or women of meane condition, educations, and callinges, should take

[1] Lowell's *Among my Books*, p. 249.

vpon them the garbe of gentlemen, by the wearinge of gold or siluer lace, or buttons or poynts at theire knees, to walke in greate bootes; or women of the same ranke to weare silk or tiffany hoodes or scarfes, which, though allowable to persons of greater estates, or more liberal education, yet we cannot but judge it intolerable in persons of such like condition." From which it will be seen that these Puritan democrats had no levelling down notions as to the "natural rights" of all men. They had notions about "dignities" which perhaps would not with perfect symmetry have fitted in with other parts of their creed.

The Jewish Theocracy the ideal of the Puritans of New England.—For these sumptuary laws and regulations the Puritans of New England pleaded the sanction of the Mosaic legislation. The Bible was their statute-book, the law of Moses their fountain of authority. The first code of laws, drawn up at the request of the General Court of Massachusetts, was taken entirely from the Old Testament. This was rejected in favour of a more liberal and discriminating code, submitted by Rev. Nathaniel Ward, who had had the advantage of a legal as well as a theological training, and thought that something could be learned from Justinian as well as Moses. This was "**The Body of Liberties**," which was adopted in 1641, and was the first Constitution of Massachusetts, and the foundation of all subsequent Constitutions. The Hebrew law of inheritance and of servitude (for slavery, as afterwards developed and practised, was expressly disallowed) were followed so far as their underlying principles were concerned. The breaking of the Sabbath, smiting and cursing parents, were not made capital offences. The punishment of death was reserved for ten kinds of misdemeanours. These were idolatry, witchcraft, when " direct, express, presumptuous, or high-handed," homicide, whether committed in malice or in passion, adultery,[1] two other crimes of lust, man stealing, false witness, " of purpose to take any man's life," and treason against the commonwealth. Lying and lechery, improper behaviour of any kind, extravagance in dress, profaneness, uncomely speeches, swearing, " either by the holy name of God or any other oath," were all made penal offences. In " The Body of Liberties " it was enacted that whosoever should blaspheme the name of God the Father, the Son, or the Holy Ghost, should be put to death. To deny the infallibility or inspiration of any book of the Old or New Testaments was to incur the penalty of fine, stripes, and, in extreme cases, even death. " A wanton gospeller " was, of all men, most exasperating to a Boston Puritan—" a kind of human vermin which he felt bound to extirpate." A wanton gospeller was one who made free with his criticism on the preacher or preached word, "making God's ways contemptible and ridiculous"; and for this offence he was to be condemned to stand in a public place for two hours upon a raised block, with the inscription " a wanton gospeller " fixed on his breast.[2] In Massachusetts and New Haven the support

[1] For the death penalty in respect of adultery was afterwards substituted the practice of the offender being compelled to stand up in some public place with the letter A in scarlet displayed conspicuously on the breast. See Hawthorne's *Scarlet Letter*.
[2] " The Boston Puritans," Bryant and Gay's *History*, vol. ii. chap. iii.

of the ministry and religious ordinances, and the duty of constant attendance upon them, were enforced by law. As in the mother country, no one was allowed to absent himself from church without lawful or reasonable excuse. In the colony of Virginia [1] this law was more stringently enforced. Church attendance was here made absolutely compulsory, " upon pain, for the first fault, to lose their provision and allowance for the whole week following; for the second, to lose said allowance, and also to be whipped; and for the third, to suffer death."

Still, the code of Massachusetts and New Haven (the latter was even sterner and more tainted with Mosaism) was mild and humane when compared with that of the mother country.[2] There were, at the close of Elizabeth's reign, thirty-one kinds of crime for which the death penalty was inflicted; afterwards they reached the enormous number of one hundred and twenty-three. The principles on which the written code of Massachusetts was framed were, at any rate, a great advance upon the chaos and unintelligibility of English jurisprudence. If they were strict, and sometimes magnified sins into crimes, they were at least intelligible, and people knew what to expect from their infraction.

In the eyes of the Boston Puritans it was the distinctive merit of their system that it sought to reproduce in the theocracy of New England the minuteness and exactitude of the laws according to which the theocracy in the wilderness was governed. It sought, in a word, to govern men in accordance with the will of God,

---

[1] Palfrey's *History of New England*, vol. ii. p. 34, note.
[2] *Ibid.* vol. i. p. 27.

by exercising an immediate supervision over the conduct of every individual in the community in all his private as well as public acts and relations. In their zeal for making men righteous by sumptuary legislation, the rulers and law-makers of New England were admonished by signs that filled them with dismay that they had overshot the mark. *Naturam expellas furcâ, tamen usque recurret.* The tide of vice and uncleanness could not be kept out of the fancied Arcadia of New England by such ineffectual dykes as they endeavoured to construct. The laws against lechery were specially severe and drastic, yet unnatural crimes were frequent, and punishment was continually inflicted for the vice of unchastity. The prevalence of this vice may be in a large measure accounted for by the influx of a heterogeneous population, made up of adventurers from Europe, and whose natural depravity was intensified by the attempted pressure of restraint. Anyhow, such doings spread great consternation throughout the colonies. " Marvilious it may be," exclaims Governor Bradford, " to see and consider how some kind of wickedness did grow and break forth here," notwithstanding the austerity of public opinion and the severity of the law, both exceeding that of any place he ever knew or heard of ; and the latter so relentless as to be " somewhat censured by moderate and good men." For such wickedness Bradford can only account on the supposition that " the divell may carrie a greater spite against the Churches of Christ and the gospell hear," and that " Satane hath more power in these heathen lands, as som have thought, then in more Christian nations, especially over God's servants in them."[1] But perhaps we may be pardoned for thinking that the overstrained character of the laws that were enacted for their suppression, and the mixed population of the colonies, as well as the publicity which was necessarily given to all flagitious offences in so small a community, these furnish a more rational explanation of the matter than the occult and malign influence of the Evil One.

Education in New England.—The colonists of New England would have subscribed to the opinion that "it is better to be unborn than untaught." They saw no security for religion or social order save as these were built round by the bulwark of cultivated intelligence. The Puritans dreaded to have an illiterate ministry. They dreaded also to have an illiterate people. A common school, public as the highway, was being projected by the Fathers at Plymouth at a very early date, just when they had succeeded in scaring away the wolf of starvation, and when the number of men, women, and children, all told, did not exceed one hundred and eighty. In 1635 the inhabitants of Boston passed a vote "that our brother Philemon Pormont be entreated to become schoolmaster for the teaching and nurturing of youth among us." The system of common schools came into existence as early as 1647, by an Act of the General Court: "To the end that learning may not be buried in the graves of our forefathers in Church and commonwealth, the Lord assisting our endeavours, it is therefore ordered by this Court and authority thereof, that every township in this

[1] *History of Plymouth Plantation*, pp. 385, 386.

jurisdiction, after the Lord hath increased them to fifty householders, shall then forthwith appoint one within their towns to teach all such children as shall resort to him to write and read." These common schools, now thickly planted down throughout the towns and villages of New England, may be said to constitute " the great discovery of our Puritan Fathers." " They were the first lawgivers who saw clearly and enforced practically the simple moral and political truth, that knowledge was not an alms to be dependent on the chance charity of private men, or the precarious pittance of a trust-fund, but a sacred debt which the commonwealth owed to every one of her children." [1]

In 1636 the famous **Harvard College**[2] was founded by John Harvard, a graduate of Cambridge, who had crossed the Atlantic to become the "minister of God's word at Charlestown." It was of his poverty that John Harvard gave to the college that immortalises his name. His endowment consisted of half of his property, namely, £400 and his library. The General Court voted to the cost of its erection a sum equal to a year's rate of the whole colony, and in honour of the mother university the name of the town was changed to Cambridge. The assembly which decreed the establishing of the college,—fitly pre-

---

[1] Lowell's *Among my Books*, p. 231. As to the origin of the common school system, whether imported from Geneva or Holland, the reader may consult Mr. Douglas Campbell. He contends earnestly, as against Mr. Bancroft and other historians, for the Netherlands as its birthplace and cradle,—*The Puritan in Holland, England, and America*, ii. pp. 338–340.

[2] Quincy, *History of Harvard University*.

sided over by an Oxonian, Henry Vane, the friend of Milton,—is said to have been "the first body in which the people, by their representatives, gave their own money to found a place of education." "The act was a memorable one, if we have regard to all the circumstances of the year in which it was done. On every side danger was in the air. Threatened at once with an Indian war, with the enmity of the home Government, and with grave dissensions among themselves, the year 1636 was a trying one indeed for the little community of Puritans, and their founding a college by public taxation just at this time is a striking illustration of their unalterable purpose to realise in this new home their ideal of an educated Christian society."[1]

[1] Fiske's *Beginnings of New England*, p. 111.

The Growth of Intolerance in New England

MEMORABLE EVENTS AND DATES

The Commonwealth in England . . 1649–1660
George Fox began his public preaching . 1648

CONTENTS OF CHAPTER VI

Spirit of Intolerance, Cromwell on—Measures against Anabaptistry—Clarke, Crandall, and Holmes—Imprisonment, fines, and whipping—Baptist Church in Charlestown—Cessation of persecution—Baptism and Anabaptism—Law-abiding Baptists protected—Quakers persecuted, imprisoned, banished, scourged, mutilated, put to death—Indignation provoked by these cruelties—Rhode Island refused to persecute, nevertheless suffered for its lenity—Quakerism provoked Roger Williams—Ranters not Quakers—Gross excesses—Error of rulers, Lodge and Lowell on—Massachusetts specially chargeable with intolerance, Goldwin Smith on—Roger Williams banished, not for religion but for political reasons—Puritan leaders intolerant, Endicott, Cotton, Ward, Winthrop, Dudley—Sir H. Vane's hatred of Intolerance—Popular feeling in Massachusetts against oppression—Massachusetts increased in tolerance as with strength—The Pilgrim Fathers not persecutors—Sewel's blunder—Growth of tolerance in New Plymouth—Puritans and Puritans—Doyle—*Saturday Review.*

CHAPTER VI

THE GROWTH OF INTOLERANCE IN NEW ENGLAND

IT would be an obvious and, indeed, inexcusable omission in a history professing even in barest outline, to exhibit the growth of the Puritan theocracy in New England, did it contain no allusion to the spirit of exclusiveness which gradually became grafted upon it, and culminated at length in active and bitter persecution. We have already seen one or two portentous manifestations of this spirit. We have seen how two of the early emigrants were banished from Salem because they were Churchmen, and how Massachusetts cast out Roger Williams, Mrs. Hutchinson, and others because their opinions had become too extreme to be tolerated. We shall find, as we investigate the matter further, fresh and melancholy confirmation of what has been often observed in connection with struggling religious parties, that those who have themselves suffered the evil and misery of oppression, are nothing loth in the day of their power to inflict like suffering upon others. "Every sect saith, 'Oh, give me liberty!' But give it to him, and (to his power) he will not yield it to anybody else. Is it ingenuous to ask liberty and not to give it? What greater hypocrisy than for those who were oppressed by the bishops to become the greatest oppressors themselves so soon as their yoke was removed?"[1]

We do not propose to attempt anything like a description of the ecclesiastical controversies which at successive periods during the seventeenth century agitated the Church life of New England. There are two, however, which we must not pass over, not only because of their importance, but because they were the occasion of much heart-burning, and have done more to excite prejudice against the Fathers of New England than all the other "evil and uncomfortable occurrents" (to use Cotton Mather's phrase) which were so rife during that century. These were the Baptist and the Quaker controversy.

Persecution of Baptists. — The first Baptist Church in America was founded, as we have seen, by Roger Williams; but independently of Williams it is manifest, from the nature of the soil, that among such a plentiful crop of heresies as Rhode Island got the credit of producing, "Anabaptistry" was not likely to be wanting. It was inevitable, too, that the seed should be carried into the colony of Massachusetts, if it did not spring there independently on its own account. Anyhow, the seed was sown there also, for in 1644 we find Winthrop writing: " Anabaptistry increased and spread in the country, which occasioned the magistrates at the last Court to draw up an order[2] for banishing such as continued obstinate after due conviction." The austere and intolerant Endicott was then governor of the

---

[1] *Cromwell's Letters and Speeches.*
[2] Palfrey's *History of New England*, vol. ii. p. 346.

colony. Some years after the passing of this order, John Clarke, who had been educated as a physician, and was now the pastor of the first Baptist Church in Newport, accompanied by two friends, Crandall and Holmes, went on a visit to the house of an old friend and fellow-Baptist at Lynn, ten miles from Boston. The sequel proved that this was indeed putting their head into the lion's den, or rather, into the lion's mouth. The next day being Sunday, they agreed to have a religious service among themselves, and while Clarke was speaking, two constables entered the house and arrested them. They were hauled off to the meeting-house of the town, and when the service was over, Clarke rose and asked leave to "propose a few things to the congregation." This was, of course, forbidden. Next morning they were all brought before the magistrate, and sentenced to be imprisoned in the jail at Boston. The day after, they were brought before Governor Endicott, who reviled them with being Anabaptists, their answer to which was summarily cut short, and they were each of them fined, Clarke £20, Holmes £30, and Crandall £5, and in default of payment, "each was to be well whipped." A friend came forward to pay the fine on behalf of Clarke; but Holmes, refusing to avail himself of help so little to his mind, was subjected to the humiliation of being whipped. It does not appear that any further penalty of the like kind was inflicted upon persons embracing and professing Baptist views. For years the law against Baptists remained practically a dead letter. In 1665, however, a Baptist Church was organised in Charlestown, which ultimately became the first Baptist Church of Boston, and its action in receiving to its communion those who had been excommunicated by other Churches appears to have led the authorities to deal with it in very summary fashion. Five of its members were disfranchised, and two were sent to prison, where they remained for nearly a year. Three of the leaders were sentenced to be banished. No further proceedings appear to have been instituted against the members of this sect, for two years after we have the testimony of the agents of the colony in England to the effect: "As for the Anabaptists, they are now subject to no other penal statutes than those of the Congregational way."[1]

It is not at first sight easy to explain why, for holding the apparently harmless opinion that infants are not fit subjects for baptism (the question of immersion does not seem to have figured in the controversy), Christian men should have been subjected to persecution or suffering. It seems to exhibit the spirit of intolerance in its very worst form. But it must be borne in mind that to the Puritans of that day baptism was not the innocuous seeming creed which it is to us. It was identified with Anabaptism, and Anabaptism had a history behind it full of terrorising significance. In the sixteenth century Baptism or Anabaptism (for practically there was no attempt to discriminate between them) gave the name to "one of the wildest and fiercest sects ever bred within the pale of the Christian Church."[2] The mem-

---

[1] Palfrey's *History*, vol. ii. p. 486.

[2] "Anabaptism," says Jeremy Taylor, in his famous argument for liberty, "is as much to be rooted out as anything that is the greatest pest and nuisance to the public interest."

bers of this sect denied the authority of the magistrates, the lawfulness of taking oaths, and many of the cardinal Christian doctrines, and were guilty of gross enormities, such as polygamy, rebellion, theft, murder, etc. Considering, then, the flagitious errors and excesses into which the Anabaptists had fallen, and by which they had acquired such an unsavoury reputation, it is little to be wondered at that the Puritans of Massachusetts should view with horror and alarm the possible recrudescence of such errors, and without making any attempt to discriminate between them should regard Baptists of every description as eminently unsafe and dangerous people.[1]

Whatever may be said in reprobation of the course they pursued, there is no doubt that the rulers of Massachusetts were sincerely perplexed as to how they should act in regard to those holding and avowing Baptist convictions. "The truth is," said the General Court in their "Declaration" in November 1646, "the great trouble we have been put into, and hazard also, by fanatistical and anabaptistical spirits, whose conscience and religion hath been only to set forth themselves and raise contentions in the country, did provoke us to provide for our safety. . . . But for such as differ from us only in judgment, and live peaceably amongst us, without occasioning

---

[1] Crosby's *History of the English Baptists*, lxxiii, xxiv, vol. i. p. 196; Palfrey's *History*, vol. i. p. 487, note, also vol. ii. p. 348; Motley's *Rise of the Dutch Republic*, vol. i. pp. 79, 80; Robertson's *History of the Reign of Charles the Fifth*, bk. v. "The 'superadding of Anabaptistry to Sans-culottism' (Carlyle's *Cromwell*, vol. ii. p. 70) alarmed the magistrates of Massachusetts, as it soon after alarmed the Dictator of England;" Palfrey's *History*, vol. ii. p. 348, note.

disturbance, etc., such have no cause to complain; for it hath never been as yet put in execution against any of them, although such are known to live amongst us."[1] They were glad of any pretext to restrain them from enforcing the law against Anabaptists. It is said that two of the presidents of Harvard College were Anabaptists.

Persecution of the Quakers.—The sufferings of the Baptists were mildness itself compared with the severities inflicted on the people called Quakers. This is the darkest and most shameful blot upon the theocracy of New England. Quakerism made its appearance in Boston in 1656, being thither imported by two unprotected women, Mary Fisher and Ann Austin, who had come from the Barbadoes. They were charged with holding " very dangerous, heretical, and blasphemous opinions"; their baggage was searched, and all their books and tracts confiscated, and after being kept in prison for five weeks they were shipped back to the Barbadoes. Two days after, another contingent of the same persuasion, eight in number, were in like manner imprisoned and then sent back to England. Nothing daunted by this treatment, some of them returned; nor could all the severities which the authorities could devise for their suppression—scourging, imprisonment, and threatenings—avail to quench their ardour or abate their "testimony." The punishment decreed against all who came within the jurisdiction of the Court was the loss of one ear on the first conviction; on the second, the cropping of the other ear; after the

---

[1] Palfrey's *History*, vol. ii. p. 348, note; Bancroft's *History*, vol. i. p. 324, revised edition, p. 350.

third conviction, the tongue was to be bored with a hot iron, and then they were to be imprisoned, with hard labour, till they could be got rid of "at their own charge." It was made criminal for any one to harbour any of "the accursed sect." Any captain of a vessel carrying a Quaker into port was to be fined £100, and in default of payment, to be imprisoned till the fine was paid. Three Quaker women were stripped to the waist and flogged through eleven towns, and this in the winter season, amid frost and snow. Persecution had the effect it has had so often on its hapless victims, and upon those who have witnessed their sufferings. It begot a strange and weird eagerness for the crown of martyrdom. The sufferers were most numerous where they were most feared. Their fortitude, their patience under suffering, their unwavering conviction in the righteousness of their cause, won for them friends and sympathisers among all classes of the community. The authorities did their utmost to restrain every manifestation of sympathy, even to the extent of sentencing any person convicted of being present at a Quaker meeting to a fine of 10s., and for taking part in any such meeting a fine of £5.

Four Quakers were hanged—William Robinson and Marmaduke Stevenson in 1659, Mary Dyer in 1660, and William Leddra in 1661. Leddra's was the last execution in Boston for the cause of religious opinion. "What do you gain," cried Wenlock Christison, "by taking Quakers' lives? For the last man that you put to death, here are five come in his room. If ye have power to take my life, God can raise up ten of His servants in my stead."

At last the pent up indignation of the people, inspired by these atrocities, broke out in such violence that the magistrates began to quail before it, and were forced to stay their hands, and to repeal the iniquitous laws. It is due to the other united colonies to say that though they were guilty of harsh and repressive measures, they did not go the length of enacting *capital* laws against the Quakers; it was only by the Puritans of Massachusetts that they were hanged. The persecution of the Quakers continued for five years, and during that time it was a great grievance to Massachusetts that no assistance was given by the towns of Narragansett Bay in extirpating the heretics who "propagate the kingdome of Sathan."

Rhode Island would have no part in Persecution. —It is to the everlasting honour of Rhode Island that, when appealed to by the commissioners of the united colonies, they replied in these terms: "As concerning these Quakers (so called) which are now among us, we have no law among us whereby to punish any for only declaring by words, etc., their minds and understanding concerning the things and ways of God as to salvation and an eternal condition." They did not deny that the doctrines of the Quakers tended "to very absolute cutting down and overturning relations and civil government among men"; nevertheless, they believed that the most effectual way of defeating their designs was to oppose them with no weapons other than arguments and moral dissuasives. To meet them with weapons of another kind would be to defeat their own object, inasmuch as they delight "to be persecuted by civil powers; and when they are so, they are like to gain more adherence by the conceit of their patient sufferings than by consent to their pernicious sayings." It is easy for us to see that the Rhode Islanders took the only right and reasonable ground; but, unfortunately for their very sound and enlightened theory, it did not receive practical illustration in the behaviour of the persecuted sect which they thus welcomed to their asylum. Rhode Island became a very cave of Adullam for Quaker refugees. They kept the whole colony in a state of constant embroilment and dispeace. There is no doubt that Roger Williams gave expression to the feeling of grievance on his own part and on the part of his fellow-colonists when he said: "We suffer for their sake, and are accounted their abettors." Wide as was his toleration and boundless his charity, he could not hold himself back from contending against their pernicious errors, their unscriptural opinions;[1] and his controversy with Fox, contained in a book of more than 300 printed pages, entitled, *George Fox Digged out of his Burrowes*, is perhaps the only controversy of his life into which he threw a spice of acrimony and bitterness, though he himself playfully describes it as "sharp Scripture language."

From the description of them just given, it will be seen that the Quakers of three hundred years ago

[1] His irrepressible zeal is shown in the fact that when he was seventy-three years old he rowed himself in a boat the whole length of Narragansett Bay to engage in a theological tournament against three Quaker champions.

had little in common with the peaceably-disposed, excellent, and irreproachable people we now know as the Society of Friends. Strictly speaking, they were not Quakers, but Ranters, the Ranters whom Fox spoke of as "*great opposers of Friends*, and disturbers of our meetings."[1] Yet these were the species of Quakers with which New England and Old England were made painfully familiar. At one time more than four thousand of them were in English jails. They were a disorderly and turbulent set of people, guilty of most censurable behaviour, the most wanton acts of outrage and indecency. They railed against ministers and magistrates when they met them on the road, interrupted public worship, harangued the people in public places with loud voice and excited gestures, and even women went naked through the public streets. A Quakeress appeared at a meeting-house in Massachusetts attired in sackcloth, and with her face painted black, in order to represent the coming of the small-pox. " The Quakers were drunk with religious zeal. They appeared naked in the streets and churches, hideous with grease and lampblack, breaking bottles, and raising riot and disturbance everywhere."

Undoubtedly the great error into which the authorities of Massachusetts fell was in attempting to extirpate them as fanatics and heretics, rather than as enemies of public order, and as disturbers of the peace. Some of the severities directed against them may be on the latter ground justly defended.[2] For the more drastic

---

[1] See chapter on "Quakerism in New England," Bryant and Gay's *History*, vol. ii. p. 175.

[2] " The magistrates took the ground that Massachusetts belonged

measures—those that were directed against dangerous, heretical, and blasphemous opinions—no apology can be offered. They are indefensible. The execution of Mary Dyer, William Robinson, Marmaduke Stevenson, and William Leddra was a piece of horrible and atrocious barbarity, and reflects upon Endicott and Norton, the principal agents concerned in it, lasting infamy and disgrace.

It is possible to reprobate and condemn the intolerance of the Puritans of Massachusetts,—rather, we should say, the *leaders* of the Puritans of Massachusetts, for it is clear that the body of opinion and feeling in the colony was not with them, but against them,—and yet to disavow all sympathy with the reckless unmeasured denunciation which has been poured out upon them in connection with their treatment of the Quakers. " It has been the fashion in these days to represent the case as if all the wrong were on one side, and all human sympathy should be with the Quakers. It seldom happens in any quarrel that all the wrong is on one side. Life would be much simpler if such were the case. In this instance wrong was largely on one side, but not entirely so."[1] Lowell's judgment upon this matter must, we think, constrain the sympathy, if it does not command the entire assent, of all who have fairly considered this question: " Whether they were right or wrong in their dealing with the Quakers is

absolutely to its people, and that they had the right now, as in earlier days, to put down opposition, and banish all malcontents. The theory was correct enough."—*History of English Colonies in America*, by Henry Cabot Lodge, p. 354.

[1] *Boston*, by Henry Cabot Lodge, pp. 46-48.

not a question to be decided glibly after two centuries' struggle towards a conception of toleration very imperfect even yet, perhaps impossible to human nature. If they did not choose what seems to us the wisest way of keeping the devil out of their household, they certainly had a very honest will to keep him out, which we might emulate with advantage." [1]

Massachusetts less advanced in regard to freedom and toleration than any other State.—"It is wrong," says Mr. Goldwin Smith, "to say that the Puritans of Massachusetts left the mother country to assert the principle of liberty of conscience, and then shamefully violated that principle by their own practice. They came out, not to assert liberty of conscience, a principle which had not dawned on their minds, but to found a religious commonwealth on their own model, and in it to live the spiritual life to which they aspired." "These men had come into the wilderness to build up a theocracy, and made no pretensions of securing liberty for anybody but themselves. They were quite as intolerant of opinions that were not their own as the most inexorable persecutor that ever 'peppered' a Puritan." [2]

[1] *Among my Books : New England Two Centuries Ago*, p. 269.
[2] Bryant and Gay's *History*, vol. i. p. 537. Perhaps there is too much pepper in this criticism, and it needs to be read side by side with the statement of Mr. Douglas Campbell, in his work, *The Puritan in Holland, England, and America*. He condemns, and that strongly, the intolerance of Massachusetts. He says : "She was the only one of the colonies except Connecticut in which witches were put to death ; she alone hanged the inoffensive (save the mark) Quakers ; and her records tell the worst tale—with the exception of those of Virginia—regarding the atrocities committed on the Indians,

We have already seen how Roger Williams was banished from Massachusetts for having "broached and divulged divers new and dangerous opinions." As this furnishes a crucial instance of the charge of exclusiveness and intolerance brought against the Puritans of Massachusetts, it will be well for us to try and ascertain what really were the grounds on which the action of the authorities was based in their treatment of Roger Williams. This raises the question,

Was Roger Williams persecuted on account of his religious opinions? And we may say at once that this is one of those questions which probably never will be settled to the satisfaction of every one concerned in it. Opposite conclusions will be formed, and opposite answers given, according as the standpoint from which men view it varies, and according as their minds are swayed by varying prepossessions. On the one side, it is contended that Roger Williams suffered what he did in the cause of *soul liberty*; in other words, that it was his zeal for toleration, the rights and liberty of conscience, that made him obnoxious to the authorities of Massa-

who were robbed of their land and constantly kidnapped and sold as slaves to the southern planters. He accounts for her obscurantism on this wise, on the theory which his work is mainly written to support, that she had come less than any other colony under the influence of the Netherlands. He adds: "Much has been said in history about the severe Puritanical laws of Massachusetts. They were severe when compared with the laws of some of the other colonies, like New York and Pennsylvania, which had come more fully under a Netherland influence. But in some features they were mildness itself with those enacted at an earlier period by the government of Virginia, a pure English settlement little tainted with Puritanism."—Vol. ii. pp. 414, 415.

chusetts, and led them to insist on his expulsion from the colony. On the other side, it is maintained that toleration and soul liberty or soul oppression had nothing whatever to do with his being banished. No question of this kind was involved in it. He was not charged with heresy; the issue as between him and the Fathers did not turn upon any religious dogma. The questions which he raised, and by raising provoked opposition, were questions relating to political rights and the administration of government. It will put the matter in a clearer light if we consider for a moment what exactly were the charges brought against Roger Williams. Happily he himself has left us in no doubt as to what these were. In *Mr. Cotton's Letter Examined and Answered*, he says: "After my public trial and answers, one of the most eminent magistrates, whose name and speech may by others be remembered, stood up and spoke. Mr. Williams holds forth these four particulars: First, That we have not our land by patent from the King, but that the natives are the true owners of it, and that we ought to repent of such a receiving it by Patent. Secondly, That it is not lawful to call a wicked person to sweare to pray as being actions of God's worship. Thirdly, That it is not lawful to hear any of the Ministers of the Parish Assemblies in England. Fourthly, That the Civil Magistrates' power extends only to the bodies and goods and outward state of men, etc. I acknowledge the particulars were rightly summed up." It is evident at a glance that it is only the last particular which contains any allusion whatever to the doctrine of toleration or "soul liberty." Such allusion, indeed, as may be detected in the third, rather points to the infraction than the maintenance of this doctrine.

We have read with considerable care a work recently published, entitled, *Roger Williams, the Pioneer of Religious Liberty*,[1] in which Mr. Straus does his best to relieve Williams from the charge of being factious and self-opinionative, etc., and to affix to the leaders in Massachusetts the odium of intolerance and persecution. We recognise the earnestness and ability with which he has discharged his task, but we cannot honestly say that his success is equal to his zeal, or that he has in any way weakened the argument or discredited the contention of those who hold that Roger Williams was banished from Salem, not for his religious opinions, but for political reasons, because he identified himself with doctrines and opinions which were believed to be subversive of the safety and even the existence of the rising commonwealth. That this was the conviction of those who were the means of his banishment, we have no manner of doubt. They may have been mistaken in so believing, to some extent it is very probable that they were, but their sincerity is unimpeachable; nor does a candid examination of their conduct constrain any other conclusion than that they were moved, not by a malignant and persecuting spirit, but by the prudent instinct of self-protection. This admission does not in any wise detract from our admiration of Roger Williams, nor lessen our conviction that he was a noble, magnanimous, broad-minded man, swayed by a

[1] By Oscar S. Straus. London: T. Fisher Unwin. New York: The Century Co. 1894.

passion for liberty as pure and intense as ever glowed in a human soul. Nay more, we confess that necessary as it seems to us that he should have been restrained from following divisive courses by propagating his opinions, our sympathies go out to him in his banishment and exile, as they do not go out to his judges and those who inflicted this sentence upon him, and we cannot but feel that his was the real triumph and the stainless and lasting glory.[1]

> "And more true joy Marcellus exiled feels
> Than Cæsar with a senate at his heels."

The spirit of intolerance was deeply ingrained in the minds of some of the Puritan leaders. John Endicott was a passionate, domineering, yet disinterested ruler, an unsparing and conscientious bigot. Cotton only disapproved of persecution when it was directed against truth; it was the duty of truth to persecute error. " Better tolerate hypocrites and tares," he said, " than thorns and briars." Nathaniel Ward, who drew up the first legal code, known as the Body of Liberties, said, " Polypiety is the greatest

[1] Dr. Dexter, in his *As to Roger Williams*, Boston 1876, has thoroughly discussed the question as to Williams being expelled from Massachusetts on account of his religious opinions, and justifies, we think, completely the verdict of Dr. Palfrey (*History of New England*, vol. i. p. 413), that " the sound and generous principle of a perfect freedom of the conscience in religious concerns can scarcely be shown to have been involved in the dispute."

We would take this opportunity of directing attention to an article on " The alleged Persecution of Massachusetts, or Justice to the Pilgrims," which appeared in 1892 in the March number of *New Englander and Yale Review*. This article is specially valuable for the sources of information and authority which it marshals and suggests.

impiety in the world. It is said that men ought to have
liberty of their conscience, and that it is persecution to
debar them of it; I can rather stand amazed than reply
to this: it is an astonishment to think that the braines
of men should be parboyl'd in such impious ignorance.
Let all the wits under heaven lay their heads together
and find an Assertion worse than this (one excepted), I will
Petition to be chosen the universal Ideal of the world." [1]
"The elder Winthrop had, I believe," says Bancroft,[2]
"relented before his death, and professed himself weary
of banishing heretics; the soul of the younger Winthrop
was incapable of harbouring a thought of intolerant
cruelty; but the rugged Dudley was not mellowed by
old age. 'God forbid,' said he, 'our love for the truth
should be grown so cold that we should tolerate errors.
I die no libertine.' Very different, however, was the
spirit of Sir Henry Vane. 'It were better,' he said,
'not to censure any persons for matters of a religious
concernment.'" With Roger Williams, with Milton, and
Cromwell, he held that persecution for the sake of religious opinion was both a blunder and a crime. It is
evident that in this Governor Vane carried with him

[1] This eminent lawyer-divine outdoes all the peculiarities of his style when writing of toleration. "We have been reputed as Colluvies of wild Opinionists, swarmed into a remote wilderness to find elbow-room for our Phanatic doctrines and practices; I trust our diligence past, and constant sedulity against such persons and courses, will plead better things for us. I dare take upon me to be the Herauld of New England so far as to proclaim to the World, in the name of our Colony, that all Familists, Antinomians, Anabaptists, and other enthusiasts, shall have free Liberty to keep away from us: and such as will come, to be gone as fast as they can, the sooner the better."—Bryant and Gay's *History*, vol. ii. pp. 59, 60.

[2] *History*, vol. i. p. 336, revised edition, p. 362.

the weight of opinion among the colonists. They rose up again and again in arraignment of and revolt against the policy of their rulers, and there can be little doubt that it was owing to the growing body of adverse public opinion that the reign of persecution ceased as soon as it did. "Massachusetts, on whom, as the most powerful of the colonies, lay the heaviest responsibility for her own safety and the safety of her allies, had used greater rigour than the rest in the maintenance of order and in the removal of dissentients. But in thirty-five years she had grown powerful enough and confident enough to dismiss or to relax some of the securities which, in her early feebleness, had been thought essential. It may fairly be reckoned to the credit of her people that they desisted from harsh measures, and were reconciled to the existence of dissent in some proportion to their becoming well organised and safe, while too often it has been observed in other communities, that the stronger they felt themselves the less freedom they allowed." [1]

The Fathers of New Plymouth free from the stain of persecution.—It has been asserted, and when not asserted has been frequently implied, that the Fathers and founders of New Plymouth were chargeable with persecuting those who differed from them in their religious opinions, and that consequently Mrs. Hemans' well-known tribute, that

> "They left unstained what there they found,
>   Freedom to worship God,"

must be taken with considerable abatement. In his

---

[1] Palfrey's *History of New England*, vol. ii. p. 493.

History of the People called Quakers, Sewel makes this charge without any qualification. Speaking of the followers of those men who suffered much for their separation from the Church of England,—Brown, Barrowe, Greenwood, and Penry,—he adds : " Very remarkable it is that even *those of that persuasion*, of which many in the reign of King Charles I. went to New England to avoid the persecution of the bishops, afterwards themselves turned cruel persecutors of pious people by inhuman whippings, etc., and, lastly, by putting some to death by the hands of a hangman."[1] It is evident at a glance that the writer has fallen into a double blunder, first in saying that the followers of Browne went out to New England in the reign of Charles I., and, secondly, in alleging that they turned out cruel persecutors. No doubt Sewel is thinking of the second band of emigrants who went out to Massachusetts, and which he mixes up with the settlers at New Plymouth.

That the Fathers of New Plymouth were innocent of the charge of persecuting the Quakers is proved by the fact that during their lifetime there were no Quakers to persecute. Upon this matter the testimony of George Fox may be held to be decisive. " In 1655," says Fox, " many went beyond the sea, where truth also sprung up (he means the truth for which he and his co-religionists contended) ; and *in 1656 it broke forth in America.*" This was thirty-five years after the landing of the Pilgrim Fathers in 1620, and by that time not a single leader whose name has come down to us was living. John Robinson, John Carver, Samuel Fuller, William Brewster, Edward Win-

[1] Vol. i. pp. 6, 7.

slow, Miles Standish, William Bradford, had all passed away. New Plymouth was no longer an independent colony, but had become confederated with Massachusetts, Connecticut, and New Haven. Clearly, then, no charge of persecution as against Friends or Quakers can be sustained against the Fathers and first settlers of New England.[1]

Reference has been already made to the prevalence of toleration in New Plymouth as compared with Massachusetts. The treatment of Quakers was far more humane. It was never guilty of the crime of hanging witches. In New Plymouth church membership was not made a condition of the elective franchise. Those larger and freer sentiments in regard to the toleration of differing opinions, which were fermenting in the minds of a large and influential section of their countrymen in England, were beginning to operate upon the minds of colonists, and they read with avidity the literature which was being continually imported into the colony. The impression that it made upon them may be gathered from a movement which was set on foot in New Plymouth: "for a full and free tolerance of religion to all men, without exception, against Turk, Jew, Papist, Arian, Socinian, Familist, or any other." Winslow, governor of the colony, writing to Governor Winthrop, says: "You would have admired to have seen how sweet the carion relished to

[1] See pamphlet entitled, *The Pilgrim Fathers neither Puritans nor Persecutors*, by the late Chamberlain of the City of London, Benjamin Scott, Esq., F.R.A.S. In this pamphlet Mr. Scott brings forward some interesting facts, showing how the sons and descendants of the Pilgrim Fathers were honourably distinguished for their hatred of, and hostility to, persecution.

the palate of most of them." The movement was defeated by delay; but it shows in what direction the mind of these Plymouth Puritans was tending.

Puritans and Puritans.—What has just been said about New Plymouth illustrates the necessity of careful discrimination when passing judgment upon the Puritans as a party or class. To their detractors and the majority of critics it never seems to occur that there were Puritans *and* Puritans; that the name stands for almost as much diversity of faith and character as the name "Protestant." Hence much that has been written about the Puritans recalls the saying of Napoleon, that "history is a fable that has been agreed on."[1] For instance, in his work on *The Puritan Colonies*, Mr. Doyle says: "To speak of the Puritan, whether in England or America, as the champion of spiritual freedom, is a proof of ignorance or worse. Toleration was abhorrent to him, even when he most needed it. He would have scorned those pleas of expediency which modern apologists have sometimes urged in his behalf. His creed on this matter was as simple as that of St. Lewis or Torquemada. He had possession of the truth, and it was his bounden duty, by whatever means, to promote the extension of that truth, and to restrain and extirpate error. In this he in no wise fell short of the moral standard of his age."

But as a specimen of wholesale reckless denunciation

[1] See *ante*, p. 112; Doyle's *English in America: Puritan Colonies*, vol. i. p. 6.

it would be difficult to match the following choice passage, taken from a leading literary English journal:[1] "The savage brutality of the American Puritans, truthfully told, would afford one of the most significant and profitable lessons that history could teach. Champions of liberty, but merciless and unprincipled tyrants; fugitives from persecution, but the most senseless and reckless of persecutors; claimants of an enlightened religion, but the last upholders of the cruel and ignorant creed of the witch doctors; whining over the ferocity of the Indian, yet outdoing that ferocity a hundredfold," etc. But probably enough has been quoted of this kind of swearing at large. It serves at least to illustrate the venomous antipathy which it has ever been the fate of the Puritans to provoke, whether in America or in England. Their enemies and critics (of this school) have never professed to be restrained by the usual urbanities of controversy, nor to be governed by the ordinary rules of literary warfare, but have gone upon the principle that any stick is good enough with which to beat a cur of a Puritan. The homage of such hate is perhaps the greatest of all tributes which has been paid to the greatness of Puritanism.

[1] *The Saturday Review*, January 29th, 1881.

Toleration and Religious Liberty: General Conclusions

CONTENTS OF CHAPTER VII

Toleration not from scepticism, ignorance, or indifference, Lecky, Froude, Morley, Dr. Johnson, Charles James Fox—Lord Herbert and Hobbes, St. Louis—Philips Brooks' definition of tolerance—Wrong views rebutted—Appeal to history—Origin of toleration—Christian Church founded on — Edict of Milan —'Tertullian, Lactantius, Athanasius—William of Occam, Marsiglio—Wyclif—Augsburg Confession—Luther—Hallam points to More and Jeremy Taylor— Masson on—Pioneers of liberty and toleration, how to be judged— Note on "The duty of persecution"—Note on "The tolerance of indifference"—Earliest apostles of toleration from among the persecuted —Masson's testimony to Independents and Baptists—English Baptist Church at Amsterdam—Dutch Anabaptists first advocates of toleration—William of Orange—Dutch Anabaptists in London—Robert Browne first to advocate toleration in England—Toleration bound up with Independency—Bishop Hooper—Robert Browne–Yet Browne's doctrine not toleration in the fullest sense—Plea that Papists might be tolerated—Principle of toleration very imperfectly understood—Roger Williams gave it widest practical application— Henry Jacob, Leonard Busher—Both allow magistrate right of interference in religious matters — Williams a fanatic for liberty— American Puritans, intolerance of—Less inexcusable, because living in age of intolerance—Note on "Does Calvinism promote intolerance?"—Bancroft quoted—Buckle, Froude, Fairbairn—Note on "Calvinism and Puritanism not identical."

CHAPTER VII

TOLERATION AND RELIGIOUS LIBERTY: GENERAL
CONCLUSIONS

I

THE question of toleration and religious liberty is so intimately bound up with the Puritan contention, and has been so identified with the struggle which has been fragmentarily recounted in the previous pages, that we feel we owe no apology for endeavouring to ascertain, with some degree of exactitude and detail, the position in which the question stands at the point we have now reached, and what has been the progress made in regard to it.[1]

---

[1] It need scarcely be pointed out that to discuss with anything like adequateness the principle of toleration and its historical development, not a few pages, but a large and elaborate treatise, would be required. In the preface to his candid and suggestive work, *Persecution and Tolerance* (being the Hulsean Lectures, delivered before the University of Cambridge in 1893-4 by the Bishop of Peterborough), Dr. Creighton says: "No one can feel more strongly than myself the triviality of this book as a contribution to the investigation of a large subject." As such an attempted contribution the following pages must seem triviality itself, but we are happy in thinking that they cannot possibly incur the risk of being thus construed. We have merely "put together some conclusions" which have occurred to us in tracing the genesis and growth of Puritanism in the Old World and in the New, and do not think it necessary to apologise for their being so "fragmentary and incomplete."

What is toleration?—Before proceeding, however, to trace the development of the idea of tolerance or toleration, it may be well to state and define what toleration really is, for the misconceptions which have prevailed and still prevail upon the subject are indeed extraordinary. Even able writers and acute critics have fallen into strange error in regard to it. Mr. Lecky, in his *Rise of the Influence of Rationalism in Europe*, contends that tolerance is the outcome of scepticism, and that intolerance was exploded, or, at all events, began to be undermined, by the rise of the rationalistic spirit. "Tolerance," says Mr. Froude, "means at bottom that no one knows anything about the matter, and that one opinion is as good as another." It is perfectly true, as Mr. John Morley has observed, that complete tolerance may mean only complete indifference, and certainly the cheapest of all virtues is tolerance on the part of men who have no faith. Speaking of certain controversialists, Dr. Johnson says: "They disputed with good humour, because they were not in earnest."[1] "The only foundation of tolerance," said Charles James Fox, "is a degree of scepticism, and without it there can be none." "It is getting to be a fashionable notion that toleration is the offspring of scepticism. If so, then Lord Herbert and Hobbes of Malmesbury ought to have been its apostles, but they were not; and the Baptists, the Independents, and the people called Quakers ought

---

[1] See note at end of this section on the tolerance of indifference. "Clerks may dispute," said St. Louis, "but the layman who hears the Christian faith spoken against ought to defend it only with his sword, which he should drive home into the gainsayer." Quoted by Bishop of Peterborough in *Persecution and Tolerance*, p. 91.

not to have been its early apostles, but they were."[1]
Even Mr. Lecky is constrained to declare that "the most illustrious of the advocates of toleration were men who were earnestly attached to positive religion, and that the writings in which they embodied their arguments are even now among the classics of the Church." Not only so, "the greatest living antichristian writer was Hobbes, who was perhaps the most unflinching of all the supporters of persecution."

No better definition of toleration, we think, has been given than that of Dr. Philips Brooks, in his admirable little work on *Tolerance*. "It is," he says, "the willing consent that other men should hold and express opinions with which we disagree, until they are convinced by reason that those opinions are untrue." This definition may not be deemed quite satisfactory from a doctrinaire or logical point of view, but as a working definition we think it leaves nothing to be desired. The tolerance which is thus defined is utterly alien from the state of mind which regards all opinions as alike,—matters of no moment,—or yields to them a mere frivolous inconsiderate assent. The very word tolerance, as applied to such a state as this, is a misnomer. Tolerance supposes that there is something to tolerate, and that some degree of strain, difficulty, and cost is involved in it. But *ex hypothesi*, this is excluded. Indifference knows no strain, to it all opinions are alike; it reminds us of what Gibbon says about the various modes of worship which prevailed in the Roman world, which were considered by the people as equally true, by the philosophers

---

[1] Dr. Stoughton, *Jubilee Lectures*.

as equally false, and by the magistrate as equally useful. To ascribe to the magistrate, the philosopher, and the people the virtue of toleration, would indeed be a glaring fallacy.[1] Not less transparent is the fallacy involved in Dr. Johnson's dictum, that controversy conducted on both sides with good humour is a proof of want of earnestness. Is it not, on the very face of it, absurd to conclude that charity and good temper must argue indifference to truth, or imply want of depth of conviction, want of firmness of principle? May we not rather say that he who feels that he has his feet firmly planted upon the rock of truth and principle, and he alone, can afford to exhibit perfect charity and good temper? The clearness of a conviction is the best preservative against its over-passionate enforcement.[2] When the Church was most catholic, and so most tolerant, then it was that the victorious certitude of her own faith was pre-eminently exhibited to the world. Toleration, it has been truly

[1] "A man of vague and uncertain opinions cannot lay claim to tolerance; he is exercising no self-restraint, he is not guiding himself towards any moral purpose; he is simply indifferent and incapable. The tolerant man, on the other hand, has decided opinions. ... He is virtuous, not because he puts his own opinions out of sight, nor because he thinks that other opinions are as good as his own, but because his opinions are so real to him that he would not have anyone else hold them with less reality."—*Persecution and Tolerance*, p. 123. "Tolerance is not merely a negative virtue. It is needful on the part of the Church as an organised body. Tolerance is needful to the individual, for it is the expression of that reverence for others which forms a great part of the lesson which Christ came to teach him. It is the means whereby he learns to curb self-conceit, and submit to the penetrating discipline imposed by Christian love."—*Ibid.* p. 137.

[2] Rothe. See Canon Mozley's fine sermon on "The unspoken judgment of mankind."

said, is not only possible, but necessary, the moment religion is made a matter for the conscience rather than the magistrate, but impossible the moment it becomes an affair of the magistrate rather than the conscience.[1]

The best answer, however, to the assertion that toleration is created by scepticism is that supplied by history.

Rise and growth of toleration. — The history of Independency is to a large extent the history of the rise and spread of the principle of toleration. By this it is not implied that it originated within the borders of Independency. Its origin, strictly speaking, is indeterminable. Like the passion for liberty, it is universal as the mind of man, and old as the first attempt to rivet fetters upon it. All through the ages the forces that have contributed to the progress and development of the world have been making for it.

> " Thou hast great allies,
> Thy friends are exultations, agonies,
> And love, and man's unconquerable mind."

Still the principle of toleration may be shown to have had a historic beginning. During the first century, as we should expect (for surely it may be said that the Christian Church was founded on toleration), and before the impulse communicated to His followers by Christ and His apostles had passed away, toleration and charity or love were almost synonymous terms, and constituted an

[1] Dr. Fairbairn's *Religion in History and in the Life of To-day*, pp. 229-231.

evidence of Christian discipleship which the heathen around were unable to resist or gainsay.[1]

Toleration we find expressly provided for in the Edict of Milan put forth by Constantine in conjunction with Licinius, A.D. 313. This rescript contained far more than the first edict of toleration published by the Emperor Galerius. By the latter, Christianity was merely received into the class of the *religiones licitæ*, while this new law implied the introduction of a universal and unconditional religious freedom and liberty of conscience—a thing, in fact, wholly new (Neander). "The rights of man and the law of nature," says Tertullian, "give everyone the power of worshipping as he thinks proper, and the religion of one man neither injures nor benefits another. Force is indeed foreign to religion." So speaks Lactantius, and Lactantius was tutor to the son of the Emperor Constantine. "Religion cannot be compelled, it is by words rather than wounds that you must bend the will. Nothing is so much a matter of free will as religion. Our God is the God of all, whether they will it or no; but we do not desire that anyone, whether he will or no, should be compelled to worship Him. Religion is the one region in which liberty has fixed its domicile and home." Says Athanasius: "It is an evidence that men want confidence in their own faith when they use force, and constrain men against their wills. It is the devil's

---

[1] "'See how these Christians love one another,' was the just and striking exclamation of the heathen in the first century. 'There are no wild beasts so ferocious as Christians who differ concerning their faith,' was the equally striking, and probably equally just, exclamation of the heathen in the fourth century."—Lecky's *Rationalism in Europe*, p. 31. See entire chapter on "History of Persecution."

method, because there is no truth in him, to work with hatchet and sword."

Among the earliest advocates of religious liberty was William of Occam, who was expelled from the Franciscan order for maintaining, against the pretensions of the Papacy, that "the Head of the Church and its foundation is one—Christ alone." The *De Monarchia* of Dante did much to clear the air. John Marsiglio of Padua, in 1327, in his epoch-making book, *The Defender of Peace,* "advanced and maintained tenets which, if heard for centuries in Christendom, had been heard only from obscure and fanatic heretics, mostly mingled up with wild and obnoxious opinions."[1] These tenets found a prepared and fruitful soil in the mind of Wyclif, and from them he elaborated his famous doctrine of the sovereignty of the people, and the universal priesthood of believers. The idea of toleration was not, perhaps, explicitly recognised by these early Reformers, but it was certainly implied and subsumed in the position which they took up.

The earliest and most explicit statement of the doctrine of toleration that we have come upon since the first centuries of the Church is that contained in that firstborn of Protestant creeds, the Augsburg Confession, which, though drawn up by Melanchthon, was doubtless drafted under the direction of Luther, and reflects the opinions of the great Reformer. In his treatise on the secular power, and how far obedience is due to it, Luther says: "Its duty is to secure external peace and order, and to protect men in their persons and property against

[1] Milman's *History of Latin Christianity,* vol. vii. p. 406. See "The Evolution of Tolerance" in *Persecution and Tolerance,* pp. 94-97.

ill-doers. . . . But God cannot, and will not, allow any one but Himself to rule the soul. Whenever, therefore, the temporal power presumes to legislate for the soul, it encroaches. No one can or shall force another to believe. Thoughts are toll-free. Heresy is a spiritual thing which no iron can hew down, no fire burn, no water drown. Body, gold, and goods God has given over to the emperor; the heart He has reserved to Himself. The Church is to be governed with the spoken sword, the rod of the mouth, which alone touches the conscience. The civil authority has nothing else than the sword of the fist and a rod of wood. They differ both as to ends and means. The end and aim of the Church is the peace of eternity; that of the State is peace on earth."

Hallam rebukes Southey for having declared, in language which at least dates after the year of the Spanish Armada, that " no Church, no sect, no individual even, had yet professed the principle of toleration," by citing the *Utopia* of Sir Thomas More and the harangues of the Chancellor l'Hospital of France. Hallam calls Jeremy Taylor's *Liberty of Prophesying* the first famous plea in England for toleration in religion. But as we have seen already the idea had a much earlier origin than this. " Who shall say," asks Professor Masson, " in the heads of what stray and solitary men scattered through Europe in the sixteenth century, *nantes rari in gurgite vasto*, some form of the idea, as a purely speculative conception, may have been lodged ?" Notwithstanding the successive struggles which have been waged on its behalf, religious toleration, or, as it is often called, liberty of conscience, " the noblest innovation of modern times,"[1] was of slow growth, and not till the close of the seventeenth century can it be said to have been recognised or clearly understood by any large body of people. It had to fight its way at first in the face of undisguised bitter hostility, and afterwards in the face of suspicion and of secret or openly avowed distrust. Ever since the Reformation there has been a slow and continuous progress in the direction of widened freedom, but it has been marked by this special peculiarity, that the progress has never been all along the line. It has been always the few, sometimes the one or two, that have stepped out of the line, and sounded the signal for the advance. " A few guiding spirits march first, and the multitude fall into line and follow after them." And even these guiding spirits have often shown themselves surprisingly backward to cast away, not merely the dregs and tatters, but the more ample habiliments of intolerance and religious bigotry. If they have struck the blow for freedom with one hand, they have helped to manacle it with the other. Of course this charge has to be brought against the various members of the vanguard with differing degrees of force, but there are very few indeed against whom it may not be to some

[1] " The principles of tolerance are no modern discovery," says the Bishop of Peterborough, *Persecution and Tolerance*, p. 97. " Men had always known that truth [that the compelling of a man to anything against his own conscience is a doing evil], but it was not always convenient to act up to their knowledge," p. 114. Dr. Creighton does not, we think, give sufficient weight to the consideration that this truth had not only become eclipsed, but had actually been *lost*, through the obfuscation of men's consciences, and through the influence of inherited traditional belief, and that in the seventeenth century it was practically *rediscovered*.

extent preferred. It were strange indeed had it been otherwise. As in judging of the morality of the Old Testament saints we recognise the propriety of applying to them, not the standard which prevails in our age, but that which prevailed in the age in which they lived; so, in like manner, the attainments of the early pioneers of freedom may fairly claim to be judged, not by an ideal standard, but by prevalent contemporary conceptions of conscience and liberty. Judged by this standard they were conspicuously in advance of the age in which they lived, and this honour must be ungrudgingly accorded to them. No doubt their theory of liberty was very defective, and was often vitiated by such unreasonable limitations and illusory safeguards, that, had it been logically carried out, it would have been nugatory, or even subversive of its avowed purpose. Happily the instincts of these zealots were better than their logic, and preserved them from drawing the practical deductions of their own theory; while their heroic struggle in what to them was the most sacred of all causes, makes it a thankless task to dwell upon their inconsistencies and errors.

NOTE ON THE DUTY OF PERSECUTION

The idea of toleration was understood neither by those who espoused the cause of the Reformation nor by those who opposed it. "Both sides believed that it was necessary to punish or even to burn a man's body to save his soul." Sir James Mackintosh says: "The toleration of heresy was deemed by men of all persuasions to be as unreasonable as it would now be thought to propose the impunity of murder." From a list of authenticated trials for heresy drawn up by Bishop Stubbs at the request of the Royal Commission on Ecclesiastical Courts (1881-1883), it appears that, beginning with Wyclif, and ending with William Balowe, who was burned in 1466, more than one hundred and twenty persons were tried for heresy ; and the number of those who were thus tried was probably far in excess of this. "Everywhere the dominant party, whichever it might be, forbade, and that in most cases under pain of death, the practice of any religion except that of the dominant party. Those who clave to the old religion forbade the practice of the new; and the professors of the new doctrines, the moment they had the power, forbade the practice of the old. . . Under Edward and Elizabeth the standard of belief was changed, so changed that only a few extreme sectaries were now in danger of the flames. But the difference simply was that the line was drawn at a different point. Those who went beyond that point were burned by those who, a few years before, might have been burned themselves."—Freeman. In the reign of Elizabeth, Hallam distinguishes five stages or degrees in restraint on religious liberty. Here is the persecutor's ladder, as it has been termed : (1) The regeneration of a test of conformity to the established religion as a condition of exercising offices of public trust. (2) Restraint of the free promulgation of opinions, especially through the press. (3) Prohibition of the open exercise of religious worship. (4) Prohibition of even private acts of devotion, or private expression of opinion. (5) Enforcement by legal penalties of conformity to the Established Church, or an abjuration of heterodox tenets." "The statutes of Elizabeth's reign," he adds, "comprehended every one of these progressive stages of restraint and persecution."—*National Rights*, by D. G. Ritchie, M.A., Professor of Logic and Metaphysics in the University of St. Andrews, pp. 199, 200, Note A, "Religious Persecution and Toleration ; some Historical Illustrations."

NOTE ON THE TOLERANCE OF INDIFFERENCE

What has been said in the preceding chapter on the persecution of the Quakers in Massachusetts furnishes a somewhat striking example of *quasi* or rather pseudo-toleration. In a tract on liberty of conscience, already referred to, written by Leonard Busher, the author says: "I read that Jews, Christians, and Turks are tolerated in Constantinople, and yet are peaceable, though so contrary the one to the other. If this be so, how much more ought Christians not to force one another to religion! And how much more ought Christians to tolerate Christians, when as the Turks do tolerate them! Shall we be less merciful than the Turks? or shall we learn the Turks to persecute Christians?" Now the humaneness of the Turk, as compared with that of the Puritans of Massachusetts, is supposed to be illustrated by the treatment to which the Quakeress Mary Fisher was subjected. Persecuted and imprisoned both in Old and New England, she found an asylum in Turkey, and there, under the protection of the Grand Turk, she was unmolested, and left free to propagate her opinions, and enjoy the fullest liberty of prophesying. "This is one of the numerous incidents," says Mr. Fiske (*Beginnings of New England*, pp. 183, 184), "that on a superficial view of history might be cited in support of the opinion that there has been, on the whole, more tolerance in the Mussulman than in the Christian world. Rightly interpreted, however, the fact has no such implication. In Massachusetts the preaching of Quaker doctrines might (and did) lead to a revolution; in Turkey it was as harmless as the barking of dogs. Governor Endicott was afraid of Mary Fisher; Mahomet III. was not."

It is said that one of the first papers laid before Charles II. after his restoration was a memorial on behalf of the oppressed Quakers in New England. The result was the despatching of a missive to Governor Endicott and the Court of Massachusetts, commanding them to desist from all further proceedings against the Quakers. Does anybody suppose that Charles cared a single straw whether the Quakers were persecuted or not? The King had the best of reasons for wishing to secure toleration for Catholics, and the securing of toleration for Quakers would, he believed, be one step towards the attaining of this object.

II

The earliest apostles of toleration.—We have distinguished from among the early Separatists those who were pioneers in the struggle for religious freedom, and those who may fairly claim to be regarded as the apostles of this doctrine. The latter, at first very few, as time went on and the struggle waxed fiercer, became more and more numerous. Professor Masson thinks that the doctrine of toleration became gradually evolved from persecution and suffering, and those whose experience of the latter was most bitter, and into whose souls the iron entered most deeply, became naturally its most strenuous upholders. A common cause, says Hallam, made toleration the doctrine of the sectaries. "The plea for liberty of conscience has always come most ardently from those to whom it was denied. Men begged to be tolerated long before they learned to tolerate." [1]

Professor Masson holds that the Church of England was more tolerant than the Church of Rome, and Scottish Presbyterianism or Scottish Puritanism was more tolerant (though the reverse is usually asserted) than the Church of England prior to 1640. He adds—and the words are a weighty and most important testimony—"Not to the

[1] Hunt's *Religious Thought in England*, vol. i. p. 353. "The meaner and more ignoble the party, the more general and comprehensive are its principles, for none but principles of universal freedom can reach the meanest condition. The serf defends the widest philanthropy, for that alone can break his bondage."—Bancroft's *History*, vol. ii. p. 687, revised edition, p. 181.

Church of England, however, nor to English Puritanism at large, does the honour of the first perception of the full principle of liberty of conscience, and its first assertion in English speech, belong. That honour has to be assigned, I believe, to the Independents generally and to the Baptists in particular."[1] The first organised Baptist Church was that formed by Smyth and Helwys at Amsterdam in 1611. It consisted of forty-two members, and the Declaration of Faith which they put forth is truly remarkable, not less for its advanced position in regard to religious liberty, than for the Arminian and anti-Calvinistic character of its doctrines. In a revised and fuller confession published afterwards by Smyth, the position is taken up: "That the magistrate, by virtue of his office, is not to meddle with religion or matters of conscience, nor to compel men to this or that form of religion or doctrine, but to leave the Christian religion to the free conscience of everyone, and to meddle only with political matters, —namely, injustice and wrong of one against another, such as murder, adultery, theft, and the like; because Christ alone is the King and Lawgiver of the Church and of the conscience." It is believed, says Professor Masson, that this is the first expression of the absolute principle of liberty of conscience in the public articles of any body of Christians. The first formulated expression in a confession adopted and put forth by

[1] Masson's *Milton*, vol. iii. p. 99. We think that the Bishop of Peterborough scarcely exhibits his usual candour when (*Persecution and Tolerance*, p. 114) he says : "Tolerance was not the doctrine of any sect or party." It certainly was the doctrine of the Independents.

a particular Church it may be, and probably is, but we have evidence that places it beyond a doubt that this principle was apprehended and acted upon by a body of Christians long anterior to the period here referred to.

This was the poor and despised sect of Dutch Anabaptists, which first appeared in Holland about the year 1522. Afterwards they became known as Mennonites, after Menno Simons, of Friesland, a leader who acquired great influence over them; but the name Anabaptist still survived, and the name Mennonites gradually disappeared. They contended resolutely for the right to enjoy perfect liberty of conscience, and held that there ought to be no alliance between the Church and the State. But even in Holland, where religious freedom was cradled, and realised and enjoyed as in no other country, these poor Mennonites did not escape persecution. They were fortunate enough, however, to obtain the protection of William of Orange. This broad-minded ruler wrote to the magistrates of Middelburg: "We declare to you that you have no right to trouble yourselves with any man's conscience so long as nothing is done to cause private harm or scandal. We thereupon expressly ordain that you desist from molesting these Baptists, from offering hindrance to their handicraft and daily trade by which they can earn bread for their wives and children, and that you permit them henceforth to open their shops and to do their work according to the custom of former days. Beware, therefore, of disobedience and of resistance to the ordinance which we now establish." This had the effect of quelling the persecution of Anabaptists in the Dutch Republic. About the year 1575 a number of Anabaptists—about twenty-seven—who had made their way to England, were apprehended in a private house in London, where they had assembled for worship, and tried for heresy before the Bishop's Court. Nine of them were banished, and two were publicly burned alive at Smithfield.[1] Allusion has been already made to the church at Norwich which Robert Browne succeeded in gathering, the main part of which was composed of refugees from the Netherlands, who at that time formed the majority of the population of Norwich. Among them were many Anabaptists.

The judgment of Professor Masson, that the honour of the first perception of the full principle of liberty of conscience has to be assigned to the Independents generally, and to the Baptists in particular, calls, we think, for some measure of revision in the light of what has been said about the Anabaptists of Holland. But it needs also to be modified in view of another person, who Professor Masson, indeed, mentions with honour in this connection, but whose real position he seems scarcely to apprehend. Yet it is a fact that the full principle of liberty of conscience had found a strenuous defender and advocate in the erratic and notorious founder of the Brownist sect.[2] Dr. Dexter holds that Robert Browne

---

[1] Motley's *Rise of the Dutch Republic*, vol. iii. p. 206; Brandt's *History of the Reformation*, bk. xi. pp. 588, 589; *Neal*, vol. i. p. 228; *Froude*, vol. xi. p. 43. See *ante*, p. 19.

[2] *Ante*, pp. 128, 192. Mr. Taylor Innes, in his valuable *Historical Handbook on Church and State*, p. 173, says: "The only controversialists who held the modern doctrines of toleration were the Brownists and

is entitled to the proud pre-eminence of having been the first writer claiming to state and defend, in the English tongue, the true and now accepted doctrine of the relation of the magistrate to the Church. This he speaks of, but more doubtfully, as "the true *modern* doctrine of toleration and of liberty of conscience."

The principle of religious liberty is almost logically bound up with the theory of the independency of particular Churches. Hallam says:[1] "The Congregational scheme leads to toleration as the National Church scheme is adverse to it, for manifold reasons which the reader will discover." "This being the principle of some of the early Protestant movements that went beyond Luther, Zwinglius, or Calvin, and perplexed these Reformers, little wonder that flashes of the fullest doctrine of liberty of conscience should be found among the records of those movements, whether on the Continent or in England. Little wonder, either, that the principle of toleration should be discernible in the writings of Robert Browne, the father of the crude English Independency of Elizabeth's reign."[2] But it is one thing, says Professor Masson, to hold a principle vaguely or latently, as implicated in a principle already avowed, and another thing to extricate the implied principle, and kindle it, as on the top of a lighthouse, on its own account.[3] He shows that

---

Barrowists, so called from their founders, whose position was like that afterwards known as Independents." Baillie, the famous chronicler of the doings of the Westminster Assembly of Divines, makes it a reproach against Browne that he held the toleration doctrine.

[1] Hallam's *Constitutional History of England*, vol. ii. p. 102n.
[2] Masson's *Milton*, vol. iii. p. 100.
[3] The difference which Professor Masson here notes is a very im-

the early Separatists, as a whole, lagged behind Browne, and looked with lively fear on the conclusions he had reached. They wanted toleration for themselves, and perhaps a general mildness in the administration of religious affairs, but they could not rid themselves of the notion, held alike by all the established Churches, whether Prelatic or Presbyterian,—that is, the duty of the prince

portant one. Among the writings of some of the Reformers it would not be difficult to find statements as advanced in regard to religious liberty and the relation of the magistrate to the Church as anything written by Robert Browne. *E.g.* in his treatise of *Reformation without Waiting for Any*, Browne says : " They, the magistrates, may doe nothing concerning the Church, but onelie civilie and as civile magistrates ; that is, they have not that authoritie over the Church as to be prophetes, or priestes, or spirituall kings, as they are magistrates over the same ; but onelie to rule the common wealth in all outwarde justice, to maintaine the right welfare and honour thereof with outwarde power, bodily punishment, and civill forcing of men." Compare with this the following extract from a letter by Bishop Hooper thirty years before, written while he was in prison, and addressed to the members of Convocation : " Cogitate apud vos ipsos, an hoc sit piorum ministrorum ecclesiæ officium, vi, metu et pavore corda hominum in vestras partes compellere. Profecto Christus non ignem, non gladium, non carceres, non vincula, non violentiam, non bonorum confiscationem, non reginæ majestatis terrorem media organa constituit quibus veritas verbi sui mundo promulgaretur, sed miti ac diligenti prædicatione evangelii sui mundum ab errore et idololatria converti præcepit." In opinion and conviction as to the inviolableness of conscience, and the unlawfulness of the civil magistrate meddling with matters of faith, Bishop Hooper seems to be quite as advanced as Robert Browne. But Hooper remained to the last an attached son of the Reformed Protestant Church, whereas Browne separated from it, and formed a " gathered " Church founded upon Separatist principles, and made it a matter of boast that for preaching against bishops, ceremonies, etc., " he had been committed to thirty-two prisons, in some of which he could not see his hand at noonday."—*Ante*, pp. 43-45, 132, 133.

or the civil power in any State to promote true religion and suppress false.

Dr. Dexter's contention, that Browne's doctrine of the relation of the magistrate to the Church is identical with the true modern doctrine of toleration and of liberty of conscience, is perhaps scarcely justified. It has been pertinently asked, would he or any of his followers in Elizabeth's time have conceded freedom of worship to Roman Catholics?[1] No one will assert that they were any of them prepared to extend to Papists the liberty which they claimed for themselves. It may be said, and doubtless with great force, that even in this free and tolerant nineteenth century there are large numbers of so-called enlightened and religious people who would conscientiously refuse to go this length. Remembering how tardily the disabilities which Roman Catholics have suffered have been removed, it is not to be wondered at that in Elizabeth's day it was regarded as eminently unsafe to accord to them any full

[1] There were some among the early Independents—though of a later period than that referred to in the text—who did not shrink even from this concession, as is evident from a Brownist petition prepared in the year 1640, praying "that every man may have freedom of conscience," not excepting Papists.—Stoughton's *History of Religion in England*, vol. i. p. 337. A pamphlet was published in the year 1644, in which the question was asked, "whether, if security be taken for civil subjection, Papists might not be tolerated?" Otherwise, it is added, "if England's government were the government of the whole world, not only they, but a world of idolators of all sorts—yea, the whole world—must be driven out of the world." —Surrey's *Congregational History*, by Dr. Waddington, and Hanbury's *Memorials*, vol. ii. p. 246. This was not, of course, in Elizabeth's time, but many years after, during which the question of toleration had wonderfully grown and ripened.

measure of civil and religious liberty. "With Jesuit priests creeping secretly from one country house to another in Norfolk and Lancashire, and inciting the Catholic gentry to revolt; with the troops of Alva in the Netherlands threatening England with invasion; with the Spanish Armada in the Channel,—even an advanced member of the Liberation Society might not have had the courage to insist on granting the Catholics perfect religious equality."[1] It would have marked a most extraordinary and, indeed, incredible advance on the part of the early Independents, if their principles had approximated more closely than they did to the true modern doctrine of toleration and of liberty of conscience. The wonder is, in an age when the authority of the civil power was so uniformly invoked in defence of religion, and deemed the only effectual safeguard for its preservation, that so many earnest-minded religious men should have been found ready to insist upon the worthlessness of this security, and to claim for the conscience of every man the sole and indefeasible right to govern his religious convictions. It need not surprise us to know that this great principle was held, even by those who first adopted it, in a very halting and hesitating manner. We find the

[1] "Even in that age, the permission to Papist, Puritan, and Anglican to exercise each his own worship, and to persuade his neighbour into the better form of practice and belief, would apparently have diminished instead of increasing the discontents of the kingdom, and would have surrounded the already absolute Queen with a barricade of enthusiastic loyalty."—Mr. Taylor Innes on *Church and State*, p. 173. We firmly believe this; but it is one thing to believe it now in the light of all the teaching of history; it would have been quite another and enormously more difficult thing to believe by the Elizabethan Puritans.

Apostle Peter, notwithstanding his emphatic and oft-repeated assertions that there was no difference between Jew and Gentile, contradicting his own principle, and, through fear of those who were of the circumcision, separating himself from those whom he had already recognised as brethren in Christ. For this he was rebuked openly by St. Paul, who says: "I withstood him to the face because he was to be blamed." It is unhappily common enough in these days for men to identify themselves with principles and doctrines which they shrink from carrying out to their logical conclusion, and not infrequently, when they are called upon to apply them, they show an incredible faithlessness and want of courage. It would have been, indeed, a miracle if there had been nothing of this vacillating temper in those who espoused for the first time the great doctrine of religious liberty. They fell into gross error and inconsistency, not simply through vacillation, but in consequence of the very imperfect way in which they apprehended and grasped the doctrine.

If in that age, when freedom's battle was being so hotly and strenuously waged, the endeavour is made to select from among the combatants one who, with fearless, uncompromising spirit, contended for toleration of the broadest and most unqualified description, the choice, it seems to us, must fall upon Roger Williams. We have already given reasons for refusing to subscribe to the opinion of Mr. Bancroft and others, that Williams was the earliest champion of religious liberty—that he was the "first person in modern Christendom to assert in its plenitude the doctrine of the liberty of conscience"; but such abatement of this estimate as we are required to make, in view of some who were before him in the field, and had already won honour and glory in the struggle for freedom and toleration, does not invalidate the conclusion that he was the first to give the principle of liberty—both religious and civil—its widest application and its most perfect embodiment. It is his unique title to pre-eminence and fame that he was the first to found an absolutely free Church in an absolutely free State, and Rhode Island and Providence Plantation remain a monument of his sagacity and daring and penetration, a centre from which the light of "soul-liberty" has radiated far and wide, till it has flooded a whole continent, and shines with concentrated splendour in the constellation of States which now form the great Western Republic.

It is scarcely necessary, after what has been previously said in reference to the Dutch Anabaptists, Robert Browne and Henry Jacob, to call attention again to their position in regard to freedom and toleration. Henry Jacob's tract, published in 1609, entitled, *An Humble Supplication for Toleration and Liberty to Enjoy and Observe the Ordinances of Jesus Christ*, has been spoken of [1] as the first work written in the English language in which the duty of toleration is explicitly advocated. But it does not appear that this plea for toleration is based upon any broad or sufficient ground. It allows to the civil magistrate a power of interference in religious matters which is incompatible with perfect liberty of conscience, and amounts merely to a plea that he, Jacob, and his followers might be protected in the enjoyment of their religious

[1] *Ante*, p. 224.

rights, privileges, and worship. A considerable advance upon this position was a treatise published by Leonard Busher, a Baptist, who had probably been a member of Smyth's congregation in Amsterdam, and had come over to England with Helwys in 1611. It is entitled, *Religious Peace; or a Plea for Liberty of Conscience*.[1] "The tract is certainly the earliest known English publication," says Professor Masson, "in which full liberty of conscience is openly advocated." Exception may, however, be taken to this encomium on the ground that the liberty contended for by Busher was by no means "full," but qualified in several directions, notably in the authority which he assigns to King and Parliament to "enact and publish the law of Christ." It is an admirable and stirring treatise against persecution, but hardly more than this can be claimed for it.

Neither Jacob nor Busher take, as did Browne, the broad ground of separation between things civil and religious. Both allow to the civil magistrate a right of interference in matters of religion of which Browne, at least, would not have approved. But the Puritans of that age—Separatists as well as others—were nearly all of them in bondage to the notion that it was the duty of the ruling powers to uphold true religion and to suppress false. To this notion Roger Williams would, as we

[1] See *Tracts on Liberty of Conscience*, published by the Hanserd Knollys Society. Hanserd Knollys was an eminent Baptist minister, born in 1598, went out to New England in 1638, returned to England in 1641, and died in London in 1691. When the Society for republishing early Baptist Writings was organised in 1845, the name of Hanserd Knollys was given to the series in recognition of his learning and of his labours and sufferings in the advocacy of Baptist doctrines.

have seen, give no quarter whatever. Like Milton, he was a fanatic for liberty, and if he could have heard the great Puritan poet declaiming his famous words, he would have hailed them with vociferous applause: "And though all the winds of doctrine were let loose to play upon the earth, so truth be in the field, we do injuriously, by licensing and prohibiting, to misdoubt her strength. Let her and falsehood grapple; who ever knew truth put to the worse in a free and open encounter?"

In the course of what has been said concerning the American Puritans, no attempt has been made to minimise, still less to excuse or justify, the spirit of intolerance which broke out in New England, and especially in Massachusetts, in connection with the persecution of Baptists and Quakers. This it is impossible to defend. But it is possible only too easily to fall into the error of imputing to the people generally the criminality of that which lies almost exclusively at the door of their leaders and rulers. "One might almost say that it was not the people of Massachusetts after all that shed the blood of the Quakers; it was Endicott and the clergy."[1] Nor must it be forgotten, as Mr. Bancroft reminds us, that the age in which these cruelties were practised was an age of intolerance. "For four centuries Europe had maintained that heresy should be punished by death. In Spain more persons have been burnt for their opinions than Massachusetts then contained inhabitants. Under Charles V., in the Netherlands alone, the number of those who were hanged, beheaded, buried alive, or burnt for religious opinion, was fifty thousand, says

---

[1] Fiske's *Beginnings of New England*, p. 187.

Father Paul; the whole carnage amounted, says Grotius, to not less than one hundred thousand. America was guilty of the death of four individuals; and they fell victims rather to the contest of will than to the opinion that Quakerism was a capital crime."[1]

NOTE

Does Calvinism Promote Intolerance?

It has been a charge not infrequently brought against the Puritan Separatists, that they were cruel and intolerant because they were Calvinists in religion and Republicans in politics. Reasoning on *à priori* grounds, it is not, perhaps, unnatural to conclude that Calvinism should make men intolerant, for it will be admitted by friends and foes alike that Calvinism is a stern and uncompromising creed. Did not Calvin himself defend the lawfulness of persecution; and was not his burning of the heretic Servetus an act applauded by all sections of Protestants? Nevertheless, the charge is one which history most persistently refuses to sustain. To all *à priori* conclusions it opposes the stern logic of facts, a body of facts so hostile and so conclusive that no theory can stand against it. It is not, of course, to be denied that many of the Puritans were intolerant. This has been admitted already; but the question to be determined is, was it their Calvinism that made them so? This, we hold, history disproves. It is disproved, in the first place, by the history of the Puritans in Holland. No one can impugn their zeal as Calvinists, nor call in question their love of liberty. Much as they suffered from persecution, they were never goaded into retaliation, even when they had the power, and their annals are (with the exception of those of the Quakers or Friends) most free from the stain of persecution. But the best answer to the charge that Calvinism tends to promote intolerance is the history of Puritanism itself. It will not be denied that the Puritans were ever found in the vanguard of the struggle for religious and civil freedom, and the Puritans were (at least up

---

[1] Bancroft's *History*, vol. i. p. 341. See Lecky's *History of Rationalism in Europe*, "History of Persecution," vol. ii. pp. 32, 33.

to the middle of the seventeenth century) all Calvinists.[1] The Reformers, and those who, like Hooper, resisted the imposition of the vestments, were Calvinists. The Separatists were Calvinists; Browne, Barrowe, Greenwood, Penry, Robinson, Johnson, Jacob were all Calvinists. The Pilgrim Fathers, not less than the first colonists of Massachusetts, were all Calvinists. Roger Williams was a Calvinist of the most thoroughgoing type.[2] "In Boston," says Mr. Bancroft (vol. ii. p. 692, revised edition, p. 184), "with Henry Vane and Anne Hutchinson, 'Calvinism ran to seed'; and the seed was 'incorruptible.' . . . The exiled doctrine, which established conscience as the highest court of appeal, fled to the island gift of Miantonomoh; and the records of Rhode Island, like the beautiful career of Henry Vane, are the commentary on the true import of the creed."

"It is an interesting fact that the doctrines which in England are called Calvinistic have been always connected with a democratic spirit, while those of Arminianism have found most favour among the aristocratic or protective party. In the republics of Switzerland, of North America, and of Holland, Calvinism was always the popular creed. On the other hand, in those evil days, immediately after the death of Elizabeth, when our liberties were in imminent peril; when the Church of England, aided by the Crown, attempted to subjugate the consciences of men; and when the monstrous claim of the divine right of Episcopacy was first put forward;—then it was that Arminianism became the cherished doctrine of the ablest and most ambitious of the ecclesiastical party. And in the sharp retribution which followed, the Puritans and Independents, by whom the punishment was inflicted, were, with scarcely an exception, Calvinists; nor should we forget that the first open movement against Charles proceeded from Scotland, where the principles of Calvin had long been in the ascendant."—Buckle's *History of Civilisation in England*, vol. ii. pp. 339, 340.

"Nothing is more remarkable in the history of the sixteenth century than the effect of Calvinism in levelling distinctions of rank, and in steeling and ennobling the character of common men. In Scotland, in the Low Countries, and in France there

---

[1] The only exception we can think of were the Baptists of Amsterdam, whose "Confession or Declaration of Faith," promulgated in 1611 (see *ante*, p. 370), is as anti-Calvinistic as it is advanced in its doctrine of religious liberty.

[2] "His theology was severely Calvinistic, typical of his generation, not in advance of it."—*Roger Williams*, by Oscar S. Straus, p. 232.

was the same phenomenon. In Scotland the Kirk was the creation of the preachers and the people, and peasants and workmen dared to stand in the field against belted knights and barons, who had trampled on their fathers for centuries. The artisans of the Low Countries had for twenty years defied the whole power of Spain. The Huguenots were not a fifth part of the French nation, yet defeat could never dishearten them. Again and again they forced Crown and nobles to make terms with them. It was the same in England."
—Froude's *English Seamen in the Sixteenth Century*, p. 127.

See also what Mr. Bancroft says on Calvinism and predestination, *History of the United States*, vol. ii. pp. 689-692, revised edition, pp. 182-185.

Let those who would realise the debt of freedom which the world owes to Calvin and Puritanism read an article by Principal Fairbairn in the *Contemporary Review* for November 1888, on "The Genesis of the Puritan Ideal": "The influence of Geneva had penetrated Germany, and, even where provoking resistance, had quickened the whole body Protestant; had converted almost the half of France, and enlisted her noblest sons in the army of reform, with the royal Condé and the gallant Coligny at their head; had gone like iron drops into the blood of the Netherland Churches, and made the heroes that broke the mighty power of Spain; it had reached England, created the Puritan spirit, the faith that was to determine her political constitution, condition her religious development, and create her most fruitful and characteristic colony; had sent Knox into Scotland with a theology that was to nurse a brawny race, civilise a people, and with a polity that was to effect the completest and happiest revolution any nation ever experienced. Without Calvin and Geneva these things would not have been; and without these things Europe and America would not have been as they are to-day—not so good, so well-ordered, or so free."

CALVINISM AND PURITANISM NOT IDENTICAL

It would be a great mistake, however, to infer from what has just been said that Calvinism and Puritanism are indissolubly bound up together. As we have previously had occasion to maintain, Puritanism was not a creed, but a spirit, an ethical force or power making for righteousness, rather than a reasoned system of belief. It allied itself with Calvinism in order that it might thereby more effectually promote the ends and righteousness of the kingdom of God; but when its ethical significance and force could be maintained unimpaired by its centre of gravity being shifted from the side of Calvinism to that of Arminianism or to that of a greatly modified Calvinism, the history of religion in our nineteenth century shows that it has exhibited the utmost readiness to enter into this new alliance. It is a favourite device with those who wish to discredit Puritanism to represent it as being identical with the most rigid and extreme form of Calvinism. But the necessity of any such identity, if it ever existed (and we cannot allow that the existence of the identity ever demonstrated its necessity), has long since passed away. The subsequent developments of Puritanism, the changes it underwent after the Commonwealth and has undergone since, show conclusively that Calvinism is no necessary integral part of it. "It cannot be too often repeated that those who use the word Puritanism merely to define a supposed temporary mood of English sanctimoniousness, or even to define the domination of Calvinist theology for a time in the British Islands, know nothing whatever of what Puritanism was historically and included intellectually. Puritanism was a revolt from authority, clothing itself at first in whatever doctrines of a fervid theology or ideas of popular Church discipline were at hand to suit, but passing on, by the usual law of development, into a multiplicity of forms and phrases, with abundant inclusion of the most abstruse scientific inquisitiveness, and the coolest philosophical freethinking."—Masson's *Milton and his Time*, vol. vi. p. 393.

But the supposed monopoly in the Calvinistic creed and system which Puritanism is represented as possessing, is refuted by the fact, which no one who has any acquaintance with the ecclesiastical history of England during the sixteenth and seventeenth centuries will venture to deny, that up to the time of James I. Calvinism was no more peculiar to Puritanism than it was to Prelacy. Nearly all the divines of the Elizabethan age were Calvinists. "It is a question which has been keenly discussed between Calvinists and Arminians, which side could claim Cranmer, Ridley, Latimer, and Hooper. If the question were to be determined by the general tone and spirit of their writings, there can be no doubt that they were Calvinists."—See entire note, p. 33, Hunt's *Religious Thought in England*, vol. i. "It is evident to every unbiassed person," says Mr. Hunt (vol. i. p. 131, note), "that all the Reformers were Calvinists in doctrine. The denial of this is the most daring thing in all ecclesiastical history." Both Parker and Grindal were Calvinists; while Archbishop Whitgift, the bitter enemy and relentless persecutor of the Puritans, was an ardent and thoroughgoing Calvinist, as is proved by the part he took in framing the Lambeth Articles, the first four of which are: 1. "God from eternity has predestinated some persons to life, and reprobated others to death." 2. "The moving or efficient cause of predestination to life is not foreseen faith or good works, or any other commendable quality in the persons predestinated, but the goodwill and pleasure of God." 3. "The number of the predestinated is fixed, and cannot be lessened or increased." 4. "They who are not predestinated to salvation shall be necessarily condemned for their sins." We must wait for Archbishop Laud before we find Arminianism allowed in the English Church. James I. was a strict Calvinist. He called Vorstius, the successor of Arminius at Leyden, a monster and a blasphemer, and said by his death only did Arminius escape the vengeance of the Most High and Mighty Prince.

Conclusion

CONCLUSION

WE have now concluded our brief survey of the rise and growth of Puritanism in the Old World and in the New. We have seen it at last firmly planted in the soil of New England, destined to grow into a great tree, sending forth its branches northward and southward, eastward and westward. But the most eventful and glorious chapter in the history of Puritanism remains as yet untouched. That chapter recounts the struggle of Puritanism in the old land, from which many of its noblest sons had been driven out, and whither some returned at length to bear their part in, and to celebrate its triumph and glory. This sequel we may endeavour to relate at some future time, should what we have attempted thus far meet with such acceptance as to encourage us to resume and continue the story.

We have now reached a point in the history of the New England theocracy when not a few signs admonish us that the golden age of Puritanism was passing away. New England was "a plantation of religion, not a plantation of trade." Such a plantation contained within itself the seed of eventual decay. In respect to States as to individuals, that is not first which is spiritual, but that which is natural, and afterwards that which is spiritual, and the attempt to invert the order will in the long-run prove a failure. There came a time in the history of the Jewish Church when the theocracy established by Jehovah Himself began to wax old, and was ready to vanish away. It was so with the theocracy of New England. Its framers sought to compass that which was impossible. "Perhaps," said Plato of that perfect republic of which he dreamed, "some image of it remaineth for us in the heavens." Yes, in heaven, but not upon earth! There is something not a little pathetic in what Cotton Mather says of Davenport, the nobleminded founder of New Haven: "After all, the Lord gave him to see that in this world a Church-State was impossible, whereinto there enters nothing which defiles." The Puritans of New England soon began to see that no dyke which they could possibly construct could keep out of their Arcadia the tide of surging corruption. Laxity, both of creed and conduct, worldly conformity, indulgence and chartered libertinism,—the scum which ever rise to the surface of a free commonwealth, and fills timid and faithless souls with panic and with dark foreboding,— these began to sap the virtue and threaten the very life of the young struggling republic. But this blotted page belongs to a chapter in the annals of New England later than that embraced within the scope of our present plan. And there are brighter pages which follow: for, if there are periods of decadence, there are also epochs of revival, resurrections of those very virtues which men deem to be dead and extinct. It has ever thus been with the soul or spirit of Puritanism. It was from the hour of its seeming downfall that its real victory began. The Restoration of 1660 seemed to deal it its death-blow, but

Mr. Green is speaking the words of truth and soberness when he says that the whole history of English progress on its moral and spiritual side has been the history of Puritanism. Puritanism never dies. The form in which it clothes itself changes, must change, from age to age, and its history both in England and America, shows that much that has seemed to be inevitably associated with it is destined to pass away; but the spirit of Puritanism lives on, and not until conscience is dethroned from its chief and controlling place in human affairs, and righteousness ceases to run down as a mighty stream, will it ever perish, or cease to be a force to be reckoned with by the rulers and peoples of the world.

INDEX

INDEX

A

Act of Supremacy, transfers Pope's authority to Crown, 52; absolutism of Crown, 53; nevertheless acceptable to people, 64.
Act of Uniformity, appoints second Prayer-Book of Edward VI., 53; fine for absence from worship, 53; Prothero's "Statutes and Constitutional Documents,"54n.; distasteful to Puritans, 64.
Admonitions to Parliament, 69, 70.
Advertisements, Parker's, 58n.
America. *See* New England.
American Democracy from Puritanism, 312n. *See* Democracy.
Anabaptists — martyrs, 176; early adopted principles of toleration, 192, 280; excesses of, 336, 337. *See* Baptists.
Anglicanism and Puritanism, 46.
Animus of Anglican writers, 193-4.
Antinomianism and Anne Hutchinson, 283-4.
Antitheses, Puritan and Anglican, 72.
Arber, on corruption of clergy, 151n.; on Martin Marprelate Controversy, 153n., 159, 167, 168; defence of Martin Marprelate, 164; authorship of Martinist Tracts, 167, 168.
Arminianism, not allowed in church till Laud, 385; Buckle on, 382.
Athanasius on persecution, 362.
Augsburg Confession, 363.

B

Bacon, Lord, *Advertisement touching Controversies*, 49; commends prophesyings, 85; would have room made in church for Puritans, 114; his opinion of Brownists, 178n.; his prejudiced testimony regarding them, 207, 209.
Bancroft, Archbishop, his *Dangerous Positions*, 74n.
Bancroft, History of United States on *Mayflower* Compact, 239n.; on Salem, 255; on Roger Williams, 279-81; on Connecticut, 291; on Puritans of New England, 306n.; on Winthrop, 349; on intolerance of Massachusetts, 380-1.
Baptists, John Smyth, founder of, 213; first English Church of General Baptists, 221; Roger Williams forms first Baptist Church in America, 277; order for banishment of, from Massachusetts, 334; fined and whipped, 335; imprisonment and banishment of, 336; commonly identified with Anabaptists, 336-8; first in struggle for religious liberty, 369-70.
Barlow, Bishop, no record of consecration, 49, 50; his unsacerdotal spirit, 50.
Barrowe, Henry, 177; arrest of, 178; examination, 178-81; writings in prison, 182; Dexter thinks him author of Marprelate Tracts, 168, 188; his execution, 183.
Barrowism, between Brownism and system of Cartwright, 184; and Brownism, 185; Congregationalism of America Barrowism, 315.
Bible, one of creative causes of Puri-

tanism, 11, 14: Wyclif's, 15; Tyndale's New Testament, 16: Great Bible, 16, 17; Genevan Version, 17; influence on people, Foxe, 17n.; Strype, Green, 18.
Bishops, Puritan, 4, 46; not necessary to Church, 47, 48; simony and peculation of, 149, 150; Latimer on, 150n.; Martinist attack on, 152; on their defence, 161; Arber on, 165.
"Body of Liberties," constitution of Massachusetts, 324.
Borgeaud's *Rise of Modern Democracy*, 22, 23; on Robert Browne, 128; "Divine Right Democracy," 129; Democracy from Independency, 312n.
Bradford, William, second Governor of New Plymouth, 243.
Brewster, William, at Scrooby, 215; New Plymouth, 243; elder, 246.
Brooks, Philips, on Tolerance, 359.
Browne, Robert, 126; at Norwich, 127; treatise and opinions, 128; flees to Holland, Middleburg, 129; with Penry in Scotland, 130; accepts living in Northamptonshire, 131; first to grasp principle of Independency, 132; in thirty-two prisons, 133; Dr. Dexter's estimate of, 133, 134; early Independents disowned, 134; sometimes attended Established Church, 185, 186; his Treatise on *Reformation without waiting for any*, 128, 374n.
Brownism, Cotton disowned, 135; Dexter says misunderstood, 135n.
Brownists, carried principles to extreme, 134; Neal on their uncharitableness, 135; "twenty thousand in England," 136, 201; Neal's distinction between Brownists and other Puritans, 137, 138; increase and persecution of, 174, 175.
Burleigh, Lord, his remonstrance against the Whitgift Articles, 98; Brownist petition to, 196-8.
Busher's *Religious Peace*, 281, 367, 379.

C

Calvinism, meant democracy in church government, 22; not intolerant, 381; early Puritans all Calvinists, 381-2; democratic, 382; Buckle, Froude, Fairbairn on, 382-3; not identical with Puritanism, 383; not peculiar to Puritanism, 384; of Whitgift and Lambeth Articles, 385.
Cambridge Platform, 313.
Campbell, Douglas, on the *Puritan in Holland, England, and America*, 140; on State Church, 141; England's debt to Holland, 206-7; intolerance of Massachusetts, 344n.
Carlyle, heroism of Puritanism, v; on libelling Puritans, 122.
Cartwright, Thomas, on Christ's Headship, 61, 62; first to systematise Puritanism, 67; position defined in six propositions, 68; founder of Presbyterianism, 69; author of second Admonition to Parliament, 70; controversy with Whitgift, 71, 72; antitheses, 72; did not approve of separatism, 76; aimed at a Presbyterian despotism, 76-9.
Carver, John, first Governor of New Plymouth, 239, 243.
Child, his *Church and State under the Tudors*, 38n.; on continuity of Church, 38-9; quotes letter by Dr. Hammond, 47n.; on Canon Dixon regarding corruption of clergy, 150n.
Chillingworth on Scripture authority, 112n.
Church, Dean, takes narrow view of Puritanism; alleged appeal of Puritans to Scripture against reason, 110.
Church, and Scripture, 63, 70, 71, 111, 112; and State, Hooker on, 115; Browne's definition of, 128, Robinson's, 217, 218, Jacob's, 222.
Church of England, had origin under Henry VIII., 31; papal character of pre-Reformation Church, 32; from quarrel with Pope, 32;

alleged continuity in England and Scotland disproved, 35; retained Popish elements, Macaulay, Zurich letters, Hallam, Strype, 40n.; Whitgift on corrupt state of, 71, 72, 145; Jewel, 146; Strype, 147.
Church of Scotland, recognised by Convocation, 48; ordination of, held valid, says Bishop Cosin; excluded by Bishop Hall, 49.
Clergy, extreme ignorance of, 46; numbers object to vestments, 56; looseness, illiteracy, and number of, 147, 148; Child on corruption of, 150n., Arber on, 151n.
Confession signed by those taking part in prophesyings, 22, 84.
Conformists and Puritans, 52, 137.
Connecticut, colonisation of, 289; T. Hooker on self-governing power of people, 289; constitution of, 290-2; ignores allegiance to British Crown, 291.
Continuity of Church of England, of Scotland, with ancient Church, alleged, 33-5; *reductio ad absurdum*, 34; confuted by Child, 38, 39.
Convocation recognised Church of Scotland, 48; majority of one against Puritans, 57.
Cooper, Bishop of Winchester, declares most part of men averse to Episcopacy, 75.
Copping, John, martyr, 177.
Cosin, Bishop, on Presbyterian ordination, 49.
Cotton, John, 259, n., 262; disowns Brownism, 135n.; his *Way of Congregational Churches cleared*, 313; disapproved not of persecution of error, 348.
Court of High Commission, its inquisitorial powers, 95; use of by Whitgift, 97; detested by laity, 97; how differing from Star Chamber, 96-7.
Creighton, Bishop, his *Persecution and Tolerance* quoted, 357n., 358n., 360n., 365n., 370n.
Cromwell, on reproach of Puritanism, 5; on refusing liberty to others, 333-4.

Curteis, Canon, on schism, 37n.; on vestments controversy, 54; on Puritan martyrs, 193-5.

D

Dale, Dr., error regarding Browne corrected by, 127n.; on Brownists, 134.
Democracy the outcome of Puritanism, 22, 23; *Rise of Modern Democracy*, 312n.
Dennis, William, martyr, 177.
Dexter, Dr., on church of Richard Fitz, 124-6; estimate of Browne, 133, 134, 192, 373; thinks H. Barrowe author of Marprelate Tracts, 168, 188; on Robinson's farewell words, 224, 225; "as to Roger Williams," 348n.; alleges Browne's toleration to be the true modern doctrine, 375.
Discipline, Book of, by Cartwright and Travers, 75; subscribed by five hundred ministers, 75; *Demonstration of Discipline* by Udall, 79, 172.
Dissenters, three classes of, 136; Brownists in second class, 137; Fuller on Nonconformists not being Separatists, 138, 139; Hooper and Philpot not Separatists, yet recommend separation, 139, 140; Anabaptists of Holland in third class, 140; Douglas Campbell on Dissent, 140, 141; Green's mistake, 141n.; Dissenters through force of circumstances, 141, 142.
Döllinger on continuity of Church, 34n.
Doyle, *The Puritan Colonies*, does Pilgrims scant justice, 245; undiscriminating censure of Puritans, 353.
Dudley, Thomas, aversion to toleration, 263, 349.

E

Edict of Milan gave universal religious freedom, 362.

Education in New England, schools, 328, 329; Harvard College, 329, 330.
Eliot, John, apostle to the Indians, 296.
Elizabeth, Queen, had no sympathy with the Reformation, 12; persecuted Puritans, 13; resisted changes, desired Popery without the Pope, 24; her short-sighted policy, her sagacity overestimated, 25-27; made separation necessary, 28; the two pillars of her ecclesiastical edifice, 52; her rigour in enforcing the vestments, 56-8; determination to suppress prophesyings, 88, 89; suspends Archbishop Grindal, 90-2.
Endicott, governor of Massachusetts, 252, 253; his character, 348.
England, "the Pope's farm," 32; not birthplace of Puritanism, population of, 201.
Episcopacy, not of the essence of the Church, Macaulay on, 47; Whitgift on, Child on, 47n.; Puritans did not object to, *per se*. 62; people averse to, 75.
Erasmus, dream realised, 16.

F

Fairbairn, Dr., on Puritan and Anglican antitheses, 72; on Hooker's theory of the Church, 116; on Jacob's humble supplication, 224; on toleration, 361; on Puritan ideal, 383.
Fisher, Mary, persecuted in New England, 338; tolerated in Turkey, 368.
Fiske, on education in New England, 330; on toleration, 368; exonerates people of Massachusetts, 380.
Fox, Charles James, on tolerance from scepticism, 358.
Fox, George, *Digged out*, 341; on origin of Quakerism in America, 351.
Foxe, John, on joy with which Bible received, 17n.; petitioned for lives of two Anabaptists, 19; *Book of Martyrs* next to Bible, 18, 19.
Freeman, says dominant party persecuted, 367.
Froude, on Calvinism, 2n.; De Silva on name Puritan, 4; first mention of name, 51n.; on prophesyings, 84n.; on young Puritans, 87, 88; toleration from indifferentism, 358.
Fuller, on name Puritan, 4; on Cartwright and Whitgift, 71; on Browne, 130-132, 174; on Nonconformists, 138.

G

Gardiner, on development of Puritanism, 66; on two classes of Puritanism, 258.
Gladstone, W. E., view of Elizabeth's policy, 25; on Reformation in Cambridge, 107n.
Green, on Neal and Strype, 6; on Bible, 16-18; spirit of inquiry, 19; his view of Elizabeth, 25, 27; on Cartwright's bigotry, 77; on those who objected to National Church, 141n.; on Puritanism and progress, 391.
Greenwood, John, in prison, 178; executed, 183; disowns Brownism, 185.
Grindal, Archbishop, succeeds Parker, 89; refuses to suppress prophesyings, 90; suspended by Queen, 91; denounced by Sacheverell, 92.

H

Hall, Bishop, his *Episcopacy by Divine Right*, 49.
Hallam, his estimate of Elizabeth, 26; on Church of England, 40n.; against enforced uniformity, 58; Puritan claims, 62n.; on Cartwright, 77 and n.; few preachers among clergy, 102; on the oath *ex officio*, 104n.; predominance of Puritan party, 106, 107; on

INDEX 399

Hooker's *Ecclesiastical Polity*, 113; on bishops, 149; on Udall's trial, 173.
Harvard, John, 263.
Harvard College, 329; two presidents Anabaptists, 338.
Headship of Christ, 62; martyrs suffered for, 190.
Higginson, Francis, disavowed separatism, 252; leader of company, 253, 262; chosen teacher, 253; drew up confession and covenant, 254.
Holland, population equal to England, 201, 202n.; England's indebtedness to, 203; Refugees from, 204, Green's estimate, 204n.; Lollardism among Walloon settlers in England, 204n.; arts and religion, 205; Douglas Campbell on indebtedness to, 266 and n.; churches, Middleburg, 129; Amsterdam, 212, Leyden, 217; Puritan emigrants poor under scholarly leaders, 211; no home for Puritans in, 233; leavetaking, 235.
Hooker, and Cartwright, 70n.; Master of Temple, 73; his genius, 108; his *Ecclesiastical Polity*, 109; supremacy of law, 110; exaggeration of ecclesiastical authority, Hallam on, 113; original source of authority same as with Puritans, 114n.; identity of Church and State, 115, criticised, 115, by Fairbairn, 116.
Hooker, Thomas, light of Western Churches, 262; pioneer in Connecticut, 289; "Father of American democracy," 290.
Hooper, John, first Nonconformist, 43; for liberty of conscience, 44; offered bishopric of Gloucester, "scrupled the vestments," 44; imprisoned, accepts conditionally, burnt at Gloucester, 45.
Hume, his sneer at Puritan scruples about vestments, 54.
Hunt, his complaint regarding spirit in which history is written, vii; on name Puritan, 4; vestments, 56.
Hutchinson, Anne, 283; her doctrines, 284; expelled from Massachusetts, 285; flees to Rhode Island, with followers founds Portsmouth and Newport, 285.

I

Independency, how developed, 119; fundamental principle held by Wyclif, 120; unlawful conventicles, 121; beginnings of, 123, 124; congregation under Richard Fitz, 124-6; Brown, Mackennal, and Stoughton on, 125, notes; Dr. Dexter's view, 126; in Middleburg, 129; in what sense Robert Browne founder of, 132; historic Independency, 220; became prevailing form in New Plymouth, 246; only system suited to new Puritan Republic, 120, 311; exception taken to temper of its apologists, democracy and, 312; the Cambridge platform, 313-5; Cotton's criticism on name, 313; American Congregationalism Barrowism, 315; growth of, in New England, 315-6.
Independent church, first permanent, 221; second in America, 253.
Independents, and R. Browne, 126n.; pioneers of religious liberty, 223-4, 370.
Innes, Taylor, his handbook on Church and State, 114n.; toleration and Independents, 372n.; toleration safest, 376n.
Intolerance, growth of, in New England, 333-54; Massachusetts, 344; of some of Puritan leaders, 348n.; of Puritans exaggerated by Doyle, 353, *Saturday Review*, 354. *See* Persecution.

J

Jacob, Henry, 221; defined Church as Independent, 222; broadminded, 223; his *Humble Supplication for Toleration*, 224, 378.

James I., his opinion of Udall, 171n.; a strict Calvinist, 385.
Jewel, Bishop, letter to Peter Martyr, 46; on worship appointed by Queen, 46; on vestiges of Popery, 57; on state of Church, 146.
Johnson, Francis, in London, in Amsterdam, 212, 213.
Johnson, Dr., good humour from want of earnestness, 358, 360.

L

Lacordaire's great saying, 50.
Lactantius, religion a matter of free will, 362.
Lambeth Articles, 385.
Latimer, Hugh, most popular preacher, 44; *Sermon of the Plough*, 150n.
Laws of New England, sumptuary regulations, tainted with Mosaism, the Body of Liberties, 320-8.
Lecky, toleration outcome of scepticism, 357.
Liberty, of conscience, growth of, 19; of prophesying, 86; political, promoted by Reformation, 19-21, but not immediately, 20; soul liberty, 280, 282n.; religious, and toleration, 357-85; principle of religious liberty involved in Congregationalism, 373; Winthrop on, 307.
Lollardism in Norfolk among Flemish weavers, 204-5.
Lowell, *Among my Books*, on Puritanism, 23, 66n.; on free education, 329; on persecution of the Quakers, 343.
Luther, and peasant war, 21; his doctrine of liberty, 35; on religious liberty, 363, 364.

M

Macaulay, on persecution and increase of Puritans, 14; on effect of Reformation, 20; on Popish elements retained, 40; Episcopacy not essential, 47; on Whitgift, 93.

Marsden, real question regarding prophesyings, 86.
Marsiglio, *The Defender of Peace*, 363.
Martin Marprelate controversy, 152; works on subject by Arber, Dexter, and Maskell, 153n.; *Epistle*, 154-8; effect of, 158; restrictions on printing, 158-9; *Epitome*, 159-61; bishops on their defence, 161; *Hay any worke for Cooper*, 161; press seized, 162; Puritans disapprove of tracts, 163; Curteis, Dexter, and Arber on, 164-5; conclusion of *Epistle*, 165-6; authorship—opinions of Arber, Maskell, and Dexter, 166-8; effect in high quarters, 168.
Martyr Peter, letter from Jewel, 46; on vestments, 55n.
Martyrs, for assembling themselves, 123; communion service interrupted, 124; John Udall died in prison, 171-4; Roger Rippon died in prison, 175; Macker and Terwoort burnt at Smithfield, 176; Dennis, Copping, Thacker, 177; Henry Barrowe and John Greenwood, 177, executed, 182-4; John Penry, 186-8, executed, 189; not for mere polity, but for Christ's supremacy, 190-1; not for "crotchet," as Curteis, 193-5; not for political offence, 195; Wakeman's judgment, 196; petition of sufferers to Lord Burghley, 196-8.
Mary, Queen, persecutions under, 51; separate meetings recommended by Hooper and Philpot, 139-40.
Maskell, his prejudice against the Puritans, 123; on Marprelate Tracts, 153n., 163n., 167n., 187n.
Massachusetts, founding of, 251; land acquired in, 252; Endicott, Governor at Salem, 252-3; new exiles with Royal charter, 251; disowns separatism, 252; Church membership a condition of franchise, 260-1; leading men, 262-4; Winthrop and Dudley joint governors, 264; large accessions to, 265; laws from Old Testa-

INDEX

ment, 324; banishes Roger Williams, 274; the Body of Liberties, 324; ten capital crimes, 325; laws humane compared with England, 326; vice prevalent, 327, causes, 328; persecutes Baptists, 334-8, and Quakers, 338-40, 342-44; more intolerant than other States, 244; more tolerant as became stronger, 350.

Masson, Professor, on Independents, R. Browne, 126n., 269, 270; on Roger Williams, 278, 279; on Anne Hutchinson, 285; origin of doctrine of toleration, 369, 370; Puritanism and Calvinism, 384.

Mayflower, 235; with *Speedwell*, sails from Southampton, 236; alone from Plymouth, 237; numbers on board, 231; compact drawn up and signed on board, 238-9; harbour of Cape Cod, 239; Plymouth Bay, 241.

Middelburg, Church in, founded by Browne, 129.

Milman — "England the Pope's farm," 32.

Milton, on Puritans, 232; on truth and liberty, 380.

Misconceptions of Puritanism, Hooker's, 110; Dean Church's, 110; Canon Curteis, 111; Matthew Arnold's, 111n.; Carlyle on, 122; Doyle, *Saturday Review*, 353-4.

Missionary labours, 295; John Eliot, 296; first Protestant Missionary corporation, 297.

Moore and Brinckmann's *Anglican Brief against the Roman claims*, 37.

Morley, John, tolerance from indifference, 358.

Motley, on Robinson's farewell address, 219.

Multitudinism in church, assailed by Browne, 128, and Barrowe, 190.

N

Neal, his classification of Puritans in reign of James I., 4; note on, 6; on Puritan confession of faith, 22; on compulsory attendance at worship, 53; differences between Puritans and their opponents stated, 62-4; early and later Puritans, 64; "why believe as King believes?" 65; Puritans desire uniformity, 65; few preachers and best Puritans, 102; on Browne, 127; Brownists, uncharitableness of, 135; distinction between Brownists and other Puritans, 137, 138.

New England, growth of, 289-308; twenty-three years' progress, 299; interference of mother country, 299; Governor-General appointed and resistance to, 300; measures to stop emigration to, 302; Council forbids clergy to transport themselves, 303; eight ships arrested, 303; Hampden and Cromwell said to be on board, 303; loss to England from emigration, 304; return tide, 305; elements of population in United States, 306n.; Governor Winthrop on liberty, 307-8; New England Way, 315; Independency in, 316; religion and social life in, 316; wholesale proscriptions, 320, 321; life laborious, 321; laws regulating smoking, width of sleeves, etc., 322, 323; exemption for persons above ordinary degree, 323, 324.

New Hampshire, 292.

New Haven, founded by Davenport and Eaton, 292; joined to Connecticut, 293.

New Plymouth, founding of, 241-8; first winter in, 242; leading men, 243; Congregationalism in, 246; money obligations cleared off, 247; description by De Rasières, 247, 248; church membership not necessary to franchise, 261, 352; Fathers of New Plymouth not guilty of persecuting Quakers, 351, 352; Sewel's double blunder, 352; toleration more prevalent than in Massachusetts, 352, 353.

Norwich, Browne gathers congregation in, 127; second city in England, 204 and n.

O

Orders — non-Episcopal valid, Macaulay on, 47; Whitgift on, Child on, 47n.; Scottish orders held valid, 48, Cosin, 49, and foreign — Hall and Bacon, 49; orders of unreformed Church—Story, 35n.
Owen on martyrs, 123.

P

Palfrey, Dr., *History of New England*, defends banishment of churchmen from Salem, 255n.; on John Cotton, 259n.; church membership and franchise, 261; on Roger Williams, 348.
Parker, Archbishop, consecrated by deprived bishops, 50, 51; requires Foxe to subscribe, 19; supports Queen in imposing vestments, 57; thirty-seven suspended from ministry, 58; *Advertisements*, 58n.; suppresses prophesyings, 88; one hundred clergymen resign their livings, 101; a Calvinist, 384.
Parkhurst, Bishop of Norwich, remonstrates against suppression of prophesyings, 88, 89.
Penry, John, 186; twice cited before High Commission, 187; flees to Scotland, 188; suspected of being author of Marprelate Tracts, 167; publisher of, 168, 188; execution of, testimony before death, 189; denies Queen's warrant to establish false religion, 191.
Pequot Indians make war, are "wiped out," 293-5.
Persecution, and tolerance, Bishop Creighton on, 357; note on duty of, 366-7; "persecutor's ladder," 367; by all parties, Freeman, 367; effect of persecution on Puritans, 14; last who suffered death—confiscation and banishment, 208-9; of Baptists in New England, 334-8; of Quakers, 338-40.

Pilgrim Fathers, 231; Robinson's address to, 218, 224n., 235; number in *Mayflower*, 237, compact, 238; at Cape Cod, 239; sufferings of, 240; at Plymouth Rock, 241; great mortality, 242; Governor Carver died, Bradford succeeds, 243; a hostile tribe—epidemic among Indians, 243-4; influence belittled by Doyle, 244-5, but real founders of the American Republic, 245-6; *The Pilgrim Fathers neither Puritans nor persecutors*, 257n.; Puritans though Separatists, 256-8.
Plymouth Rock, "corner-stone" of American Republic, 232; object of veneration, 242.
Preachers, scarcity of, 85, 86, 102.
Presbyterianism, rise of, 66, 67; Cartwright, founder of, 69; first presbytery at Wandsworth, 74; short-lived in England, 79; under Commonwealth in London and Lancashire, 80.
Presbyterians not Separatists, 76.
Printing, Reformation helped by, 15; Caxton's, 15; restrictions on, 122n., 158-9.
Prophesyings, 83; confession of faith of those taking part, 22, 84; commended by Bacon and Strype, 85; liberty of, 86; benefits of, 87-8; suppressed, 88.
Protestantism, Elizabeth's attitude towards, 12-14; developed and justified by Puritanism, 36.
Prothero's *Statutes and Constitutional Documents*, 54n.
Providence, town of, founded by Roger Williams, 275, 282; a harbourage for all sorts of consciences, 283.
Puritan, and Anglican antitheses, 72; bishops, 4, 46; demands, 57; literature, vi.
Puritanism, "last of all our heroisms," v; spirit of, 1; not a system but a force, 2, 3, 383; name, 2, 4; zeal for purity, under James I., 4, 5; causes of, 11; offspring of Reformation, 13; led to democracy, 23; had origin in Holland, 43, 206; rise in

England, 43–58 ; growth, 107, 208, 201 ; hatred provoked by it, 354 ; not indissolubly bound up with Calvinism, 383–4 ; spirit of, imperishable, 391.

Puritans, causes of increase, 4, 5 ; Elizabeth's hatred of, 27 ; and Reformation settlement, 36 ; rose into power, 51 ; Fuller on, 4, 5, 51, n. ; about eight hundred fled to Continent, 51 ; returned threadbare, 52; points of divergence from ruling powers, 62–4 ; early and later, 64 ; desired uniformity, 65 ; Gardiner on development of, 66 ; numbers, 106–7, how accounted for, 201 ; continued oppression of, 207 ; banishment and confiscation, 208–9 ; exile made necessary, 209, 210 ; poor under scholarly leaders, 210–12 ; Puritans and Puritans, 353 ; denunciations of—Doyle, 353, and *Saturday Review*, 354 ; to middle of seventeenth century Calvinists, 381–3 ; yet Calvinism not more essential to Puritanism than to Prelacy, 383–4 ; decay of Puritanism in New England, 389 ; resurrection power, 390–1.

Q

Quakers, shameful treatment of, in Massachusetts, 338–9 ; four hanged, 339 ; indignation of the people, 340 ; Rhode Island refuses to persecute, 340 ; Williams writes against errors of, 341 ; gross excesses of, 342 ; Lodge's view and Lowell's, 343, 344 ; Goldwin Smith, 344 ; and Douglas Campbell, 344n. ; Charles II. befriends Quakers, 368.

R

Raleigh, Sir W., on number of Brownists, 136, 201.

Reformation, relation to Puritanism, 11–14 ; alleged indifference of English people to, 12 ; Elizabeth no sympathy with, 12 ; resisted, 12, 25 ; wanted leaders, 13 ; promoted by printing, 15 ; not at first favourable to liberty, 20 ; highest point under Edward VI., 25 ; settlement a compromise, 36.

Reformers, continental, took a less extreme view of vestments, 55.

Rhode Island, 282 ; Roger Williams obtains charter, 298 ; perils of, 283 ; progress of, 298.

Rippon, Roger, died in prison, 175.

Robinson, John, 213 ; at Norwich, 214 ; justified separation, 214 ; at Gainsborough and Scrooby, 215 ; at Amsterdam and Leyden ; 217 ; definition of church, 217–8 ; farewell address to Pilgrims, 218, 219 ; Dexter's view of, criticised, 224n. ; death, 219 ; tablet to memory, 220n. ; influence on New Plymouth, 246 ; advice to shake off name of Brownists, 258.

S

Sabbath, place of worship, 247, 248, 317 ; preparation for, 317–8 ; strict observance of, 318–9 ; Miss Earle on the *Sabbath in Puritan New England*, 319, 320.

Sacerdotalism and vestments, 55.

Salem, Skelton, pastor, and Higginson, teacher, 253 ; covenant, 254 ; worship on basis of Independency, 254–5 ; two objecting Churchmen banished, 255, this defended by Dr. Palfrey, 255n. ; democracy and the ballot from the first, 260.

Sampson deprived of deanery, 58.

Sandys, Bishop of Worcester, on scarcity of preaching, 86.

Saturday Review on "savage brutality" of American Puritans, 354.

Schism, the right of, 35 ; the "sin of," 36n. ; Anglican schism denied—Moore and Brinckmann, 37, and Curteis, 37n. ; *Spectator* on foolish dread of word "schism," 38.

Schools in New England, 328–9.

Scriptures, supremacy recognised by Puritans, 22, 84; not sole organ of Holy Ghost, 111; only rule of all things, say some, 111, 112, but not against reason, 112-3; Chillingworth, 112n. *See* Bible.
Separation, necessity of, 23-5, 27, 28; right of, 35, 36.
Separatism, Puritanism advanced to, 23, 28; arose out of vestiarian controversy, 61; points of divergence between Separatists and Reformers, 62-3; three classes of dissenters, 136; Brownists, Separatists, 137; brethren of the second separation, 138; in Queen Mary's reign, 139; few objected to principle of Establishment, Anabaptists did, 140; doubtful statements of Douglas Campbell and Green, 140, 141; originated by force of circumstances, 141-2.
Sewall, Judge, his communion service experiences, 319.
Skeat, Professor, on Dutch and English, 203.
Skelton, Pastor, at Salem, 253.
Smith, Goldwin, 241, 244, 290, 295, 302, 344.
Smyth, John, at Gainsborough and Amsterdam, became Baptist, 213.
Spectator on dread of word "schism," 38.
Speedwell, purchased, 235; sailed, 236; discharged as unfit, 237.
Spenser, a Puritan, 108.
Standish, Miles, 243, 262.
Story, Dr., quoted, 35n.
Stoughton's History — Brownist petition for freedom of conscience, 375n.
Straus, on Roger Williams, 280.
Strype, on thirst for Scriptures, 18; Annals quoted, 27n.; Life of Grindal, 40n.; letter of Whitgift's, 47n.: return of Puritans, 52; Fellows and scholars of St. John's, 56; on separatism, 61; on prophesyings, 85; on Grindal, 91; on state of religion, 147.
Stubbs, Bishop, quoted, 32; trials for heresy, 367.
Supplication of Puritan ministers 148n.
Supremacy of Scriptures. *See* Scriptures.
Sutton, Archbishop, his advice to Bishop Heber, 88.

T

Tertullian, on religious freedom, 362.
Test Articles, 93-5.
Thacker, Elias, martyr, 177.
Tolerance, *Persecution and Tolerance* by Bishop of Peterborough, 357n.; of indifference, 367; of Mahomet III. and Charles II., 368; Lecky and others, as outcome of scepticism, 357-8; Philips Brooks' definition, 359; good temper from firmness of conviction, 360; not a negative virtue, 360n.
Toleration, 191, 357-85; Browne, Barrowe, and Greenwood, 192; Roger Williams claimed complete, 279, preceded by Anabaptists and Prince of Orange, 280, also by Browne, Busher, and English Baptists of Amsterdam, 281; Rhode Island practised, 282, 340; Christian Church founded on, 361; Edict of Milan, Tertullian, Athanasius, Lactantius, 362; William of Occam, Wyclif, Augsburg Confession, 363; Luther, 363-4; Jeremy Taylor's Liberty of Prophesying, 364; few in favour of before close of seventeenth century, 365; Dr. Creighton, 365n.; pioneers to be judged not by ideal standard, 366; evolved among persecuted, Masson and Hallam, 369; Bancroft, 369n.; Masson on Independents, specially Articles of English Baptist Church at Amsterdam, 370; but Anabaptists and Browne held doctrine, 371-3, Hooper also, but Browne suffered for it, 373n.; Brownists later desired Roman Catholics included. *See* Stoughton, 375n.; Browne's not modern doctrine, 375-6; full really

INDEX   405

safest, Taylor Innes, 376n. ; but experience of then wanting, 376-7 ; Roger Williams most fully grasped, 377-8 ; Jacob and Busher did not distinguish civil and religious, 378-80 ; Massachusetts rulers criminal, 380, but compare hundred thousand martyrs in Europe, 381.
Travers, Walter, the "neck" of the Presbyterian party, 72, 73; lecturer at Temple, silenced by Whitgift, 73; his Work on Discipline, 75.

U

Udall, John, cited before High Commission, 171 ; *Diotrephes*, 172; *Demonstration of Discipline*, 79, 172; Hallam's opinion of trial, 173; Udall's declaration, 173; death in prison, 174.
United Colonies of New England, 297.
United States, elements of population, 306n.

V

Vane, Henry, one of the greatest of Puritan statesmen, 263 ; regarded persecution as a crime, 349.
Vestments, Hooper scrupled, 45 ; controversy, Hume's sneer, 54; underlying meaning, 55 ; Zurich Letters, 55; aversion to, at Lambeth, 56 ; opposition at Cambridge, 56; Queen resolute, 56-8 ; majority of one in Convocation against Puritans, 57 ; thirty-seven ministers suspended, 58; Hallam's moderate view, 58.
Voluntaryism, Roger Williams apostle of, 279.

W

Wakeman's appreciation of Puritans, 196.
Ward, Nathaniel, author of Body of Liberties, 324 ; intolerant spirit, 348, 349n.
Whitgift, Archbishop, on name Puritan, 2n.; bishops not indispensable, 47n.; signed petition against vestments, 57 ; controversy with Cartwright, 70-72 ; on state of Church, 71, 72, 145; silences Travers, 73; saved England from democratical pontificate, 79 ; appointed archbishop, 92; character of, Macaulay on, 93; Test Articles, 93-5 ; prosecuted heretics in Court of High Commission, 97; Lord Burleigh scandalised, 98 ; two hundred and thirty-three ministers suspended, 101 ; Lords of Council wrote remonstrance, 103 ; Commons petition Lords, 104 ; petition to Queen, 105; Queen inexorable, 106 : at Barrowe's examination, 178-81 ; signed Penry's death warrant, 189 ; a Calvinist, 384 ; took part in framing Lambeth Articles, 385.
William of Occam, an early advocate of toleration, 363.
William of Orange, 280, 371.
Williams, Roger, 270 ; pain in leaving England, 271 ; at Nantasket, 271 ; extreme Independent and arch individualist, 272; claimed universal toleration, 273; of most amiable character, 273; called to church at Salem, 274; sentence of exile, 274 ; wanders among Indians, 275 ; lands in Rhode Island, founds Providence, 275 ; acquires land, 276 ; becomes Baptist, founds first Baptist church in America, 277 ; deposed by Salem Church, 277; tract on *The Bloody Tenet of Persecution*, 279 ; others had held doctrine of toleration, 280-1 ; first to set up government on principle of, 282 ; Slate Rock and Providence, 282, statue to founder, 282n., a harbour for all sorts of consciences, 283 ; dissolves alliance of Pequots and Naragansetts, 294 ; four particulars for which tried, 346 ; not

persecuted for religious opinion, 347-8.
Winthrop, John, 263; governor of Massachusetts, 264; ideas on liberty, 307-8; weary of banishing heretics, 349.
Witches put to death in Massachusetts and Connecticut, 314n.
Wyclif, raised spirit of liberty, 20; a Puritan of Puritans, 51; held fundamental principle of Independency, 120; his opinions implied doctrine of religious toleration, 363.
Wyclif's Bible, 15, 16.

Z

Zurich Letters, 40n.; on vestments, 55n.

www.ingramcontent.com/pod-product-compliance
Lightning Source LLC
Chambersburg PA
CBHW030556300426
44111CB00009B/996